QUEEN VICTORIA

First Media Monarch

QUEEN VICTORIA

First Media Monarch

JOHN PLUNKETT

OXFORD
UNIVERSITY PRESS

OXFORD

UNIVERSITY PRESS

Great Clarendon Street, Oxford OX2 6DP

Oxford University Press is a department of the University of Oxford.
It furthers the University's objective of excellence in research, scholarship,
and education by publishing worldwide in

Oxford New York

Auckland Bangkok Buenos Aires Cape Town Chennai
Dar es Salaam Delhi Hong Kong Istanbul Karachi Kolkata
Kuala Lumpur Madrid Melbourne Mexico City Mumbai Nairobi
São Paulo Shanghai Taipei Tokyo Toronto

Oxford is a registered trade mark of Oxford University Press
in the UK and in certain other countries

Published in the United States
by Oxford University Press Inc., New York

British Library Cataloguing in Publication Data

Data available

Library of Congress Cataloging in Publication Data

Data available

ISBN 0-19-925392-7

1 3 5 7 9 10 8 6 4 2

Typeset by SNP Best-set Typesetter Ltd., Hong Kong
Printed in Great Britain
on acid-free paper by
T.J. International Ltd,
Padstow, Cornwall

PREFACE

This book would not have been possible without the support of many people. My special thanks go to Isobel Armstrong who, as a supervisor, was both an inspiration and a model of critical elegance. My Ph.D. examiners, Regenia Gagnier and Catherine Hall, also provided a wealth of useful guidance and suggestions for improvement. Chris Brooks and Grace Moore likewise made important contributions to the existence of this project. Grace first suggested the subject of Queen Victoria and for this, as well as all her subsequent and previous help, I remain in her debt. Chris was a source of encouragement from my first days as an undergraduate. He subsequently became a generous partner in conversations upon Victoria, Albert, and much else besides. His untimely death, just as this book was nearing completion, means he will never read an argument that he did much to shape.

Numerous others provided invaluable help and discussion at different stages, particularly Laurel Brake, Hester Higton, Andrew King, Sally Ledger, Ana Parejo Vadillo, and Andrew Wyllie. I am also grateful for the receipt of an AHRB studentship and for all the assistance provided by the staff at the British Library, Collindale, the National Portrait Gallery, the Public Record Office, and the Victoria and Albert Museum.

Finally, I would like to thank Kyriaki Hadjiafxendi for reading each word of the manuscript with precision, patience, and a great deal of love. The completed version was much improved by her criticism; and yet this is undoubtedly the least of what I owe her. Nevertheless, my greatest thanks have to go my parents. They have provided unwavering support of every kind. This book is dedicated to them with much love: their labour made this labour possible.

J.P.

ACKNOWLEDGEMENTS

For permission to reproduce images, I am grateful to the following institutions. Figs. 1, 12, 22, 23, Courtesy of University of London Library, Fig. 2, By Permission of the British Library; Figs. 3, 4, 5, 6, 7, 8, 9, 14, 24, 29, 40, 41, 42, By Permission of Exeter University Library; Figs. 10 (EXEBD70192), 21 (EXEBD74920), 27 (EXEBD61885), 31 (EXEBD62225), 34 (EXEBD61903, 68673, 58744, 58750), 36 (EXEBD74877), 43 (EXEBD17537), Courtesy of the Bill Douglas Centre for the History of Cinema and Popular Culture; Figs. 11, 13, 15, 17, 18, 37, 38, 39, Courtesy of the National Portrait Gallery; Figs. 25, 26, 32, 33, 35, Courtesy of Her Majesty the Queen; Figs. 16, 19, Courtesy of British Museum; Fig. 30, author's collection.

CONTENTS

LIST OF ILLUSTRATIONS

TABLE

LIST OF ABBREVIATIONS

BJP	*British Journal of Photography*
BM Add. MS	British Library Manuscripts Collection
GL	Guildhall Library, Department of Prints and Drawings
ILN	*Illustrated London News*
JoPS	*Journal of the Photographic Society*
LMPJ	*Liverpool and Manchester Photographic Journal*
NPG	National Portrait Gallery, Prints and Drawings Archive
PN	*Photographic News*

INTRODUCTION

> Will they ever say of me as they say of 'Good Queen Bess'—Ah, that was
> in the days of 'Good Queen Vick'. There is one thing sure enough, that
> posterity will know far more about us than about Bess; for all our move-
> ments are recorded in the papers—our balls, our dinners, our visits to the
> Opera, the French Plays, or the legitimate—all are in print, to last as long
> as England herself. Only the time may come when even these records
> may come to be interesting and moulder on the shelves of a national
> library.
>
> (*Penny Satirist*, 19 July 1845)[1]

The media is one of the principal means by which the British monarchy
maintains its traditional prominence. Yet, as my epigraph demonstrates, the
relationship between these two institutions is anything but a new concern.
This book argues that the growth of a mass print and visual culture in the
nineteenth century was a vital influence upon the development of the British
monarchy. Queen Victoria was the first monarch to preside over conditions
approaching a mass urban and industrial society. During her reign, she was
subject to both the political demands of a partially enfranchised public and
the public demands of a nascent mass media. These pressures, and the symbiotic links between them, are crucial for understanding Victoria's creation as
a populist sovereign. In conjunction with the far-reaching social changes of
the century, a burgeoning publishing industry helped to reinvent the position
of the monarchy in national life.

Since Victoria's death in January 1901, there has been a regular flow of
complimentary biographies. As David Cannadine has archly noted, Victoria's
reputation is still very much *regina intacta*.[2] Only within the last ten years has
the accretion of myth and deference begun to be slowly unpicked. A renewed
scholarly interest in the nineteenth-century British monarchy has resulted in
several literary and historical studies.[3] However, despite their value, recent

---

[1] 'Court Circular', *Penny Satirist*, 19 July 1845, 1.
[2] David Cannadine, *The Pleasure of the Past* (London: Collins, 1989), 24.
[3] Richard Williams, *The Contentious Crown: Public Discussion of the British Monarchy in the Reign of
Queen Victoria* (Aldershot: Ashgate, 1997); Margaret Homans, *Royal Representations: Queen Victoria and*

books have nevertheless failed to capture fully how Queen Victoria kept the monarchy a potent institution. Literary critics have concentrated on interpreting Victoria's various manifestations. In contrast, historians have focused on the broader structural issues of anti-monarchism, popular politics, and constitutional discourse. No study has yet come close to the aesthetic character of Victoria's reign. This is because the role of print and visual culture has been neglected. Not enough attention has been paid to either the novelty of the various newspapers and periodicals disseminating royal news, or to the dramatic changes in graphic reproduction that meant a large growth in the print trade and the advent of photography and the illustrated press. Thus, Margaret Homans, in a feminist attempt to reclaim the influence of Victoria, declares that 'Seeing, appearing, or being represented are instances of the Queen's agency, regardless of whether self-representation can be said to have been chosen or actively undertaken.'[4] Such an assertion makes Victoria the personal agent for all her manifestations, from the most lewd attack to the most unctuous toadying. Such an approach abnegates the need to understand the forces constituting her position.

During Victoria's reign, the British monarchy could never hope to control the political and commercial pressures that shaped its public character. The number of contradictory portrayals demonstrates that the royal family was far from having any self-fashioned representation. Victoria inhabited her subjects' lives to a remarkable degree—but only through their appropriation and propagation of her presence. This condition is the key to both her power and her powerlessness. Only by tracing the media structures through which her figure came into being can we understand her overarching presence. Like a Russian Doll, the large icon of Queen Victoria was built up out of countless different smaller versions. It is because the growth of a material culture and a popular publishing industry were primarily responsible for Victoria's almost limitless plasticity, her diffuse proliferation, that they form the core of this work.

The central argument of this book is that, for radicals and royalists alike, the media making of the monarchy was crucial to its nineteenth-century formation. Throughout Victoria's reign, the royal family enjoyed an exceptional degree of publicity. The royal image was constantly available on a diverse assortment of media, ranging from engravings and magic lantern shows to

British Culture 1837–1867 (Chicago: Chicago University Press, 1998); Adrienne Munich, *Queen Victoria's Secrets* (New York: Columbia University Press, 1996); Frank Prochaska, *Royal Bounty: The Making of a Welfare Monarchy* (New Haven: Yale University Press, 1995); Frank Prochaska, *The Republic of Britain 1760–2000* (London: Allen Lane, 2000); Antony Taylor, *'Down with the Crown': British Anti-Monarchism and Debates about Royalty since 1790* (London: Reaktion, 1999). David Nash and Antony Taylor (eds.), *Republicanism in Victorian Britain* (London: Sutton, 2000).

[4]   Homans, *Royal Representations*, p. xix.

street ballads and photographs. Moreover, the expansiveness of the royal culture industry was such that contemporary commentators invariably ascribed to it an overdetermined political agency. Victoria's relationship with the press was a frequent subject in journals like *Punch* and the *Penny Satirist*, and its political implications were discussed by figures such as Benjamin Disraeli, Douglas Jerrold, and Walter Bagehot. There was a crucial osmosis between the making of a media monarchy and the evolving conception of Victoria's role as a constitutional monarch—the consequences of which remain with us today.

A charged relationship between print media and the British royal family is obviously a long-standing phenomenon. The perceived impact of nineteenth-century newspapers and prints was the product of an accumulated political inheritance involving both the aesthetics of the monarchy and the role of the press. The weight of this legacy goes back to the newsbooks published during the Civil War period between 1641 and 1649.[5] These appeared after the breakdown of the Star Chamber censorship laws that forbade the printing of domestic news. The publication of domestic news had previously been made illegal because of fears that it would demystify government and the King. The first Civil War newsbook, *The Heads of Severall Proceedings in the Present Parliament*, included the Remonstrance of the Long Parliament against Charles I. Thus, although newsbooks were subsequently produced both by parliamentarian and royalist factions, the advent of the modern English newspaper was heavily influenced by a republican movement in favour of the liberty of ideas. Where the British monarchy is concerned, the press has never entirely lost this democratic function. Its ability to encourage widespread participation in political events—in opposition to the secrecy of absolutist control—align it with the civic virtues of classical republicanism. Aspects of this discourse certainly provided the basis for nineteenth-century perceptions of the scope and limits of royal news. The press was both criticized and celebrated for the way it removed royal mystique and involved its readers in the lives of the royal family.

The importance her contemporaries attached to Victoria's media figure was a direct consequence of the tremendous expansion in the market for newspapers, books, periodicals, and engravings.[6] This growth was itself fostered by

---

[5] Joad Raymond (ed.), *Making the News: An Anthology of the Newsbooks of Revolutionary England 1641–1649* (Moreton-in-Marsh: Windrush Press, 1993).

[6] On these changes see Michael Twyman, *Printing 1770–1970: An Illustrated History of its Development and Uses in England* (London: Eyre and Spotiswoode, 1970); Lucy Brown, *Victorian News and Newspapers* (Oxford: Clarendon Press, 1985); Michael Twyman, *Lithography 1800–1850* (London: Oxford University Press, 1970); Patricia Anderson, *The Printed Image and the Transformation of Popular Culture 1790–1860* (Oxford: Clarendon Press, 1991); Richard Altick, *The English Common Reader* (Columbus, Oh.: Ohio University Press, 1957); Louis James, *Fiction for the Working Man 1830–1850* (London: Oxford University Press, 1963).

large-scale societal changes, especially the creation of large urban markets, gradually rising incomes and literacy levels, and the transport infrastructure provided by the railways. Victoria's rejection of the aristocratic mores of her predecessors is well known. Yet her appropriation by new modes of publication was an equally important part of the progressive character of her reign. The one factor that dynamically increased the supply of printed matter was industrialization. The mechanization of production improved all aspects of print manufacture from the making of the paper to the speed of the printing. To take just one example, wooden hand-held presses were displaced by metal steam presses, which, in their turn, were superseded by the introduction of the rotary press. The first edition of *The Times* to be printed on a steam press, capable of printing 1,100 sheets an hour, appeared on 29 November 1814. By the late 1850s, *The Times* and *Lloyd's Weekly Newspaper* were using Hoe rotary machines capable of nearly 20,000 impressions an hour. Technological advances made newspapers, books, and serial fiction increasingly affordable. The dissemination of a range of reading material was also aided by a network of penny reading rooms, Athenaeums, Mechanics' Institutes, and circulating libraries.

The exponential growth of the newspaper and periodical press underpinned the modernity of Victoria's figure. This growth was also responsible for a series of key qualitative shifts that fed into the changing character of the monarchy. As is well known, government regulation, especially the Newspaper Stamp Duties Act of 1819, had a strong impact upon the circulation and price of newspapers. In the 1820s and 1830s any provision of cheap news was significantly impeded by the paper tax, the 4*d*. Stamp Duty, and the 3*s*. 6*d*. tax on advertisements. State regulation was principally aimed at the cheap radical press and led to the concerted prosecution of unstamped newspapers between 1830 and 1836. The reduction in Stamp Duty from 4*d*. to 1*d*. in 1836, and its hard-fought-for abolition in 1855, were the most notable successes in the battle by publishers against the 'taxes on knowledge'.

Victoria's accession thus coincided both with the end of the political turmoil associated with the unstamped press and a growing awareness of the possibilities offered by a potential mass readership. Popular publishing gained a new commercial impetus, and the 1830s saw the first rage for penny-issue serial fiction and periodicals. By the end of the decade, cheap magazines, many aimed at a working-class readership, had replaced radical journals like the *Poor Man's Guardian* (1831–5). John Wilson, writing in the *London Journal* in 1845, hailed 'a new coming epoch in the world of letters— ECONOMIC LITERATURE'.[7] In the 1830s and 1840s, there were obviously sig-

---

[7] James, *Fiction for the Working Man*, 33.

nificant differences in the large number of new publications and their target readerships. Yet, they were generally more supportive towards Victoria than towards William IV and George IV. The monarchy's shift away from party political involvement was both mirrored and aided by the type of apolitical attention Victoria received from the rash of innovative popular weekly newspapers, women's journals, and 'improving' periodicals.

The royal family was also one of the principal beneficiaries of a similar and interrelated expansion that took place in the reproduction of the visual image. In the eighteenth century, virtually all illustrations that demanded precision or sought refinement were engraved on copper plates. Even using mezzotint as opposed to line-engraving, the employment of copper plates was often a long and expensive process. Prior to the 1820s, cheap illustration was restricted to the woodcuts accompanying ballads, chapbooks, and broadsheets. The most famous publisher of these street ballads was the Catnach Press of Seven Dials. Often recording the latest execution, murder, disaster, or royal event, Catnach's illustrations came from a common stock and were frequently reused for different occasions. The beginning of a rapid expansion in graphic culture took place with the introduction of steel-plate engraving in the early 1820s, particularly as embodied through its use for illustrating the literary annuals and the Books of Beauty. The 1820s and 1830s also saw lithography establishing itself. This is evident in the number of coloured lithographs commemorating Victoria's coronation. Their sumptuousness emphasized both the spectacle of the occasion and their own eye-catching distinction.

Lithography, like steel-engraving, was cheaper than copper-engraving owing to its longer print-runs. Nevertheless, neither could match the advantages of letter-press printing. The most far-reaching development to influence the graphic representation of Victoria before the advent of photography was a revival in wood-engraving and the subsequent development of an illustrated press in the early 1840s. The beginnings of the revival can be traced to Thomas and John Bewick's publication of their *General History of Quadrupeds* in 1790. It was not until the 1820s and 1830s, however, that its use became widespread. The 1820s saw the introduction of 2*d.* illustrated miscellanies that played an important role in the development of a cheap periodical press. *The Portfolio* (1823–5) and *The Mirror of Literature, Amusement and Instruction* (1823–41) adapted the 6*d.* miscellany format for a wider readership.[8] They were precursors to the remarkable success of two illustrated periodicals that commenced in 1832. These were the *Penny Magazine* (1832–45) and the *Saturday Magazine* (1832–44). With coloured prints like H. B.'s political sketches selling at two shillings each, the illustrations of the penny journals

[8] Brian Maidment, *Into the 1830s: Some Origins of Victorian Illustrated Journalism* (Manchester: Manchester Polytechnic Library, 1992), 5–7.

were an important element of their attraction. At the height of its circulation in 1833 and 1834, the *Penny Magazine* was reputedly selling 200,000 copies, although its actual readership would have been several times higher.[9] Integral to the resurgence of wood-engraving was its ability to reproduce cheaply large numbers of impressions. The print-runs of many of the engravings produced by the fine art printsellers were limited to around a thousand good impressions before the copper-plate became worn. In contrast, wood-blocks were said to yield up to two or three hundred thousand impressions.[10] As a form of relief printing, wood-engraving could also be printed alongside typeface; hence its utilization by the illustrated press.

The increasing affordability of prints also produced a new ideological emphasis on the social benefits of disseminating high-quality artistic engravings. The London Art Union was set up in 1837, for example, to promote a popular taste for fine art. In periodicals and newspapers, there was also a significant rise in the coverage of the annual exhibitions and in the number of reviews of contemporary British paintings.[11] Two obvious signs of this discursive expansion are the formation of the *Art Union* in 1839, the first periodical exclusively devoted to news on the fine arts, and Thackeray's invention of the persona of Michaelangelo Titchmarsh. Thackeray's mock reviews of the Royal Academy in *Fraser's Magazine* between 1837 and 1845 gloriously burlesque the pretensions of both artists and reviewers. There was a new self-consciousness towards graphic culture, the expression of which ranged from a belief in the moral influence of cheap illustration to satires upon the highfalutin language of critical reviews. It was at this critical juncture that Victoria's accession took place.

Victoria's public presence was made up of a wealth of heterogeneous representations. Behind each print or newspaper report cited here, there stand many, many others. An insistent accumulation of artefacts and images created a cluster of dominant royalist tropes. Subsequent chapters often focus on large-scale events because this is where the iterative impact of the media was at its most intense and discernible. The symbolic nature of these occasions is also when they were at their most formative in promoting Victoria's position as a national figurehead. However, equally as important is the day to day reiteration created through the inherent regularity of newspapers and periodicals. The ephemeral nature of any single royal photograph or souvenir should not disguise the cultural work carried out by their abundant presence, as can be seen when individual photographs or news stories are located against a backdrop that indexes their volume of sales and consequent dominance of the

---

[9] James, *Fiction for the Working Man*, 17.
[10] Henry Cole, 'Modern Wood Engraving', *London and Westminster Review*, 31 (1838), 268.
[11] See John Charles Olmsted (ed.), *Victorian Painting: Essays and Reviews* (London: Garland, 1980).

market. As John Thompson has noted, ideology is as much about the fixing of meaning as its creation.[12] Quantifying the fulsome coverage of the monarchy demonstrates its privileged position in the public sphere. The weight of reverent royal attention forcibly located Victoria at the heart of an imagined and imaginary community.

This book is not simply a study of the cultural production of Victoria. Rather, it is devoted to the media making of the monarchy. The term owes much to the conception of making argued for by Michel De Certeau:

The 'making' in question is a production, a *poiēsis*, but a hidden one, because it is scattered over areas defined and occupied by systems of 'production' (television, urban development, commerce, etc), and because the steadily increasing expansion of these systems no longer leaves 'consumers' any place in which they make or do with the products of these systems.[13]

Victoria's media making obviously includes an examination of the impact of large-scale developments in print and visual culture. The character of royal image was determined by the way it was reproduced according to the conventions of photography, newspapers, and engraving. It was not that Victoria's image was disseminated through photographs. The royal image itself became photographic. This condition holds true both at the level of the technological format of the different media and their broader aesthetic status. Responses to Victoria's portrayal were invariably influenced by concerns that already existed over the role of newspapers, prints, and photography. The gamut of reactions was also firmly linked to specific political and institutional standpoints. Commentaries in the periodical press, for example, often stressed the benefits derived from the press's ability to disseminate the royal image. Such claims have to be seen as including a large element of self-promotion. Victoria's media making was as much about the media's making of its own mythology.

The royal culture industry had a seemingly relentless presence. The second strand of this book therefore traces the insinuating nature of Victoria's imaginative and affective impact. Victoria's endless materialization was so important because it was a bridge between individual experience and the type of mass collectivity created by industrialism. Two different definitions of 'the media', whereby it functions as both noun and verb, pertain to this. As noun, 'the media' stands for an institutional bloc, a shorthand and overly homogeneous term for a diverse ensemble of newspapers, periodicals, prints, and broadsheets. Yet the term also refers to the epistemological process of

---

[12] Quoted in Terry Eagleton, *Ideology: An Introduction* (London: Verso, 1991), 195.
[13] Michel de Certeau, *The Practice of Everyday Life*, trans. Steven Randall (Berkeley: California University Press, 1984), p. xii.

mediation, an act of linking and connection. The most important feature of Victoria's media making was thus not the precise parameters of her portrayal, where the same tropes were repeated with monotonous regularity. Rather, it was the individual and collective experience provided by the different media. The wealth of newspapers, prints, and photographs offered Victoria's subjects an intimate and personal interaction with the monarchy. The monarchy's prominence within national life was the sum product of Victoria's position within the interior lives of her subjects. De Certeau emphasizes, however, that making never equates directly with production. There was always space to appropriate, reject, or simply ignore Victoria's overweening figure. Thus her media making helps to explain why she was simultaneously revered, reviled, fetishized, ignored, and gossiped about. An extensive examination of the assimilation of the monarchy into individual subjectivities, as revealed through diaries and letters, is not possible here. Nevertheless, through examining practices like the collection of royal photographs, we can see that Victoria was continually spilling beyond the pages of the newspapers and beyond the frame of her portraits.

A third major concern is the reflexive awareness of Victoria-as-image, and, concomitantly, with the constitutional politics that the royal press coverage helped to promote. There was an ongoing critique of the benefits the royal family derived from the inordinate attention it received. These commentaries stem from a long-standing political concern over the monarchy's ability to appeal to popular sentiment and imagination. Republican critics have traditionally disparaged the means by which royalty occupies the attention of the masses. Thomas Paine, for example, repeatedly attacked the use of 'king-craft' to create governance by 'fraud, effigy and show'.[14] Tropes of showmanship, simulacra, and spectacle recur throughout Paine's republican writings. In *The Rights of Man*, he famously derided Edmund Burke for letting his imagination be captivated by the grand theatricality of the *ancien régime*, and by the character of Marie-Antoinette in particular:

He is not affected by the reality of distress touching his heart but by the showy resemblance of it striking his imagination. He pities the plumage but forgets the dying bird. Accustomed to kiss the aristocratical hand that hath purloined him from himself, he degenerates into a composition of art, and the genuine soul of nature forsakes him. His hero or heroine must be a tragedy-victim expiring in show, and not the real prisoner of misery, sliding into death in the silence of a dungeon.[15]

John Barrell has argued that Paine's attack was part of a much larger discursive conflict over the political role of the imagination during the 1790s. Paine,

[14]   Thomas Paine, *The Thomas Paine Reader*, ed. Michael Foot and Isaac Kramnick (Harmondsworth: Penguin, 1987), 275.
[15]   Ibid. 213.

for example, portrayed the *ancien régime* as an 'entirely fictive system of government and society, entirely without substance, because entirely the creature of the imagination'.[16] For Paine, hereditary monarchy was a thing surviving by its imaginative appeal. It was necessarily wholly fabricated because of the insubstantial nature of its existence.

Numerous opponents to Burke's *Reflections on the Revolution in France*, not least Mary Wollstonecraft, castigated the excesses of his imagination and his lack of rationality. An important element in the rejection of Burke stemmed from his use of the language of sentiment to revere the *ancien régime*. Paine accused Burke of being too overwhelmed by the tragic paintings of his own imagination. His rhetoric attempted to evoke a corresponding sympathetic feeling among his readers, whereby 'facts are manufactured for the sake of show, and accommodated to produce, through the weakness of sympathy, a weeping effect'.[17] The language of sentiment was likewise widely used to evoke sympathy for, and empathy with, George III. Indeed, Barrell argues it played an important role in the anxieties that the revolutionary events in France caused with regard to the British monarchy. The language of sentiment protected the monarchy by encouraging relations between George and his subjects to be imagined in familiar, affective, and personal terms.

The conflicts of the 1790s are significant because they influenced reactions to the importance of Queen Victoria's dissemination through print and visual media. They provided a discursive inheritance for interpreting the nature of Victoria's popular presence. Newspapers and periodicals were given a political agency because of their willingness to imagine Victoria, and their concomitant ability to encourage an imaginative identification with her. In the years prior to her accession, there was also an ongoing concern with the dominant vocabulary of loyalism vis-à-vis the courtier-like language of the press. In his *History of the Regency and Reign of George IV*, a typically indignant Cobbett attacked newspapers' slavish imitations of court phraseology. He declared that 'baseness such as was exhibited in the press, during the last ten years of this reign, never was equalled before in the world'.[18] Cobbett viewed the royalist language of newspapers as another form of Old Corruption, and Victoria's relationship with the press encouraged similar reactions.

George IV's love of extravagant ceremony also did much to further Paine's accusation that the monarchy was nothing but a sham spectacle. This mode of critique was subsequently applied to Victoria because of the rapid expansion of popular publishing in the 1830s and 1840s. Attacks upon her ubiquitous

---

[16] John Barrell, *Imagining the King's Death: Figurative Treason, Fantasies of Regicide 1793–1796* (Oxford: Oxford University Press, 2000), 20.

[17] Paine, *Reader*, 211.

[18] William Cobbett, *History of the Regency and Reign of George IV* (London: William Cobbett, 1830), para. 492.

image exploited the notion that the monarch was an invented figure without any material substance. Commentators claimed that prints and newspapers offered an unprecedented immediacy with Victoria. Yet, to use Hegel's terms, Victoria's figure was never in-itself. It was always for-itself, always aware of its own fabrication. Such a strong reflexive awareness suggests a previously unexamined continuity in anti-monarchist writing: Victoria's media making was one of the principal areas through which radicals contested support for the monarchy.

The extent of Victoria's ubiquitous presence has to be continually set against the critiques and satire that it aroused. Radical and Chartist publications strongly attacked the sycophantic coverage of Victoria by the metropolitan press. They conceived of it as another form of aristocratic mummery and a preservation of the existing aristocratic hierarchy. Royal journalism and the *Court Circular* were also stock satirical targets for periodicals ranging from *Punch* to *Reynolds's Newspaper*. Conversely, the nature of Victoria's representation was frequently politicized as a means of celebrating her disdain for pomp and circumstance. In the 1860s, for example, periodicals like *All the Year Round* and *Once a Week* lauded the equalizing and unadorned realism of Victoria's photographs because of the ordinary monarch that they revealed. Thus many of the critiques and celebrations of Victoria had their origin in the mediated nature of her depiction. The populist status Victoria achieved was a product of the aesthetics of different media interacting with long-standing political discourses surrounding the monarchy.

I have chosen to concentrate on the first half of Victoria's reign, from 1837 to 1870, because this period covers a distinctive phase in her sovereignty. After the death of Prince Albert in December 1861, Victoria remained in widowed seclusion for several years. Her behaviour then was a significant departure from the high-profile tours and visits that punctuated the previous decade. The period around 1870 marks a useful endpoint because of two contemporary events that are minor culminations of the political and media developments affecting Victoria's position. The passing of the Second Reform Act in 1867 and the publication of *Leaves from the Journal of Our Life in the Highlands* in 1868 exemplify the changed character of the monarchy. Moreover, following Victoria's creation as Empress of India in 1876, there was an imperial reinvention of the monarchy that deserves a study in its own right. The second reason for concentrating on the first half of the reign is that it covers the most significant developments in print and visual culture. Although a truly mass culture did not exist until the end of the century, it was the working out of a dynamic that had started several decades previously. This book focuses on such moments as the success of the first published royal photographs in the 1860s. The reactions they aroused testify to the way that new media provided a novel and modern experience of the monarchy. Once royal photographs became an accepted part of the everyday they rarely provoked a reaction, even though their influence continued to be pervasive.

The five chapters proceed in broadly chronological terms and concentrate on different media. Yet they are also organized to illustrate the way that the same ideological concerns resurface again and again. The first chapter argues that the coverage of Victoria and Albert's numerous civic visits was instrumental in the promotion of a populist monarchy. Chapters 2 and 3 focus more specifically on the growth of print and visual culture from the late 1830s, and trace the ubiquity of Victoria's presence and the self-consciousness towards her media figuring. Chapter 4 examines the first royal photographs and the way in which the camera became caught up in the same constitutional discourses that characterized the 1840s and 1850s. The final chapter ranges over all of the individual media to provide a genealogy of royal journalism. It details both the procedural minutiae of reporting royal events and the widespread derision attendant upon it. Taken together, the five chapters provide an understanding of why, when the political influence of the monarchy was waning, Victoria remained an overarching yet intimate figure. To misquote the opening of *David Copperfield*, the following pages tell the story of how Queen Victoria was made into the hero of her own life; and, indeed, of the Victorian Age itself.

1

CIVIC PUBLICNESS

Assuredly, the reign of Victoria will be known as the reign of royal visits;
it seems to have established an era of royal and imperial sociability.

(*Illustrated London News*, June 1844)[1]

What does a British constitutional monarch do? Month on month, year on
year, what provides worthy employment for a sovereign, particularly one supposedly above the machinations of party politics? In the profession of royalty,
the public engagement reigns supreme. Whether patronizing diverse charities, touring countries in the Commonwealth, or honouring the latest newly
built hospital or battleship, civic visits loom large in the modern conception
of royal duties. This chapter argues that Queen Victoria and Prince Albert,
through the impact of a burgeoning print and visual culture, set the model for
the serious duties and pleasurable diversions that we have come to expect
from a constitutional monarchy. They undertook an unprecedented number of
regional tours, foreign visits, and civic engagements, forging a role that would
be successfully followed by future British monarchs. Their work ranged from
an earnest social concern, as in Albert assuming the Presidency of the Society
for Improvement of the Labouring Classes in 1848, to the more enlivening
nature of their marine jaunts to Louis-Philippe and Napoleon III in 1843 and
1855 respectively.

The thread that binds together the diverse activities of Victoria and Albert
is the extensive attention that they received. Royal occasions, whether an
exclusive court levee at Windsor or one of the many parish dinners given to
commemorate the monarch's birthday, had traditionally occupied a privileged
position in the official calendar of national events. Industrialism and mass
society wrought vast changes to the make-up of nineteenth-century Britain.
Yet the cumulative regularity of Victoria and Albert's activities, along with
the media attention they received, ensured that the monarchy continued to

---

[1] 'The Royal Guests', *ILN* 8 June 1844, 361.

dominate the public sphere. Royal events were increasingly indivisible from the way in which they were experienced through their media coverage. There was a new style of royalty that was as much inaugurated around Victoria and Albert as by them. The roles they created were inseparable from the modernity of their lives existing as royal news, disseminated as never before by prints, periodicals, and newspapers.

The engagements carried out by Victoria and Albert were keyed into the simultaneous development of popular weekly newspapers and the first periodicals devoted primarily to graphic news. The *News of the World*, *Lloyd's Weekly Newspaper*, and the *Weekly Times*, along with the more expensive 6d. illustrated periodicals such as the *Illustrated London News* and the *Illustrated Times*, all commenced publication during the 1840s. The reduction in Stamp Duty in 1855 and the repeal of paper tax in 1860 meant that the circulation of metropolitan daily newspapers also underwent a significant jump. These well-known changes in print culture, a shift not only in quantity but in kind, became bound up with a new style of monarchy. They did so because in contrast to Victoria's consultations with her ministers—which invariably took place behind closed doors—her tours and visits took place as a series of specifically 'public' duties. There was a crucial symbiotic relationship between the civic publicness of Victoria and the publicity that these events received. The very nature of the events fostered the royal news coverage that facilitated the domination of the public sphere. Tellingly, one of most common truisms concerning Victoria was that her political influence was greater than was commonly realized. Only brief episodes bought to light her proactive relationship with her governments and threatened to interrupt the procession of tours and visits. Instead of loyalty towards the Crown being played out primarily through the customary local ceremonies, the movements of Victoria and Albert provided an ever-greater individual focus on their lives.

Attacks and commentary upon the nineteenth-century monarchy as an institution have to be continually set against the much larger number of column inches engendered by the Queen's engagements. By its *ipso facto* success, Victoria and Albert's civic publicness set the agenda for a royalist popular politics. Publicness is used here in the sense defined by John Thompson, meaning not just making visible but the making of the experience of an event available to an audience not immediately present.[2] Coinciding with the aftermath of the Reform Bill turmoil and the changing balance of power between the Crown, the Lords, and the Commons, royal civic activities were invested with the discourse of popular constitutionalism. They were integral to the coterminous creation of Victoria as both a popular and a con-

---

[2] John Thompson, *The Media and Modernity* (Cambridge: Polity, 1995), 120–5.

stitutional monarch, defining her royal role as well as producing a label that inspired endless platitudes.

Recently, there has been an upsurge of interest in nineteenth-century populism and the discourse of constitutionalism. As part of a movement away from class-based subjectivities, studies by Patrick Joyce, James Vernon, and James Epstein have all drawn attention to the multiple ways in which notions of the People and the constitution were deployed.[3] Of particular relevance to this study is Vernon's claim that the language of constitutionalism was the principal narrative of English popular political culture up until at least 1867. Vernon argues that, from the 1820s, there was a series of legislative attempts to impose an official public sphere through the use of increasingly exclusive definitions of citizenship. Thus, legislation like the Seditious Meetings Act of 1819, the Reform Bill of 1832, and the Municipal Reform Act of 1835 sought to make the political arena the legal preserve of propertied men, particularly at the level of parish, municipal, and county politics. Vernon argues that, as a consequence of these more restrictive legal definitions, increasing stress was attached to generating support from the very People legally excluded by official political culture. From parish meetings and civic ceremonies to parliamentary elections, popular participation was conceived as being increasingly important at precisely the same time as it was constituted in a way that would reinforce the status quo. The presence of the People upon such occasions was thereby turned into their acceptance of the disenfranchised position that was already imposed upon them.

Against such inclusive moves, radicals sought to turn the People into a sign of the excluded: a group whose constitutional rights for freedom of assembly and parliamentary presence were being denied. Despite the liminality, even the potential vacuity, of a term like 'the People', it was a crucial mobilizing idiom and the cause of much controversy. Indeed, its very pervasiveness meant that it was appropriated by a large number of political groupings. At radical dinners it was common to toast, 'The People the Source of All Power'. Cobbett was among those who frequently employed the rhetoric of the People as part of the call for political reform: 'The Bill of Rights declares that the Laws of England are the birthright of the people. It does not say, of the rich, of the nobles, of the priesthood, the yeomanry cavalry, the members of corporation, the borough-workers—but of the PEOPLE.'[4] This was a radical language that was used to demand political inclusion, an assertion of the constitutional

[3] James Vernon, *Politics and the People: A Study in English Political Culture, c.1815–1867* (Cambridge: Cambridge University Press, 1993); Patrick Joyce, *Visions of the People: Industrial England and the Question of Class, 1840–1914* (Cambridge: Cambridge University Press, 1991); James Epstein, *Radical Expression: Political Language, Ritual, and Symbol in England 1790–1850* (Oxford: Oxford University Press, 1994).

[4] Quoted in Vernon, *Politics and the People*, 303.

rights of citizenship in opposition to those legally defined by the imposition of an official public sphere. Republicans were also part of this cumulatively dense discourse. The *Northern Tribune*, run by two of the most prominent republicans of the late 1840s, W. J. Linton and Joseph Cowen, was wholly typical in its definition of republicanism as the 'Sovereignty of the people, untrammelled by birthright'.[5] English republicans promoted their own constitutional genealogy, celebrating Cromwell and the Commonwealth alongside the poetry of later republicans such as Shelley and Byron.[6]

One of the proclaimed impulses behind the renewed attention to the language of constitutionalism is the reappraisal of E. P. Thompson's focus on the influence of Paineite republicanism in the making of a specifically working-class subjectivity.[7] Thompson stressed the need for early nineteenth-century radicalism to break through the pervasive rhetoric of constitutionalism because 'it implied the absolute sanctity of certain conventions: respect for the institution of monarchy, for the hereditary principle, for the traditional rights of the great landowners and the established church'.[8] Despite the recent attention to populism and its various cognates such as patriotism and melodrama, little attention has been devoted to the impact of popular constitutionalism upon one of its most obvious beneficiaries: the monarchy and Queen Victoria herself.

One of the most oft-repeated platitudes concerning Victoria was that she had overseen the transition to a constitutional monarchy. At Victoria's death in January 1901, even the republican *Reynolds's Newspaper* felt able to assert that she was 'the example of a constitutional ruler and the founder of the Modern British Monarchy . . . she reduced meddling to the lowest terms and never imposed her will in an arrogant manner on her Ministers'.[9] As the monarch who had elevated the Crown above party politics, Victoria basked in the long afterglow of the Magna Carta and the Glorious Revolution. Later, the Reform Acts of 1832, 1867, and 1884 became part of the same constitutional mythology. This was a narrative whose potent hold was political, imaginative, historic. Moreover, it is vital to emphasize that it seeped into every aspect of Victoria's role. It was through the interlinked discourses around the People and the constitution that Victoria's first tours and visits were endlessly played out. Their prominence established her role as a national figurehead and simultaneously downplayed the high politics between Victoria and her ministers.

---

[5] *Northern Tribune*, 2 (1855), 116–17.

[6] Richard Williams, *The Contentious Crown* (Aldershot: Ashgate, 1997), 22.

[7] James Vernon, 'Notes Towards an Introduction', in *Re-Reading the Constitution: New Narratives in the Political History of England's Long Nineteenth Century* (Cambridge: Cambridge University Press, 1996), 5.

[8] E. P. Thompson, *The Making of the English Working Class* (Harmondsworth: Penguin, 1968), 96.

[9] 'Our Glorious Constitution', *Reynolds's Newspaper*, 27 Jan. 1901, 4.

The populist invention of the British monarchy is often dated from the latter years of Victoria's reign. David Cannadine has contrasted the lack of grandiose royal ritual in the first half of the reign with the imperial extravaganzas of Victoria's Golden and Diamond Jubilees (1887, 1897), and the coronation of Edward VII (1902).[10] The pomp and circumstance of these late set-pieces is taken to exemplify Victoria's apotheosis as an imperial and national figurehead. Such an interpretation invariably downplays the significance of the Queen's activities during the first twenty years of the reign. In my view, the years between 1837 and 1861 were crucial in creating a successful model for the month-to-month duties of the British monarch. Pervading the multitudinous reports of the royal engagements of this period is the discourse of popular constitutionalism. Tours and visits were cast as a recognition of Victoria's reliance on the approval of her subjects, a celebration of the inclusivity and participation of the People in the political nation. Time and time again, the freely given support of the People was placed over and against the role of the organized pageantry. The large crowds in attendance at royal occasions were turned into a confirmation of the strength of support enjoyed by the monarchy. Royal events between 1837 and 1861 had an imaginative potency precisely because they were not overladen with militaristic or aristocratic ceremony.

Although Victoria was certainly a well-supported monarch, a weighty ideological significance was ascribed to her popular status. The term 'royal populism' is thus used throughout this chapter to describe the meanings attached to Victoria's public role. One defining index to the importance of royal populism during the 1840s and 1850s is the extent to which its claims were contested by a range of radicals, republicans, and Chartists. Victoria and Albert's civic publicness was conceived as being the monarchy maintaining its position in the face of its declining political and social importance. Tours and visits were perceived to be reliant on a restricted and pre-defined political participation: radicals criticized the way in which royal populism prescribed the position of the People for them. Good old plebeian John Bull was often portrayed as the most loyal of royals. And there was certainly no shortage of deep-rooted deference and long-standing customs. Conversely, anti-monarchists frequently argued that the discourse of the People was used to overdetermine the meaning of royal occasions. Victoria's support was cast as heavily populist; it was both manipulated and exaggerated, rather than the genuine expression of cross-class feeling. Opposition to royal events was only partially motivated by an outright republicanism. This is important because it

---

[10] David Cannadine, 'The Context, Performance and Meaning of Ritual: The British Monarchy and the "Invention of Tradition", *c.*1820–1977', in E. Hobsbawm and T. Ranger (eds.), *The Invention of Tradition* (Cambridge: Cambridge University Press, 1983), 101–64.

indicates that these protests formed part of a larger battle over the role of citizenship and the nature of participation in popular politics. Whether to be passive subjects or active citizens was the issue.

The press played a key role in creating a sense of participation or alienation around Victoria's tours and visits. Radical journals attacked the way most newspapers celebrated Victoria's visits as a validation of the existing political status quo. In 1855, *Reynolds's Newspaper* declared, albeit with a large element of self-promotion, that it was the 'only paper in the kingdom that has the courage to speak the truth in regard to royalty—the only one that dares to look the execrable tyranny in the face'.[11] Newspapers and prints, already conceived of as a foundational element of the public sphere, were caught up in a contest over the meaning of royal events, where the role of print media was an integral part of the struggle.

It is in the first three years of Victoria's reign that we can see the contours of royal populism begin to take shape. Victoria's coronation and marriage were both significant departures from precedent and aroused a large degree of controversy. Examining the tension around Victoria's coronation and marriage locates the civic publicness of the 1840s and 1850s within a reformist trajectory that the earlier two events had helped to initiate. The weight of constitutional discourse around Victoria's tours and visits was such that it actually migrated back into a broad conception of the monarch's constitutional role. In Walter Bagehot's *The English Constitution*, a treatise notable for its subsequent status, we can trace the impact of Victoria's media making upon Bagehot's conception of the Queen's political function.

Princess Alexandrina Victoria acceded to the British throne on 20 June 1837, less than a month after her eighteenth birthday and the attainment of her legal majority. Circumstances contrived to maximize the promise of the new reign. With the end of the seven-year rule of William IV and with the reactionary Duke of Cumberland succeeding to the throne of Hanover—Victoria being debarred by Salic law—her accession ended the long and uninspiring affiliation with the throne by the sons of George III. Young, female, attractive, politically innocent yet with decidedly Whiggish sympathies, the new Queen seemed far removed from the excesses of her aged Hanoverian uncles. Laetitia Landon described it as the advent of a 'spring-like reign'.[12] Scores of poems, prints, and street ballads were produced, all effusively idealizing Victoria. *Figaro in London*, a popular satirical journal, claimed that John Bull was so pleased at the idea of being governed by a girl,

---

[11] 'Monarchs and their Rights—Divine or Diabolical? Which?', *Reynolds's Newspaper*, 9 Sept. 1855, 8.
[12] Laetitia Landon, 'To Victoria', *Flowers of Loveliness; Twelve Groups of Female Figures, Emblematic of Flowers* (London: Ackerman & Co., 1838), n.pag.

he would cut off his ears if her little Majesty required them.[13] Victoria basked in the tangible freshness of a revivified royalism, comparable in the magnitude of its sentiment to that aroused by Queen Caroline in 1820: only this time it was in support of the monarchy.

Crucial to the fervour around Victoria's accession was its reliance on, and exploitation of, the anticipated political climate of the new reign. The sentiment Victoria aroused was founded on her supposedly reforming sympathies. As well as her very obvious differences in age and gender from her predecessors, Victoria's accession reorientated the monarchy around the impulse for political reform. Several factors ensured that the death of William IV would be a significant party political event. William IV and Queen Adelaide were both renowned Tories. Their opposition to the Reform Bill and to the succeeding Whig government was common knowledge. Conversely, the Duchess of Kent, Victoria's mother and sole surviving parent, was well known for her Whig sympathies. It was widely believed that Victoria had been brought up to follow the same principles. Further constitutional and religious reform seemed to be promised under the auspices of a liberal Queen. *Figaro in London* was happy to proclaim that 'we, as regular radicals of the right sort, hail Victoria as one of us'.[14] In July 1837, the radical-leaning *Tait's Edinburgh Review* likewise hinted that Lord Durham—the head of the committee responsible for drafting the Reform Bill and a close confidant of the Duchess—had already been approached to head up a new government pledged to household suffrage, triennial parliaments, and the ballot.[15] Victoria was very much regarded as a political innocent to be guided by the Duchess of Kent: she would be in office but not in power. As *Tait's Edinburgh Journal* eagerly noted 'it would augur unfavourably of her character and the prospects of her reign, were she not so submissive of the guidance of her mother'.[16] Victoria's youth and femininity meant that she was not personally aligned with the oppressive power of the monarchy.

The patriarchal assumptions inherent in the enthusiastic response to Victoria's accession are epitomized by a pseudonymous pamphlet published in December 1838. Written by Lord Brougham, it was an open *Letter to the Queen on the State of the Monarchy*. Brougham warned Victoria that reform was an unstoppable tide. Before developing his argument, he set out the credentials that he felt rendered him qualified to proffer his advice:

---

[13] 'The Queen Riding the Bull', *Figaro in London*, 20 Jan. 1838, 9. *Figaro in London* (1831–9) is best known as one of the forerunners to *Punch*, its writers included Douglas Jerrold, Gilbert A'Beckett, and Henry Mayhew. Despite being radical in tone and selling at only 1*d*., its market was principally affluent and metropolitan. It was reputed to have a circulation of 70,000 copies. See Richard Altick, *Punch: The Lively Youth of a British Institution 1841–1851* (Columbus, Oh.: Ohio University Press, 1997), 1–9.

[14] 'What is the Young Queen?', *Figaro in London*, 22 July 1837, 113.

[15] William Tait, 'Long Live the Queen!', *Tait's Edinburgh Review*, 4 (1837), 399.   [16] Ibid. 399.

I am an experienced man, well stricken in years. I hold myself before *you*, a girl of eighteen, who, in my own or any other family in Europe, would be treated as a child, ordered to do as was most agreeable or convenient to others—whose inclinations would never be consulted—whose opinion would never be thought of—whose consent would never be asked upon any one thing appertaining to any other human being but yourself, beyond the choice of gown or cap, nor always upon that: yet before you I humble myself . . .[17]

Brougham's ambivalent homage captures the extreme dissonance between Victoria's state body and her private body. Much of Victoria's attraction stemmed from the fact that, at the same time as her personal sympathies were often dwelt upon, her femininity meant that she was regarded as being politically innocent.

In 1837 it was still the case that parliament was dissolved upon the accession of a new sovereign. During the subsequent elections, royal favour and further reform were the primary issues. Despite the contempt of radical candidates, Whig grandees claimed to be the party of reform. Throughout the election campaign Victoria's name was constantly yoked with the Whigs. Election addresses by Whig candidates referred constantly to the Queen's support. In his election address at North Durham, Lord Durham declared 'Let our Watchwords Be, the Queen and Liberty! The Queen and the Constitution! The Queen and Reform!'[18] The Tory-leaning *Blackwood's Magazine* drew attention to the sheer geographical ubiquity of the use of the Queen's name as an election slogan:

'The Queen' echoed all the Whig Radicals, from John O'Groats to Land's End; 'the Queen' faintly murmured the Radicals hypocritical of the metropolitan burghs, of sanctified Leeds and unitarian Manchester; 'the Queen' bellowed O'Connell and his satellites through all the bogs of Ireland . . . Queen or no Queen 'that is the question', gently whispered the more Really honest and truly destructive Radicals of Bath, of Westminster, and of Southwark.[19]

In attempting to associate themselves with the Queen's popularity, the Whigs linked Victoria with reform to an extent that was out of all proportion with her political sympathies.

Victoria's sympathy for the People had a far broader existence than mere party political machination. Ballads promoted Victoria as both a remover of corruption and an instigator of constitutional reform. Victoria was to be innocently outside the oppressive corruption of government, while simultaneously using the most autocratic power of all to reform it from within. Royal populism

---

[17] A Friend of the People, *A Letter to the Queen on the State of the Monarchy* (London: Simpkin and Marshall, 1838), 6.

[18] 'Lord Durham's Advice to Reformers', *The Examiner*, 16 July 1837, 449.

[19] 'Court and Cabinet Gossip of a New Reign', *Blackwood's Magazine*, 43 (1838), 513.

was not ideologically coherent but it was wholly consistent in the capacious agency it invested in Victoria. At the opening of the parliamentary theatre in September 1837, *Figaro in London* hoped that the 'School of Reform' would begin the action, with the abolition of the House of Lords at the top of the bill.[20] To coincide with the Queen's opening of parliament, *Figaro in London* printed a spoof speech claiming that it contained what Victoria really wished to have said:

> To business, for oh! I'll not have any shirking,
> Of popular measures there shall be no lurking,
> They tell me I ought not to dictate to you,
> But who's to prevent it, good folks, if I do?
> If I can deter you from doing what's ill,
> I can and I ought, and I must and I will!
> I'm not going to be like some of your kings,
> A mere puppet to move, just as you pull the strings,
> So I tell you at once, I *am* on the throne
> And mind if I don't have a will of my own.
> You Tories that sit on the benches out there,
> I'll just give you warning so you'd better take care![21]

Street ballads similarly presented Victoria not merely as a Whig Reformer but as a committed radical. One ballad claimed that the Poor Law amendment would be revoked, before going on to note that 'She doth declare it her intent | To extend Reform in Parliament'.[22] Another ballad portrayed Victoria as a dictatorial but reforming Queen who would not be beguiled by either the tricks of the Whigs or the Tories:

> I'll make some alterations,
> I'll gain the people's right,
> I will have a radical parliament,
> Or they don't lodge here tonight.[23]

The explicitly political assertions of the ballads form part of a broader promise that Victoria's reign, in a folklore-style tradition, would provide a universal fount of milk and honey. Ballads exploited to the full the feel good factor of the new reign:

[20] 'Opening of Parliamentary Theatre', *Figaro in London*, 30 Sept. 1837, 154.
[21] 'The Queen's Speech', *Figaro in London*, 18 Nov. 1837, 183.
[22] 'Queen Victoria's Accession', in John Ashton (ed.), *Modern Street Ballads* (London: Chatto & Windus, 1888), 273.
[23] Robert Collison, *The Story of Street Literature: Forerunner of the Popular Press* (London: Dent, 1973), 95.

> Says she, I'll try my utmost skill
> That the poor may have their fill,
> Forsake them!—no I never will,
> When I am Queen of England.[24]

Personal and political veneration of Victoria subverted the issue of monarchical power, skewing the reform of a system that had the monarchy at its apex. Even the *Northern Star* emphatically stated 'We love the Queen . . . None can desire more ardently than we do the happiness of the Throne',[25] although it went on to warn her that such happiness could only rest securely on the universal happiness of her subjects. It is a revealing index to the extent of the populist sympathies around Victoria that there is no contradiction between the achievement of reform and its accomplishment by the very form of power it was designed to proscribe.

The coronation of Queen Victoria was celebrated with a plethora of local parades, fairs, and dinners. The occasion, however, was far from being a national communion, a ceremonial affirmation of the status quo. The coronation, on 28 June 1838, was caught up in the fervid antagonism between Whigs and Tories. Controversy arose because the arrangements for the coronation broke with precedent in several important ways. Tories conducted a vociferous campaign complaining that the revised ceremony had been shorn of majesty by Benthamite utilitarianism. For Tories, the revised style of Victoria's coronation was further evidence of the radical assault on the constitutional role of the Crown. Simultaneously, however, Chartists attacked the cost and irrationality of the coronation's feudal mummery. These contrary criticisms are testimony to the different political perceptions of royal occasions at the start of Victoria's reign.

The revised organization of Victoria's coronation ceremony is part of the reforming populism that dominated her initial representation. The eschewing of excessive ceremony, with its long-standing connotations of self-indulgent expense, meant that Victoria's coronation was conceived of as an attempt to apply the common touch. It allowed the metropolitan and provincial press, small though they were, to build a royalist rhetoric out of the inclusive participation of the People. This rhetoric was crucial in giving the impression of a new style of monarchy. Despite the coronation being too entrenched in party politics to embody the same consensus as later royal events, out of its success would emerge the public and populist monarchy of the 1840s. Significantly, it was the meaning drawn from popular participation in the coronation that Chartists and radicals most sought to undermine. Chartists challenged the

---

[24]   Ashton (ed.), *Modern Street Ballads*, 273.
[25]   'The Coronation', *Northern Star*, 30 June 1838, 4.

way in which the various coronation celebrations—both discursively in the press and materially through the local processions—positioned them as passive subjects within a public sphere dominated by royal occasions. In a conflation of the mediate and immediate, radicals rejected the constitution of the People as a mob of plebeian John Bulls. They did so in order to stress that the People were rational citizens deserving enfranchisement.

In April 1838, the ceremonial arrangements for the coronation were announced. Rather than reverting to the grossly lavish arrangements with which George IV was crowned, the pageant followed the relatively spartan principles introduced by William IV. Instead of the £240,000 expended by George IV, Victoria's coronation would eventually cost £70,000. A declaration by the Queen stated that the Privy Council had been directed to make the arrangements 'as much abridged and as economical as might be compatible with a strict regard to the solemnity and importance of the coronation'.[26] The walking procession of all the estates of realm from Westminster Hall to Westminster Abbey would not take place, nor would there be a post-coronation banquet. Hereditary sinecures pertaining to various antiquarian rites were to be suspended, most notably that of the Queen's champion. At the banquet it was still the practice for the champion to enter Westminster Hall dressed in full armour, throw down his gauntlet, and challenge to combat any whom dared to gainsay the Sovereign's right to rule. Victoria's coronation was also the first in which the House of Commons participated in the service at Westminster Abbey. With these revisions, the *Gentleman's Magazine* commented significantly that the ceremony followed 'in most respects after the *reformed* mode of her immediate predecessor'.[27] In the same way as the Reform Bill transformed the position of the House of Commons, the coronation of Queen Victoria saw the public role of royalty undergo a correspondingly 'democratic' shift.

In its pared down ceremonial, the coronation prefigures the civic visits of the 1840s and 1850s. As Greville noted, 'the great merit about this coronation is that so much has been done for the people'.[28] Although initially the day was to consist merely of the Westminster service, the centrepiece of the proceedings became a long procession commencing from Buckingham Palace. There was also a large fair in Hyde Park. According to the *Gentleman's Magazine* the last monarch to employ such a coronation procession had been King Charles II.[29] Contemporary responses to these revisions emphasize their novelty.

---

[26] 'By the Queen. A proclamation', *The Times*, 6 Apr. 1838, 4.
[27] 'The Coronation', *Gentleman's Magazine*, 10 (1838), 188.
[28] Charles Greville, *Greville's Memoirs of the Reign of Queen Victoria 1837–1852*, ed. Henry Reeve (London: Longmans, Green & Co., 1888), iv. 236.
[29] 'The Coronation', 188.

When many of the visiting foreign attachés were asked to join the cavalcade, an article in *Blackwood's* by George Croly noted that the decision was an 'unheard of innovation'.[30] The endeavour to enhance the spectacle was not an unqualified success because it actually resulted in the carriages of the foreign dignitaries outstripping, in both numbers and grandeur, those of the British monarchy and its entourage. *Figaro in London*, whilst critical of the governmental penny-pinching, similarly objected to the novelty of the roundabout route. It complained of the importunate treatment of Victoria by the new-fangled 'system of lugging, pulling, hauling, and dragging the Sovereign about through all the bye-streets of London'.[31] Nevertheless, after the event, it caught the reforming impulse of royal populism by suggesting that, in order for everyone to be able to witness the coronation, the trappings and properties of the abbey should be taken on a theatrical tour and shown as tableaux at venues around the country.[32]

It was the desire for economy at the coronation, with the consequent effects on the accompanying majesty of the pageant, which created the shift in political focus. Victoria's coronation was poorly organized and was overshadowed by Tory criticism. Yet it is the very nature and extent of that criticism which provides the key to understanding the future success of her public role. As the comments of *Figaro in London* emphasize, the diminution in ceremony went hand in hand with making Victoria more available to her subjects. Unsurprisingly, the revised arrangements were the chief source of controversy between radicals and Tories. The downsizing was, in part, conducted out of respect to widespread economic hardship and simmering political discontent. The Tories nevertheless believed that a miserly coronation represented an affront to its aristocratic participants. On 2 May, the Tory Marquis of Londonderry sent an open letter to the Lord Mayor, Alderman, and Tradesmen of the City of London, complaining that the alterations were the removal of the ancient splendour expected from London.[33] At a protest meeting in London on 12 May, Capt. W. Jones MP declared that 'the interests of a great country had been sacrificed, the interests of the aristocracy, the interests of the gentry, and the landed interest, had been assaulted'.[34] Numerous meetings were held in London in May to protest against the paltry nature of the coronation. The campaign culminated in the Marquis of Londonderry moving an address in the House of Lords imploring the Queen to postpone the coronation until 1 August, and for there to be no diminution in its splendour.

---

[30]   George Croly, 'Letters of an Attaché; The Coronation', *Blackwood's Magazine*, 43 (1838), 374.
[31]   'Coronation Procession', *Figaro in London*, 26 May 1838, 83.
[32]   'A Suggestion to the Queen', *Figaro in London*, 14 July 1838, 108.
[33]   Marquis of Londonderry, 'The Coronation. To Lord Mayor, Alderman, Tradesmen of the City of London', *The Times*, 2 May 1838, 6.
[34]   'Meeting on the Subject of the Postponement of the Coronation', *The Times*, 12 May 1838, 5.

The reportage of Victoria's coronation demonstrates that its revised organization was as much symbolic as pragmatic. Royal populism saturated the narratives disseminated by Tory and Whig metropolitan newspapers. In a swipe at the Whiggish organization of the event, the Tory *Standard* declared that, with the pageantry of the court being meanly and offensively arranged, the grandeur of 'this sublime spectacle was due solely to the *people*'.[35] The Whiggish monthly, the *Examiner*, similarly viewed the coronation as a success created by the crowds. It described the event as a 'national ovation, in which they were actors as well as their Sovereign'.[36] More explicit than many others about the politically encoded nature of its own reporting was the weekly *Spectator*, which had a strongly utilitarian and dissenting outlook. It proudly announced its preference for describing fully only 'that part of the celebration in which the multitudinous people of England . . . the hundreds of thousands out-of-doors shared so eagerly'.[37] The hallowed coronation service in Westminster Abbey, designed for a favoured few, was regarded as having as little novelty as it did genuine importance. In a discursive move that would recur throughout the next two decades, the *Spectator*, through its reporting, self-consciously enacted the religious compact between God, the Crown, and the Peers being superseded by a public sphere founded on an enfranchised popular participation. The crowd was a politicized subject whose actions played a primary role in making the meaning of the event. The *Spectator*'s explicit focus on the People, setting itself against the ritual inside the Abbey, was facilitated by the revised arrangements governing the coronation as a whole.

Despite Tory grievances, radicals were not stirred into celebrating any concessions to economy. Instead, they pilloried the coronation for its expense. The utilitarian criticism employed by much of the Whig and radical press was both extensive and forceful. Described by the *Examiner* as a 'thing opposed to the growing sense of the times',[38] the coronation was derided as feudal and antiquarian. In similar terms, the *Sunday Times* forthrightly declared that if the pageant 'cannot be simplified, adapted to the manners, laws and habits of the present time, it were better be abolished altogether'.[39] Individual witnesses to the occasion also shared this aversion to the ceremony. Harriet Martineau, well known for her utilitarian views, found herself repulsed and offended by the events inside the Abbey. In her journal, Martineau describes the aged peeresses as old hags, their court dresses requiring them to wear their hair dyed and drawn to the top of their heads in order that they could put

---

[35] Editorial, *Standard*, 29 June 1838, 2.   [36] 'The Coronation', *Examiner*, 1 July 1838, 405.
[37] 'Postscript', *Spectator*, 28 June 1838, 607.
[38] 'The Queen's Coronation', *Examiner*, 1 July 1838, 402.
[39] Editorial, *Sunday Times*, 1 July 1838, 4.

on their coronets. She recoiled from the profusion of arms and necks covered with diamonds and yet 'so brown and wrinkled as to make one sick; or dusted over with white powder that was worse than what it disguised'.[40] The religious service fared no better. The dissenting Martineau perceived the correlation of divine right and royal rank as worthy of only the old Pharaonic times in Egypt, 'it was offensive as offered to the God of the nineteenth-century in the Western world'.[41] Out of these trenchant critiques of royal ceremony would emerge the discursive contours of royal populism. Unlike the latter years of Victoria's reign, where the grandiloquence of her jubilees was in keeping with her imperial matriarchy, Victoria was initially construed as a populist monarch precisely because she distanced herself from excessive pageantry.

In the manufacturing districts of northern England, suffering under a severe trade depression, the coronation was not an opportunity to affirm, literally or figuratively, the roast beef and plum pudding of Olde England. Coronation day was commemorated with a series of co-ordinated demonstrations, fuelled by economic unrest and calls for the Charter. Over the next twenty years, radicals and republicans would continually contest the dominant position enjoyed by royal occasions, both in themselves and through the publicity they received. Victoria's accession encouraged radical critiques that foreground the media making of the British monarchy.

The protests by Chartists and other radical groups at the coronation betray a self-conscious comprehension of their need to work against their disenfranchisement in a mediated public sphere. Since the repression of the radical press through the Newspaper Stamp Duties Act of 1819, print culture had, of course, been an important arena of conflict. Kevin Gilmartin has argued that radical newspapers of the 1820s and 1830s frequently defined themselves against a corrupt establishment press.[42] The *Poor Man's Guardian*, one of the most prominent unstamped publications, declared that, before its commencement in 1832, 'the whole Newspaper Press was in the hands of the monied and trading classes; the wants, the wishes, the sufferings of the working man were unknown and unheard'.[43] This conception of the press, where it is allied to the interests of the state and ruling classes, fed into the coronation demonstrations. The protests clearly functioned at an immediate local and physical level. Yet they were also premised on the Chartists' awareness of a mediated level of representation. As well as simply voicing their discontent, the Chartists specifically aimed at contesting the accounts of

[40] Harriet Martineau, *Autobiography* (Boston: J. R. Osgood, 1877), i. 421.

[41] Ibid. 423.

[42] Kevin Gilmartin, *Print Politics: The Press and Radical Opposition in Early Nineteenth-Century England* (Cambridge: Cambridge University Press, 1996), 93–5.

[43] 'The Real Authors and Objects of the Late Seizures of the Property of the Unstamped', *Poor Man's Guardian*, 16 Aug. 1835, 631.

the metropolitan press. Instead of accepting the disenfranchising narrative imposed upon them, accepting their own fashioning as a crowd of dimly ple-beian John Bulls persuaded by the glittering gewgaws into huzzaing for the Queen, Chartists sought to portray themselves as rational citizens. They sought to reappropriate the enlightenment values which, as James Vernon has argued, were promoted as one of the key properties required for participation in official political culture.[44] The various critiques of the coronation empha-sized its barbarity and irrationality. The Chartists likewise denounced any hint of the carnivalesque.

Protests against Victoria's coronation took place throughout the north. The most significant was that which took place in Manchester, a city whose cotton manufacturing and unfamiliar class system made it the 'shock city' of the age. On coronation day, despite a supreme effort by the local authorities to make the festivities a success, they could not overcome what *The Times* described as the 'listless feeling which pervaded the working classes'.[45] It was common practice for guilds, associations, and tradesmen to join the militia and muni-cipal dignitaries for the local coronation procession. However, not one-third of those who joined the event at the two previous coronations participated in Manchester's procession for Queen Victoria.[46] The meagre attendance was primarily the result of an orchestrated campaign. On 23 June, an open letter was addressed to all officers and members of the Trade Unions in Manchester and Salford. Signed by twenty-three Trades Councils and supported by the Manchester Universal Suffrage Association the letter epitomizes the response to the coronation by Chartists and artisan radicals. The expense of the coro-nation was seen as endemic of a profligate political system that was paid for by the constant persecution of the poor. Insisting upon their status as rational beings, the Chartists refused to become the 'dupes of our oppressors, the passive instruments for creating by shows and gewgaws' the image of a false social prosperity.[47]

The letter from the Manchester Trades Councils is premised on the notion that the coronation was an official celebration in support of the status quo. It justifies its call for the non-involvement of the Trade Societies because of the interpretation that would be placed upon their large-scale participation:

We therefore hope that Trade Societies will on no account allow themselves to be duped by their employers with gifts of money, drink and feasts, in order to induce them to join the procession: such conduct would betray their weakness, and afford the

[44] Vernon, 105.

[45] 'Manchester and Salford', *The Times*, 30 June 1838, 7.

[46] Ibid. 7.

[47] 'Coronation. To the Officers and Members of the Trades' Union in Manchester and Salford', *The Times*, 23 June 1838, 5.

venal press an opportunity to boast of prosperity which every thinking man knows full well does not exist. Let the authorities send their delegates in vain, join neither procession or idle throng that gapes on it; but betake yourself of some more rational mode of testifying your loyalty to the Queen.[48]

At many locations around the country subscriptions were raised to provide coronation dinners for the poor, aged, and infirm of the community. Parish dinners and other organized festivities were often arranged by large employers, landowners, or local dignitaries. For the Trades Councils, joining such celebrations would confirm their place in the social hierarchy through the highly visible acceptance of a benevolent paternalism. This was very much a long-standing radical position. At the jubilee of George III in 1809, William Cobbett used his *Political Register* to protest that subscription dinners marked out the recipients as 'a degraded cast, as if they had badges put upon their clothes, or, as some of the American negroes have, a burnt mark on their cheek'.[49] However, in 1838, while the non-attendance of the Trades Councils clearly worked as an immediate and local series of protests, the letter also reveals that they were conceived of with the press in mind. Widespread participation would provide the 'venal press' with the opportunity to promote prosperity and consensus. The Trades Councils' participation would be turned into an expression of their support for the monarchy and a validation of their disenfranchised role. Significantly, the letter is also careful to call for a more rational way of testifying to their loyalty towards the Queen. These were not so much republican protests as a rejection of the populist discourses invested in royal occasions.

The demonstration at Manchester was replicated throughout northern England, with the *Northern Star*, which had commenced publication in November 1837, magnifying the articulation of the Chartist dissent. The *Northern Star*, with a circulation boasted to be as high as 42,000 in the late 1830s, was able to constitute its own narrative of royal occasions.[50] Like the letter from the Manchester Trades Council, the *Northern Star* was committed to fashioning a collectivity opposed to the vision of the People proffered by the coronation celebrations. The reports of the *Northern Star* present a moving series of localized protests. Against the disenfranchising discourse of royal populism, each protest constituted its own solidarity of constitutional values, its own form of intervention in the public sphere. In Wakefield, a group of protesters bearing placards with the slogans 'No Bastilles' and 'Universal

---

[48] 'Coronation. The Address of the Trades' Unions of Manchester and Salford to the Working Men of Great Britain and Northern Ireland', *Sun*, 25 June 1838, 4.

[49] William Cobbett, 'The Jubilee', *Political Register*, 21 Oct. 1809, 576.

[50] Stephen Koss, *The Rise and Fall of the Political Press in Britain* (London: Hamish Hamilton, 1981) i. 60.

Suffrage' attempted to join the local coronation procession.[51] In Keighley not one voice was heard to exclaim Long Live Victoria![52] The socialists of Oldham, following to the hilt the rational utility of Bentham, resolved not to join any state-licensed carnivalesque. Instead, they organized their own social festival for the day 'without intoxication, useless ceremony, or idle conversation'.[53] Details of the local actions, when published together in the *Northern Star*, present an alternative narrative to the holistic social cohesion promoted by royal populism.

If the coronation could not but be heavily orchestrated by precedent, Victoria's marriage to Prince Albert, the first wedding of a Queen Regnant in historical memory, was not so hindered by the weight of the past. Like the coronation, the tensions provoked by the event throw into relief the evolution of Victoria's high-profile presence. The wedding of an attractive virgin Queen to a dashing young prince provided ideal material for the promotion of a captivating royal romance. With the Queen Caroline affair a not so distant memory, newspaper editorials went out of their way to emphasize how far the Queen had been able to depart from the prescribed norm of diplomatic royal marriages. In the House of Commons, Peel congratulated Victoria on being able to marry according to her own wishes because it often occurred in royal marriages that 'the happiness of the contracting parties was sacrificed and their feelings rendered secondary to political views'.[54] Importantly, however, royal weddings were not then the grand affairs that they later became. The wedding ceremonies of George III and George IV were held in the Chapel Royal at St James's Palace in the evening. Similarly, the Duke of Kent and William IV, then only the Duke of Clarence, took part in a joint wedding in 1818 at Kew Palace. They rushed together to the altar in unseemly haste, hoping to provide a legal heir after the death of Princess Charlotte. Both left long-time mistresses trailing in their wake. In contrast to these inauspicious affairs, Victoria's wedding was held at 1 p.m., from whence the royal couple proceeded to Windsor. There was another procession of the kind inaugurated for the coronation, even though it consisted only of the Queen travelling the short distance from Buckingham Palace to the Chapel Royal. Victoria's wedding was still a relatively low-key affair in many respects (its date was not even confirmed in the *London Gazette* until 5 February, five days before the marriage took place). Yet there are important aspects of its organization that locate it as part of a movement towards royal populism.

Critiques of Victoria's wedding are notable for the way that they honed in upon the public nature of the occasion. As such, they are akin to attacks upon

---

[51] 'Wakefield', *Northern Star*, 7 July 1838, 5.   [52] 'Keighley', *Northern Star*, 7 July 1838, 5.
[53] 'Oldham', *Northern Star*, 7 July 1838, 5.
[54] 'Her Majesty's Speech', *The Times*, 17 Jan. 1840, 5.

the revised organization of the coronation. There were two principal modes of critique, both of which throw into relief the difficulties around Victoria forging a clearly defined and high-profile role for herself. Given the fierce dislike of aristocratic pomp, making the wedding into a large royal spectacle risked turning it into a cold state affair—merely another gilded but unfeeling aristocratic marriage. Equally, the prominence given to her wedding accentuated Victoria's independence and threatened a transgression of the increasingly gendered distinction between public and private space. Partly, this is because, as a ruling Sovereign, Victoria had to choose a Consort and ask for his hand in marriage. Court etiquette did not permit the various royal suitors to make their own advances. As Lynda Nead has commented, 'independence was unnatural, it signified boldness and sexual deviancy'.[55] The high-profile nature of Victoria's wedding consequently provoked attacks on the uncomfortable and deviant visibility of her sexuality. These were themselves part of a larger suspicion directed towards her feminine independence.

Alongside utilitarian dislike of royal events, there was an ongoing mode of irreverent critique that Iain McCalman has called 'obscene populism'. During the 1830s and 1840s, a number of London radical pressmen, usually based in and around Hollywell Street, were involved in a range of bawdy and semi-pornographic publications. McCalman argues that this is evidence of the continuing importance of a Regency-style satire, which, 'whatever its commercial objective, intended to amuse, shock or disgust readers by exposing the crimes, vices, and hypocrisies of the ruling classes'.[56] Certainly the way the *Satirist* critiqued the excessively public nature of Victoria's wedding by playing upon her lack of feminine propriety can be seen in this context. The *Satirist* was a 6*d.* stamped weekly publication that was one of the principal periodicals in the milieu of scandalous journalism. Devoted to whatever lurid squibs and slanderous gossip came its way, its style was very much inherited from the scurrilous satire of the Regency years. In 1840, it was selling approximately the same number of copies as the *Spectator*.[57]

Radical and Tory critiques of Victoria's marriage consistently deployed the image of a wedding arranged by a foreign confederacy. There was certainly pressure on Victoria to marry early, and, in August 1838, a cartoon in *Figaro in London* criticized the constant succession of available princes that were being set out for Victoria's inspection. Showing the Belgian King Leopold car-

[55] Lynda Nead, *Myths of Sexuality* (Oxford: Basil Blackwell, 1988), 28.
[56] Iain McCalman, *Radical Underworld: Prophets, Revolutionaries and Pornographers 1795–1840* (1988; Oxford: Clarendon Press, 1993), 206.
[57] Donald Grey, 'Early Victorian Scandalous Journalism: Renton Nicholson's *The Town* (1837–1842)', in Joanne Shattock and Michael Woolf (eds.), *The Victorian Periodical Press: Samplings and Soundings* (Leicester: Leicester University Press, 1982), 316–48.

Fig. 1. 'The Queen and her Courtiers', *Figaro in London*, 4 August 1838, 118

rying a baby basket of foreign princes, the engraving is aimed at the machinations attempting to foist a pre-selected husband on to Victoria (see Fig. 1).
Similarly, the *Satirist* unfavourably compared Victoria's predicament with
that of Elizabeth I. All that Elizabeth's parliament had asked of her was a decision on whether she had an intention of marrying whereas the current Queen
was being given no choice at all:

How very differently is our young lady treated. It is carried *nem. com.* by the Coburgs
and the Orleans that she ought to be in the family way, and forthwith somebody is sent
over for the purpose. When the animal is caught, he is brought over here just like a
parish bull and the poor little heifer is taught to receive his polite attentions without
having a word to say upon the subject, and without supposing for a moment that it was

ever in the nature of things that she could have any choice between one piece of mortality than another.[58]

The *Satirist* bawdily deconstructs the genteel romantic verbiage heaped upon the match. The portrayal of Albert as no more than the fecund German stud reduces Victoria's marriage to its most basic dynastic function—the production of an heir who would help to ensure a stable monarchy.

The novelty of the wedding's royal publicness, and the corresponding conflict over whether it was a personal romantic event or a state occasion, is most explicit in the criticism of Victoria's honeymoon behaviour. Instead of retiring in newly wedded bliss for several weeks and putting aside all court society, Victoria held large parties at Windsor on the evenings immediately following her wedding. Within three days the couple had returned to London and Victoria had resumed her state duties. According to Greville, Victoria's friends were allegedly shocked that she was not conforming more to English customs and continuing in the retirement which 'natural modesty and native delicacy generally prescribe'.[59] A letter by Thackeray similarly comments upon the fact that the couple were walking on the Windsor slopes at 8 a.m. on the morning after the marriage. Thackeray wondered why the Tories had not seized on it 'as a sign of the horrible immorality of the court'.[60] By not retiring for a respectable period of time, Victoria very firmly demonstrated an adherence to her royal duties. However, with her wedding regarded as very much a sexual rite of passage, it also bought to the fore her sexuality and independence.

Always on the look-out for a whiff of court impropriety, the *Satirist* seized on Victoria's honeymoon and conflated it with the nature of the wedding as a whole. The very publicness of the event made Victoria seem unduly brazen. Her independence was attacked because she had refused to be a suitably blushing bride and had put herself wantonly on display. For several weeks following the event, the *Satirist* railed against the sexual indelicacy of the overly public nature of Victoria's wedding and honeymoon:

Doings such as these, so much at variance with the candour and propriety of middle-life, has made it a general topic of conversation; and it is not a little creditable to those who serve us, even in the capacity of servants, that their remarks upon the subject are, if possible, stronger than that of those immediately above them. Can anyone pass through a crowded thoroughfare, and have his ears assaulted with offensive observations connected with this matter? and had any of *those* persons been then contracted,

---

[58] 'Prince Albert and the Queen', *Satirist*, 13 Oct. 1839, 325.
[59] Charles Greville, *The Greville Diary Including Passages Hitherto Withheld from Publication*, ed. Philip Whitwell Wilson (New York: Doubleday, 1927), ii. 131.
[60] William Thackeray, *The Letters and Private Papers of William Makepeace Thackeray*, ed. Gordon Ray (Oxford: Oxford University Press, 1946), i. 434.

their conduct upon and following the solemn ceremony would have partaken of greater decency and had been attended with a delicacy far more apparent.[61]

The Queen's flaunting of her sexuality is associated with long-standing conceptions of the lax nature of aristocratic sexuality. The *Satirist* declared that the marriage appeared to be like a marriage amongst the Hottentot or Abyssinians, 'where the husbands enjoy the women in public'.[62] For the *Satirist*, the only way for a royal marriage to manage the wedding respectfully was for the couple to have disappeared off to Windsor in complete secrecy and contracted a private marriage. The rest of the world should only have been informed a week after the event, thereby avoiding the indecency of what it described as an almost public consummation. There is a contradiction, however, in the *Satirist's* sustained attacks on Victoria's moral conduct. The very same periodical was far from unabashed in printing numerous scurrilous wedding-night squibs, thereby helping to engender the very lurid attention to Victoria's sexuality that it was protesting against.

Despite the criticism of Victoria's wedding, her marriage did transform the way in which her feminine role was regarded. Her wedding created a shift from maiden monarch to matron monarch, and, in so doing, downplayed her regal independence. Prior to her marriage, even the public nature of Victoria's announcement of her marriage to the Privy Council could be turned into a form of aberrant female sexuality, as demonstrated by an anonymous satire entitled *The German Bridegroom*:

> But Queen's have self-possession which defies
> Ev'n blushing cheeks and tear-besprinkled eyes.
> Down comes our maiden monarch in full state
> To tell her nobles of her happy state
>
> .   .   .   .
>
> Paints her anticipations with a smile,
> Heedless of Melbourne leering all the while,
> Hopes the consummation may be soon,
> And prays with rapture for the honeymoon.
> Well, be it so; in humbler life we deem
> That chaste reserve bestows a brighter beam
> On maiden loveliness; but Royal charms,
> We see, content not with such vulgar arms;
> And he who seeks for modesty must own,
> He seeks in vain to find it on the Throne.[63]

---

[61] 'The Force of Example', *Satirist*, 1 Mar. 1840, 70.
[62] 'London, February 16, 1840', *Satirist*, 16 Feb. 1840, 52.
[63] HonBle ***, *The German Bridegroom; A Satire* (London: J. W. Southgate, 1840), 13–14.

The Field-Marshal of the British Empire.

Queen.—Come on, my ducks, that's the way to step. Men could not lift the leg so !—nothing like the petticoat for a march, and a cool seat on a saddle, this hot weather. We'll shame the old army. Nothing like liberty, my heroines, and women's legs are the very emblems of liberty all the world over.
Soldier.—But petticoats are bad for running, your Majesty.
Queen.—Oh ! never mind that—all the better—you don't mean to run, do you? Your business is to make others run, not to run yourself.
Soldier.—But should the enemy run before us, it is our duty to run after them.
Queen.—Aye ; and if they are in breeches and you in petticoats they may possibly escape ! Well ! that's a subject for consideration, but the evil can easily be remedied by shortening the dress—don't be disheartened. Huzza ! for the petticoat ! three cheers for the petticoat ! come on my heroines !
[*Purchaser of the Penny Satirist.*—Vy ! vat a guy they're made of her—quite an old agg, vith a vite svellin' on her neck—it's too bad ; blowed if it a'n't—to trent the young lady so.—'Cause the lady's old in hexperience and visdom that ain't no reason vy they should make her hold in hears and looks, I says !]

Fig. 2. Charles Grant, 'The Field Marshall of the British Empire', *Penny Satirist*, 29 July 1837, 1

The connection between Victoria's female independence and an overt sexuality explains why both were downplayed after her marriage. A caricature published by the *Penny Satirist* in July 1837 is typical of the initial conflation of her sexual and political freedom (see Fig. 2). In the woodcut by Charles Grant, Victoria is shown in the guise of a warrior Queen. She is leading an army of women whose outstretched and partially bare legs signify their new authority. As Victoria states, 'women's legs are the very emblems of liberty the world over'.[64] However, despite such claims, the very incongruity of the petticoat-

---

[64] The *Penny Satirist* was reportedly one of the first penny broadsheets produced after the reduction of the Stamp Duty in 1836. Subtitled 'A cheap substitute for a weekly newspaper', it contained a mixture of news commentary as well as a large woodcut on the front page. Moderately radical in its politics, its circulation in June 1837 has been claimed at the relatively high figure of 15,000. W. Anderson Smith, *Shepherd Smith the Universalist* (London: Sampson Low, Master & Co., 1892), 164.

warriors undermines any emancipatory pretensions. The *Penny Satirist* plays upon Victoria's subversion of gender roles only in order to deride and contain her potential influence as feminine exemplar. Victoria's subsequent marriage and motherhood served to downplay her regal and sexual independence, enabling her to undertake her future tours and visits without laying herself open to the type of criticism made by the *Satirist*.

Chartists also sought to turn the Queen's marriage to their own purposes, forging a counter-theatre to the officially sanctioned events. In November 1839, a protest in Newport over an imprisoned Chartist turned into a riot when a crowd attacked the hotel in which the Mayor and the local troops were taking refuge. In the ensuing mêlée, ten of the rioters were killed and fifty were injured. Three Chartists, Frost, Williams, and Jones, were subsequently convicted of high treason and sentenced to death. Just prior to Victoria's wedding a large Chartist delegation, led by Fergus O'Connor, met in Manchester in order to try to decide how best to secure a free pardon for the three men. On the day of the wedding it was decided that meetings were to be held throughout the land in order to memorialize Victoria. It was to be 'a day for giving national council and advice to the sovereign, through the medium of public opinion'.[65] Meetings in aid of securing pardons were held in locations as diverse as Leeds, Huddersfield, Hull, Newcastle, Cheltenham, Oldham, Bath, Dundee, and Forfar.

The constitutional right to petition the monarch was one of the foundational tenets of Whiggism and Protestant dissent. However, upon the occasion of Victoria's marriage, the Chartists' meetings were heavily inflected with royal populism and the idealization of the Queen's femininity. An editorial in the *Northern Star* claimed that if Mrs Frost could only meet the Queen personally and plead for her husband, the feminine bond between them would mean that she would not be refused. It asserted its belief that Victoria, 'imbued with all the soft and kindly feelings of her sex . . . could she, on the day after her marriage, refuse the application of Mrs Frost and her lovely daughters'.[66] Natural feminine sympathy for her subjects, one of the most prominent factors in Victoria's portrayal throughout her reign, was the premiss for political action. The Chartist meetings did more than simply recruit Victoria for their cause in a form of radical patriotism. They express a faithful belief in her character that reproduces the traditional notion of a benevolent monarch. In a fashion that eerily echoes some of the claims of the street ballads, the Queen is invested with a beneficent agency by the Chartists.

Slowly emerging out of the tension of Victoria's coronation and marriage,

---

[65] 'The Address of the Delegates Assembled at Manchester, for the Purpose of Devising the Best Means of Providing a Free Pardon for Frost, Williams and Jones', *Northern Star*, 8 Feb. 1840, 1.
[66] 'The Queen and Mrs Frost', *Northern Star*, 8 Feb. 1840, 4.

and the political turmoil of the 1830s, was a new role for royalty. It is the reinvented publicness of Victoria's coronation and marriage, and their corresponding association with a reforming populism, which provides the discursive framework through which we can understand the potency of Victoria's activities during the 1840s and 1850s. In a recent book, Frank Prochaska has argued that much scholarship on the monarchy has neglected its substantive role in civil society. Prochaska's work focuses on the creation of what he describes as the welfare monarchy—the vital role played by royal philanthropy through the patronage of numerous charities and individuals. Given the importance of a paternalistic *noblesse oblige* at a time when the role of government remained limited, the good causes adopted by Victoria and Albert were an uncontentious way of demonstrating their compassion and concern for their subjects. Victoria was a patron of, and not just a contributor to, 150 institutions, three times as many as George IV. Between 1831 and 1871, donations to institutions and individuals were equivalent to 15 per cent of Victoria's income from the Privy Purse.[67]

Charity work nevertheless comprised only part of the revivified prominence that Victoria and Albert enjoyed. The initial excitement occasioned by the new reign, which had been fostered by a regular procession of royal events, settled down only in the sense that the Queen's marriage did not see any diminution in her high-profile role. Between 1840 and 1861, it is crucial to the whole style of Victoria's monarchy that she undertook a wide range of public engagements, and that she was seen to be doing them. Royal ceremonial may have been downsized but amongst radicals and Tories alike there was a desire for Victoria and Albert to adopt an industrious public role. For Tories, royal visits harked back to the progresses of Elizabeth I, a reinforcement of the monarch's traditional pre-eminence in the midst of disorientating change. For Benthamite critics, they satisfied the demand for a more utilitarian monarchy: one that was at least being put to work for its handsome remuneration. As the *Penny Satirist* declared in 1843: 'She is kept by the nation as a spectacle and it is right that she should be seen. In fact it is her duty to come out and show herself, that we may have value for our money; and if she should do anything very ridiculous so much the better.'[68] Royal visits provided an outlet for municipal pride in conjunction with an endorsement of Britain's new industrial achievements. Above all, they were an enactment of the reciprocal interest present between Victoria and her subjects. As the *Illustrated London News* fawningly put it on the Queen's first tour of Scotland: 'Abstractedly, the desire of a sovereign to hold communion with all classes of her people without regard to local or national distinctions, is an indication of a

---

[67]   Frank Prochaska, *Royal Bounty* (New Haven: Yale University Press, 1995), 77.
[68]   'The Royal Visitations, and Learned Foolery', *Penny Satirist*, 18 Nov. 1843, 2.

love of justice, and of that beautiful maternal affection which, in domestic life, cherishes no favourite in a family, but sheds its holy love on all alike.'[69] The comment is exemplary of the populist discourse attached to the Queen's activities. In 1843, *The Times* similarly declared that Victoria's visits 'cement the union between the Crown and the people by a reciprocity of confidence'.[70] Again and again and again, royal visits were made to signify a popular constitutionalism—the monarch willingly placing herself before her People. Furthermore, it is significant that the *Illustrated London News* saw the visits as an extension of Victoria's maternal beneficence. The feelings inscribed into the visits are intimate and personal rather than a form of state duty. Instead of any contradiction between Victoria's femininity and her 'public' role, they are conflated together by the *Illustrated London News* so that each becomes the rationale of the other. Making the monarchy available to the People gave royal events an inclusive rhetoric that mitigated much potential criticism.

The majority of the metropolitan and provincial press echoed the *Illustrated London News*'s sentiments. The extensiveness of the discourse of royal populism cannot be underestimated. On Victoria's tour of the midlands in November 1843, the *News of the World* claimed that her visits were only nominally visits to Sir Robert Peel, the Duke of Devonshire, and the Duke of Rutland. They were in fact 'intended as visits to the people—all the working people as well as the burgesses in the different localities'.[71] For the *News of the World*, it was the Queen's most agreeable pleasure to see and to be seen. The *News of the World* itself had only begun publication in October 1843. It was one of the first of the new 3*d.* Sunday newspapers aimed at a broad readership unwilling to afford a metropolitan daily paper or without the leisure time to read one. Predominantly liberal in outlook, the royal coverage of the new weekly press was far removed from the radicalism of the *Northern Star* or the scabrous satire of the *Satirist*. Publications like the *News of the World* and the *Illustrated London News* were replacing the Regency-inspired style of the *Satirist*. The latter finally ceased publication in 1846. The *Northern Star*, too, was at its most influential with the growth of Chartism in the late 1830s and early 1840s.

The *News of the World*'s comments upon Victoria's midlands tour are from its reporting of the first significant royal event to take place following its commencement. They exemplify much of the future coverage given to Victoria by papers like *Lloyd's Weekly Newspaper* and the *Weekly Times*, which began publication in January 1843 and January 1847 respectively. Upon Victoria's visit to Louis Napoleon in 1855, for example, *Lloyd's Weekly Newspaper*, which had

---

[69] 'The Royal Visit to Scotland', *ILN* 3 Sept. 1842, 257.
[70] Quoted in Williams, *Contentious Crown*, 198.
[71] 'The Queen's Visit to Her People', *News of the World*, 3 Dec. 1843, 4.

a predominantly artisan readership, made the typical declaration that 'it is not Victoria who visits Louis Napoleon, but England who visits France. It is not potentate embracing potentate, but people grasping people.'[72] The coverage of these weekly newspapers is all the more significant because they were amongst the most widely circulated of the period. By 1855, the *Illustrated London News* was selling 155,000 copies a week, the *News of the World* 110,000, *Lloyd's Weekly Newspaper* 92,000, and the *Weekly Times* 76,000.[73] These figures place them in advance of the majority of daily newspapers. Only *The Times* and, after 1855, the *Daily Telegraph* remotely approached such circulation. In 1861, the daily circulation of *The Times* was approximately 65,000 copies and the *Daily Telegraph* 141,000.[74]

The almost wholly supportive coverage of the monarchy by the new Sunday newspapers, the new illustrated press, and the existing metropolitan daily newspapers was crucial for materially embodying the discursive claims of royal populism. Victoria's visits shaped a civic role for the monarchy but they were equally important through being turned into pleasurable reading or viewing matter. Francis Mulhern has argued that communities are 'not places but *practices* of collective identification'.[75] Reading about the monarchy in a newspaper, or viewing a print or photograph, were increasingly important everyday practices of collective identification. The promotion of Victoria's relationship with the People; the assertion of an unprecedented bond of intimacy between her and her subjects; the placing of her at the centre of an imagined national community—all these were achieved, at least partially, through the extensive coverage that was given to Victoria. There was a mutually supportive reciprocity between the cultural work carried out by the growth of newspapers, prints, and periodicals, and the political claims of royal populism. Newspapers and periodicals had an essentially self-fulfilling function; they constantly enacted what they claimed simply to describe.

The number of newspapers commencing in the 1840s accentuated the impact of the number of engagements undertaken by Victoria and Albert. It is important to emphasize that their activities were a significant departure from those of the previous three monarchs. The madness of George III had ensured his long closeting away at Windsor. George IV had visited Dublin in 1821 and toured Scotland in 1822. Ill health and unpopularity, however, meant his last years were notable for a similar reclusiveness. Although George IV had been an enthusiastic supporter of art and architecture, his patronage was never

[72] 'England Meets France', *Lloyd's Weekly Newspaper*, 19 Aug. 1855, 1.
[73] Quoted in Peter Sinnema, *Dynamics of the Printed Page: Representing the Nation in the Illustrated London News* (Aldershot: Ashgate, 1998), 16.
[74] Lucy Brown, *Victorian News and Newspapers* (Oxford: Clarendon Press, 1985), 52.
[75] Quoted in Terry Eagleton, *The Idea of Culture* (Oxford: Blackwell, 2000), 80.

couched within the same framework of moral and civic progress as that of Victoria and Albert. Exhibiting more of a dilettante indulgence than a concern with industrialism and the manufacturing poor, projects such as the Brighton Pavilion seemed only to guarantee more courtly extravagance and debt. The Queen Caroline affair and the debacle of his coronation hardly encouraged the type of civic visits undertaken by Victoria. William IV did not plumb the same depths of unpopularity as George IV, but he ascended the throne in 1830 at the age of 65. His age and his involvement in the Reform Bill prevented the type of popular constitutionalism that became so significant in Victoria's reign.

Commentators in the 1840s frequently used Victoria's visits to substantiate the break between her sovereignty and that of her Hanoverian predecessors. Comparing the movements of Victoria with their seclusion, the *Illustrated London News* was typical in its approval of the new royal openness: 'the people of England had for many years been accustomed to look to their Sovereign as a fixture, which it would have been something astounding to have found out of its place, or moving out of its orbit, which was the rather circumscribed one, including Windsor, Buckingham Palace, St James, or now and then, Ascot.'[76] Instead of confining the court to a single location, Victoria was lauded for bringing its economic benefits, and sharing its attractiveness, with her subjects. In conjunction with the development of an illustrated and a popular press, Victoria and Albert inaugurated a new style of royalty. A young couple touring different areas of the nation without the trappings of pageantry, frequently accompanied by their infant family, their visits could be invested with a heady mixture of romantic sentiment, family propriety, royal patronage, and local civic pride. And, of course, it was all broadcast as a constant stream of royal news. As indeed it still is.

The Queen's first tour of Scotland, including visits to Perth, Stirling, Taymouth, and Edinburgh, took place in September 1842, the same year in which the *Illustrated London News* began publication. Much of the success of these first tours was due to their novelty. In September 1843, when it was announced that Victoria and Albert were to make an impending visit to Louis-Philippe, the reaction was one of surprise, bewilderment, and uneasiness. The *Illustrated London News*'s commentary on the startling nature of the announcement sums up the general response:

The speculations of the learned waxed many, and were mysteriously inquisitive mid the general amaze. Was it not contrary to the principle of the English constitution that Her Majesty should leave her dominions without the consent of parliament? And, on the other hand, was not her Parliament prorogued? Had she even applied for the

---

[76] 'Royal Visits', *ILN* 31 Aug. 1844, 128.

permission of Her Privy Council? Could she go? Rumours were afloat that the Duke of Wellington and others high in office had strongly, but respectfully, protested against the step.[77]

The last reigning sovereign to leave British shores had been George IV in 1821 on a coronation visit to Hanover, the British Crown then still being joined with that of the German state. The visit of Victoria and Albert to a traditional enemy was unprecedented, the first since Henry VIII met Francis I at the Field of the Cloth of Gold in 1520. Given that Victoria was meeting Louis-Philippe at Chateau D'Eu, his country retreat in Normandy, it was also a visit without any of the trappings of state. The *Illustrated London News* described it as an episode of royal adventure that assumed 'the friendly call on a neighbour whom she knows and respects'.[78] The tours were so successful because they were not ostensibly motivated by royal statecraft: they were pleasurable diversions from politics and not its source.

Despite the praise heaped upon her first engagements, it is important to emphasize that they did not simply emerge as fully fledged successes. Their novelty afflicted the participants as much as the spectators. Alex Tyrell and Yvonne Ward have noted that Victoria's first tours were characterized by numerous incidents where the royal couple exhibited a marked reluctance to fulfil the duties expected of them.[79] On their first visit to Edinburgh, the Queen's party arrived unexpectedly early. They passed quickly through the empty streets and went straight to their temporary residence at Dalkeith Castle. Many of the city's inhabitants were dismayed that their elaborate preparations had been so bypassed. Members of the Town Council went to see Robert Peel, who was travelling with the Queen's party, and a reluctant Victoria was persuaded to progress through the streets two days later. Similar incidents occurred on a marine tour around the south coast in 1843, when Victoria declined to receive addresses from various port towns.

The political pressure was very much upon the Crown to perform a worthwhile role. The making and the receiving of state visits, along with a plethora of minor civic engagements, consequently came to dominate the public activities of Victoria and Albert throughout the 1840s and 1850s. Given that their nine children were also born during this period, their domesticity combined with their diligence in a wholesome mixture to which the newspaper and periodical press gave fulsome attention. The couple established a precedent of royal duties, consisting of civic visits, military reviews, meetings, and benevolent charity work. They set a successful model for the duties of a British

---

[77] 'The Queen's Visit to France', *ILN* 2 Sept. 1843, 155.
[78] Ibid. 155.
[79] Alex Tyrell and Yvonne Ward, 'God Bless Her Little Majesty: The Popularity of Monarchy in the 1840s', *National Identities*, 2.2 (2000), 109–26.

constitutional monarch. Visits and engagements followed on from one another in quick succession. The latter half of 1844 was typical in that there was a second tour of the Scottish highlands in September, closely followed by the return visit of Louis-Philippe and the opening of the new Royal Exchange in October. November then saw an excursion to Burghley House and a tour of Northampton and the surrounding district.

In addition to the visits to and from Louis-Philippe, the first half of the 1840s saw visits from the Kings of Saxony, Belgium, Prussia, and the Czar of Russia, along with a visit to Saxe-Coburg by Victoria and Albert. A wryly amused *Punch* noted Victoria's propensity for visitations by publishing, in two separate articles, a list of the prospective marine excursions and distinguished visitors over the next five years.[80] Marine journeys were to include calling on St Petersburg, New York, and the South Pole, while projected visitors ranged from Mehmet Ali in 1847 to the Emperor of Lapland in 1852. A full-page engraving captures the packed schedule of Victoria and Albert and *Punch*'s breathless attempts to keep up with their movements (see Fig. 3). Produced upon Victoria and Albert's return from Saxe-Coburg in 1845, the engraving neatly combines their travels with their tender regard for the royal hearth.

One of the most notable features of the tours was the sheer labour that they involved. Each tour could last for a week or more, with an itinerary packed full of receptions, addresses, and dinners. The visit to the midlands in 1843 was typical in that it lasted for nine days and took in Nottingham, Derby, Chesterfield, Belvoir Castle, Lichfield Cathedral, Coventry, and Leicester. There was also an excursion to Birmingham for Prince Albert, which managed to cram in guided tours of six factories before moving on to visit the town hall and the Free Grammar School.[81] Significantly, the visit was one of the first occasions on which Victoria and Albert travelled by train. The number of subsequent tours, and the number of places they were able to visit on those tours, was, in part, a product of the railways' ability to transport the Queen with relative rapidity. Industrial precision allowed a carefully orchestrated series of receptions as Victoria would be briefly cheered at every station along the route.

Simply on her midlands train trip from Watford to Tamworth in 1843, Victoria passed through seven stations. And at each station the concourse was thronged. Crowds gathered near the railway line just to watch the royal train pass. At Weedon station the buildings were decorated with flags bearing inscriptions such as 'Victoria, England's Hope'. The national anthem was

---

[80] 'Victoria's Voyages for the Next Ten Years', *Punch*, 5 (1843), 128; 'The Queen's Illustrious Visitors', *Punch*, 7 (1844), 182.
[81] 'Visit of Prince Albert to Birmingham', *ILN* 2 Dec. 1843, 362.

"THERE'S NO PLACE LIKE HOME!"
OR, THE RETURN TO BUCKINGHAM PALACE.

Fig. 3. 'There's No Place Like Home', *Punch*, 9 (1845), 109

played as the train approached and, in the four minutes that it took for the engine to take on water, the soldiers lining the platform presented arms. There would be countless such four minutes in the years ahead. The concurrent development of the electronic telegraph meant that the Queen's arrival and departure at each location were transmitted back to London, where newspaper offices eagerly awaited the succession of royal bulletins. (It is apt that the first news story carried by telegraph was the birth of the Queen's second son, Prince Alfred, in August 1844.)[82] Victoria and Albert did more than place themselves on the side of progress through their patronage of manufacturing: they were the unconscious beneficiaries of its forces.

The visit to the midlands in 1843 is indicative of what was seen to be the Queen's willingness to patronize every part of the nation with her presence, honouring the industrial areas of Britain as well as the inhabitants of London and Windsor. Each tour of a manufacturing area was given a weighty political symbolism on top of the more pragmatic pleasures of a general holiday for many of the local inhabitants. The opening of the Royal Exchange in 1844 by Victoria and Albert was seen as one of their many acknowledgements of the power of commerce. Their tour of Lancashire in late 1851 accorded the same respect to northern industrialism. The tour of Lancashire, which took in Salford, Liverpool, Carlisle, and Manchester, shows that these visits were enormous occasions for those cities so graced. Manchester had only been incorporated in 1838 and would be made a city in 1852. Being honoured by a royal visit was an important episode in these cities' sense of their own status and development. When Victoria opened Leeds Town Hall in 1858, the corporation wore civic robes for the first time in their history.[83]

The scale of preparations attendant upon a royal visit is indicative of the importance with which they were regarded. Banners, grandstands, triumphal arches, and illuminations were the staple components of any royal visit. In a crucial shift of emphasis, local committees and dignitaries provided the pageantry on these occasions rather than the court. In 1851, Manchester spent between £100,000 and £150,000 on its entertainment for the Queen.[84] The Queen had visited Liverpool only a few days previously and, with the local rivalry between the two cities, Manchester was determined to outdo the greeting that Liverpool had given to the Queen. One member of the Manchester Corporation allegedly declared that for each thousand pounds spent by Liverpool they would spend ten.[85] Many local mayors were knighted for their loyal efforts on these occasions, a fact that must have encouraged the enthusiasm of the local corporation. A brief survey of Manchester's decorations testifies to the effort and time involved. The four miles of the Queen's route through Manchester were decorated with banners, transparencies, wreaths, and emblematic devices. Numerous triumphal arches were built, the largest of which was 60 ft high, while the arch in St Anne's Square was decorated with 4,000 variegated oil lamps. Viewing platforms were constructed on

[82] Donald Read, *The Power of News: The History of Reuters 1849–1989* (Oxford: Oxford University Press, 1992), 7.

[83] See Williams, *Contentious Crown*, 97.

[84] 'Great Reception of Her Majesty at Manchester', *ILN* 18 Oct. 1851, 478.

[85] Ibid. 478.

the line of the route, each of which could hold several hundred people. Many of the streets through which Victoria would pass were also repainted and repaved. As a final touch, Manchester's reception included the gathering together of 80,000 local Sunday school scholars in Peel Park to sing the national anthem to Victoria.[86] Civic pride replaced aristocratic ceremony in the consolidation of a mode of royal publicness that was clearly emerging out of the disputes around Victoria's coronation and marriage.

The impact of Victoria and Albert's civic publicness is particularly evident in the way their visits helped to forge a local consensus around the Crown. The provincial press's coverage of Victoria's visits to their own locality emphasizes the iterative nature of royal populism. On Victoria and Albert's aforementioned visit to Birmingham in 1843, the *Birmingham Journal* declared that their presence would 'hardly fail to operate favourably on the somewhat conflicting materials that have, for a long time, constituted that capital's population'.[87] Radical, Tory, and Whig came together to organize the welcome to the Prince. Similarly, when Victoria and Albert visited Birmingham again in June 1858, this time to open Aston Park, the *Birmingham Daily Post* took great pride in declaring that 'The most democratic town in England must also be the most orderly in its loyalty'.[88] The very contrariness of the comment is telling. Birmingham's consciousness of its own civic pride meant that it went out of its way to prove its loyalty. In a situation that is akin to the Chartist demonstrations of their enlightened loyalty at Victoria's coronation, Birmingham's fêting of Victoria confirmed not its deference but the dignity of its democratic civic identity.

The various local prints and newspapers produced to commemorate a royal visit were never simply representations of the event. They were part of the communicative encounter between the monarchy and the press that helped to shape the nature of the monarchy itself. In the days before Victoria's visits in 1858, the *Birmingham Daily Post* was full of adverts for commemorative sonnets and lithographic prints of Aston Hall. There was even a satire, *The Great Avatar*, providing anecdotes of the local dignitaries and promising to be 'incomparably more entertaining than any newspaper details can possibly be'.[89] As well as giving fulsome coverage to the event itself, the *Birmingham Daily Post* produced an extra commemorative edition in order to meet the enormous demand for an account of the occasion. Although the print-run of the commemorative edition was double the normal run of the newspaper, all copies were sold by four o'clock on the day of publication. The narrative con-

---

[86] 'Preparations in Salford', *Manchester Guardian*, 11 Oct. 1851, 5.
[87] 'Saturday, December 2', *Birmingham Journal*, 2 Dec. 1843, 4.
[88] 'The Royal Visit', *Birmingham Daily Post*, 11 June 1858, 2.
[89] 'The Great Avatar', *Birmingham Daily Post*, 10 June 1858, 2.

sequently had to be inserted in its evening journal.[90] With a national press not yet in existence, the prominence of the provincial press was vital for perpetuating the narrative of royal populism. Tellingly, the only point of dissent around the opening of Aston Hall was a protest by members of the council against their being coerced into wearing ceremonial robes.[91] Feelings were strong enough for a petition to be presented to the Mayor, signed by thirty-six Alderman and Councillors. The reluctance to adopt any form of pomp and circumstance emphasizes the continuing importance of the style in which Victoria and Albert made their visits. The more the barriers of aristocratic ceremony were perceived to have been removed, the greater the ostensible transparency of the relationship between Victoria and the People.

One particularly revealing example of the social compact symbolized by these civic engagements is a speech made by Prince Albert at his inauguration of the Grimsby Docks in April 1849. Congratulating the great spirit of English commercial enterprise for undertaking the project, Albert noted that it also shared another prominent national trait:

that other feature so peculiar to the enterprise of Englishmen, that strongly attached as they were to the institutions of the country, gratefully acknowledging the protection of those laws under which those enterprises commenced and prospered, they loved to connect them in some manner with the authority of the Crown and the person of the Sovereign, and it is the appreciation of this circumstance which has impelled me to respond to your call, as the readiest mode of testifying to you how strongly her Majesty the Queen values and reciprocates this feeling.[92]

The desire to bask in a warm royal glow meant that Victoria and Albert entered a mutually beneficial compact with the achievements of industrialism, and with the men who ran it. Their presence acknowledged the economic and social power of manufacturing, while the still expanding industrial cities reciprocated the compliment by deferentially acknowledging the continued centrality of the monarchy. Each performed a symbolic touching of the forelock.

The particular importance of municipal pride in this period meant that Victoria's visits were far from being frivolously decorative. They were constitutive of Victoria and Albert's role. In terms that prefigure those of Bagehot in the *English Constitution*, *The Times* saw Albert's opening of the Royal Exchange in 1844 as an essential part of the post-Reform Bill political landscape: 'These great occasions are not far from being an integral part of our

---

[90] 'To Our Readers', *Birmingham Daily Post*, 14 June 1858, 2.
[91] 'The Royal Visit', *Birmingham Daily Post*, 11 June 1858, 2.
[92] Prince Albert, *Addresses delivered on Different Public Occasions by HRH Prince Albert* (London: Society of Arts, 1857), 27.

constitution. To the middle-classes, who may now almost be considered the ruling class of England, it has become nearly a right . . . that the great men of the country should pay them the compliment—we might say the homage—of appearing periodically.'[93] *The Times* is typical of the way in which these royal events were signified as a new position for the Crown, an *entente cordial* between the monarchy and the middle class. Moreover, as *The Times* unconsciously expresses, thanks to the newspapers and journals, the monarchy did indeed appear periodically (*sic*). Albert's involvement with the Great Exhibition and Victoria's opening of the event was only the crowning glory of a constitutional role that encompassed a multitude of dinners, reviews, and meetings. Ranging from enormous set-piece occasions to the briefest passing through of the royal train and the receiving of yet another platitudinous address from local dignitaries, the dutiful labour of Victoria and Albert was being never-endingly displayed for all to see.

Albert had been a frequent butt of satire in the first half of the 1840s and the role that he carved out for himself is consequently particularly important. Albert's position as Consort was fraught with difficulties. Ridiculed for being purely decorative, he nevertheless risked even more severe criticism if he was perceived to be interfering in state affairs. Yet, by 1843, even the *Penny Satirist* was arguing that he should take on a more fulfilling public role. In a mock conversation between Victoria and Albert, she harangues him for not making any speeches or attending any dinners, 'you should accomplish or perpetrate something great—somehow or other, and that shortly. I insist upon it, Albert—I shall have nothing to do with you if you don't—mind that.'[94] Over the next decade, he would more than fulfil this injunction, especially through his interest in arts and manufacturing. The Great Exhibition, for example, included amongst its attractions two model homes designed by Prince Albert, which were intended to promote better working-class housing. An approving poem in *Punch* from 1853—a journal that was far from kindly to Albert in his early years—exemplifies his devotion to his duties and the journal's acceptance of the role that he had created for himself:

> Foundation stone past calculation,
> Workmanlike, you have laid, true and square,
> And a curiously dinner-rid nation
> Has still found you a saint in the chair.[95]

A well-known cartoon by John Leech from 1847 similarly plays upon Albert's undertaking of a bewildering number of official roles and appointments (see

---

[93] Quoted in Williams, *Contentious Crown*, 196.
[94] 'Court Circular', *Penny Satirist*, 15 July 1843, 1.
[95] 'Prince *Punch* to Prince Albert', *Punch*, 25 (1853), 216.

PRINCE ALBERT "AT HOME."
WHEN HE WILL SUSTAIN (NO END OF) DIFFERENT CHARACTERS.

Fig. 4.　John Leech, 'Prince Albert At Home', *Punch*, 12 (1847), 118

Fig. 4). Albert is presented in his robes as Chancellor of Cambridge University, surrounded by his other guises as Field Marshall, huntsman, Colonel of the Hussars, and in the medieval and eighteenth-century dress associated with Victoria's costume balls. *Punch*'s cartoon satires the lack of any coherent sense of Albert's appropriate role. As Chris Brooks has argued, this cartoon is an 'ironic antithesis of formal portraiture's attempt to fix an authentic image of the Consort: instead of defining identity, Leech dissipates it.'[96] The cartoon can also be read as a reflexive critique of Albert's media profile. The solidification of an acceptable public role for Albert was inseparable from the creation of a stable representation.

Like Leech's cartoon of Albert, the establishment of Victoria's tours and visits as an accepted norm saw the conventions of royal populism become increasingly fixed. If the coronation was noteworthy in its concern for the People, then the royal visits were that ideology writ large, at least according to the majority of the metropolitan and provincial press. Only the opening of

[96] Chris Brooks, 'Representing Albert', in Chris Brooks (ed.), *The Albert Memorial* (New Haven: Yale University Press, 2000), 41.

parliament and the occasional court levee punctuated the predominantly civic focus of the monarchy. The seeming lack of any militaristic or aristo-cratic ceremony also remained crucial to the interpretations that could be imposed upon the tours and visits. They were publicness without the pageantry. As the *Pictorial Times* declared: 'Victoria and her military escort is far less acceptable than Victoria "enthroned in the hearts of her people". The former is undoubtedly gay and alluring, but the latter is sublime: the former typifies the monarch's apprehension; the latter is the symbol of her confi-dence.'[97] No *ancien régime* here. Such rhetoric is exemplary of the constitu-tional semantic that was invested in Victoria's public role because of the fashion in which her visits were carried out.

Engravings of royal events reinforce the ideological stress upon royal populism. Prints and graphic reportage deployed the same inclusiveness as the written journalism of most newspapers. In the illustrated press there were innumerable depictions of Victoria and Albert either passing through triumphal arches in their carriage, arriving by the royal train, or stepping off the royal yacht, invariably surrounded by loyal and cheering crowds (see Fig. 5). This was popular constitutionalism at its strongest: the position of Victoria and Albert validated not by ceremony but by the approval of their subjects. When Victoria and Albert visited Louis Napoleon in 1855, the *Illustrated London News* contrasted the informality with which they were greeted in Britain to the grand ceremonial reception that they would receive in Paris:

The French love shows, are accustomed to and excel in them . . . The whole aspect of the streets and public buildings offers itself to aid and impress the efforts of the Government when it desires to impress the imagination of the spectators. In London the spectators are themselves the show . . . Nothing but the presence of good-humoured, orderly, and rejoicing multitudes, can impart a ray of grandeur to them [the London streets]; and these, it must be said, are never wanting at the call of Loyalty or Duty.[98]

The mob versus the loyal People, despotic state pageantry versus consensual civic pride, the foreignness of spectacle versus English constitutional liberty, these were the series of ideological binaries that were endlessly deployed in articles and illustrations.

An engraving from the *Illustrated London News* of the Queen's visit to Birmingham in 1858 is typical of the standpoint adopted by the illustrated press (see Fig. 6). The royal couple are small figures. They are recognizable only by Victoria's bonnet and parasol, and by Albert lifting his top hat to the crowd. This was a visual grammar repeated so often that it became icono-

---

[97] 'Her Majesty's Visit to Scotland', *Pictorial Times*, 21 Aug. 1847, 113.
[98] 'Her Majesty's Visit to Paris', *ILN* 4 Aug. 1855, 130.

Fig. 5. 'Queen Victoria on a Visit to Leeds', *Illustrated London News*, 26 September 1858, 291

Fig. 6. 'Queen Victoria's Visit to Birmingham, 1858', *Illustrated London News*, 3 July 1858, 1

Fig. 7. 'Queen Victoria's Visit to Liverpool', *Illustrated London News*, 18 October 1851, 489

graphic. The magnificence of the arch is in marked contrast to the unostentatious appearance of Victoria and Albert themselves. Their spartan coach, accompanied by only a small contingent of riders, is similarly set against the backdrop of the packed grandstands. Victoria and Albert are not the spectacle here: the spectacle is of popular constitutionalism and a public political sphere in which royalty is legitimated. Two exemplary engravings, the first of Victoria's visit to Liverpool in 1851, the second of the Prince of Wales's passage through London with his bride-to-be, replicate the same visual rhetoric. In Fig. 7, Victoria and Albert are no more than minuscule figures on the balcony of Liverpool exchange. What the engraving actually displays is the populist support for the Crown: the thousands of people huddled together in the pouring rain emphasize both the appeal of Victoria and the ordered loyalty inspired by the Crown. In Fig. 8, the coach of Edward and Alexandra occupies a similarly insignificant position as they progress their way through London. And, perhaps disturbingly, it is possible to read these two engravings as symbolizing the extent to which these occasions went far beyond being about Victoria and Albert, Edward and Alexandra. In both engravings, the royal couple have been very literally effaced. The more engravings and journalism sought to make Victoria a representative figurehead, to promote her as a national focal point, the more she herself tended to disappear personally

Fig. 8. 'The Reception of Princess Alexandra in St Paul's Churchyard', *Illustrated London News*, 28 March 1863, 280

under the weight of that very investment. These engravings dramatize the dialectic between the power and powerlessness of the royal family, a tension that is at the heart of the monarchy's media making.

At the same time as such engravings were being repeated endlessly, the monarchies of continental Europe were being overthrown in the revolutionary year of 1848. Beginning with the overthrow of Louis-Philippe in February, revolution eventually engulfed a large part of Europe. These events filled the pages, week after week, of the newspaper and periodical press. The contrast between the fate of the European monarchies and the reception of Victoria could not have been more acute. Barricades, chaos, and insurrection as opposed to banners, cheers, and illuminations: the benefits of a constitutional monarchy could not have been thrown into greater relief. It was a lesson to which the *Illustrated London News* for one was keen to draw attention. At Victoria's opening of the Great Exhibition it pointedly declared that such a scene could not have been possible in any other capital in Europe.[99] In its graphic and written accounts of royal news, the established metropolitan press, through its own dominant market position and social prestige, effectively imposed a consensus on the nature of royal representation.

By the late 1850s the novelty of the first royal tours had faded and civic engagements had become very much the accustomed duties of the Sovereign and her Consort. Foundation stones continued to be laid with monotonous regularity and patronage continued to be given to the arts and manufacturing. Notable events of these years—amidst a plethora of minor engagements—include the couple's visit to Napoleon III and Empress Eugenie in August 1855, Albert's opening of the Manchester Art Treasures Exhibition in 1857, and the marriage of the Princess Royal in January 1858. These events continued to comprise the staple royal coverage of the press. As the *Illustrated Times* tellingly commented in 1859, the actions of Victoria ranked among the lighter topics of the country because 'so little does the action of the Court obtrude itself on the nation, that we scarcely hear of her Majesty except when she is bestowing some honour or assisting in some work of charity'.[100] Royalty was now defined increasingly by its 'public' engagements rather than its involvement in high politics. Or, rather, the type of coverage that the monarchy was receiving from the majority of newspapers and periodicals helped to downplay Victoria's continued badgering of her ministers. Radical criticism did continue to emphasize the political influence of Victoria and, far more ferociously, of the Germanic Albert. Yet only a volatile furore during the bullish nationalism of the Crimean War, when Albert was accused of meddling in state affairs and of pro-Russian intriguing, threatened seriously to mar the stable industry of the royal family. The monarch's public duties were established by the late 1850s and, in so doing, precedents were set for the activities of future members of the British royal family.

A sign of the success of royal populism is that it constituted a standard upon which the work of the monarchy could be judged. The extent to which the desirability of interaction between Victoria and her subjects fed back into the organization of royal events, rather than being interpreted out of them, is evident in the principal complaints over the marriages of the Princess Royal

---

[99] 'The Queen's Visit to the City', *ILN* 12 July 1851, 160–1.
[100] 'Marriage of the Princess Royal', *Illustrated Times*, 23 Jan. 1858, 73.

and the Prince of Wales. The weddings took place in January 1858 and March 1863 respectively. Both caused a concerted grumbling over their failure to cater suitably for the thousands of people who wished to participate in the occasion. The dissent they aroused is similar to the friction around Victoria's very first visits and her reluctance to fulfil the role demanded of her. In January 1858, the *Daily Telegraph* complained of the 'growing system of reserving the exclusive enjoyment of State ceremonials and spectacles for particular classes'.[101] Even *Reynolds's Newspaper* agreed that there was some validity in *The Times*'s argument that the marriage of the Princess Royal would be worth the expense if Londoners were given a decent glimpse of the couple.[102]

The organization of the Prince of Wales's wedding provoked similar attacks from newspapers associated with a broad social range of readers and party political support. The *Daily Telegraph*, *Punch*, *Morning Advertiser*, *Morning Chronicle*, *News of the World*, and the *Illustrated London News* all protested against the fact that the marriage was going to be held in the seclusion of St George's Chapel, Windsor, rather than in Westminster Abbey.[103] The reason given for the restricted arrangements regarding the Prince of Wales's wedding was that the Queen was still too grief-stricken to cope with any form of procession through London. With even normally supportive newspapers like the *Illustrated London News* being scathing towards the high-handedness of the court officials, the monarchy found itself subject to a discourse it had helped to create. The manifold complaints around the two weddings should not be seen as a crude desire for more grandiose ceremony. Rather, they are part of a trajectory that stretches back to at least the coronation, for a more open monarchy. The wedding arrangements of the Prince of Wales were actually changed in response to a protest from the Corporation of London.

Initially, the journey of the Prince of Wales and Princess Alexandra through London on their way to Windsor, after the arrival of the latter from her native Denmark, was not to be attended with any ceremony. It was to be a pared down cortege of six carriages with the most meagre of military escorts. Only after the City of London authorities complained were the arrangements changed. On 5 February there was an announcement from Windsor that Princess Alexandra would arrive at Bricklayer's Arms station on 7 March. She would then proceed through the City on her way to Paddington via London Bridge, Trafalgar Square, and Hyde Park. Grandstands erected in St Paul's churchyard were alone to accommodate 10,000 people. The *Spectator* tri-

---

[101] 'London, Tuesday, January 26', *Daily Telegraph*, 26 Jan. 1858, 3.
[102] 'Gossip of the Week', *Reynolds's Newspaper*, 3 Jan. 1858, 4.
[103] 'The Politician', *News of the World*, 8 Mar. 1863, 1; 'The Royal Marriage', *ILN* 23 Jan. 1858, 73–4.

umphantly commented that the arrangements had 'at last been brought within the rules of royal etiquette—rules as binding upon the dynasty as upon the people'.[104] Royal populism may have worked to uphold the Crown but its political support was by no means unconditional. Submission to its momentum was the necessary cost of placing such an ideological charge on the free involvement of the People. As it was, the crowds greeting the Prince and Princess were so large that their carriages could barely make their way through the London throng, despite the zealous and often violent efforts of the police to ensure their passage. On the evening of 10 March, when London was illuminated following the wedding at Windsor, poor management of the celebrations meant six people died and many more were injured because of overcrowding in the streets.

The late 1850s saw the focus of attention moving away from Victoria and Albert in favour of their sons and daughters. Only so many triumphal arches could be engraved and only so many loyal addresses could be depicted before some of the gloss began to wear off. Significantly, however, when the Prince of Wales and the Princess Royal came of age the roles they adopted followed the precedents set by their parents. The first public engagement of the Prince of Wales was the laying of the foundation stone for a school of art at Vauxhall in June 1860. The birth of the Princess Royal's first son, and the Queen's first grandson, in March 1859; the enrolment of Prince Alfred as a midshipman in the Royal Navy and his first foreign voyage in November 1858; the tour of the Prince of Wales to Canada and North America in 1860; these were all episodes that continued the industrious, moral, and high-profile existence of the royal family. A *Punch* cartoon of the Prince of Wales's American tour exemplifies the appeal of youth. Edward is the brash young traveller, full of new habits, while Albert is the staid parent. With the growing dissent in the 1860s over Victoria's continued seclusion, Disraeli and Gladstone both emphasized the importance of monarchy continuing to have a public face. Upon several occasions in 1871 and 1872, Gladstone broached with Victoria the suggestion that the Prince of Wales could be made Viceroy of Ireland. His aim was to strengthen the throne through 'a new means of putting forward the Royal Family in the visible discharge of public duty. The desirableness & necessity of any plan likely to have this effect the Queen readily admitted.'[105] Victoria did not approve of Gladstone's specific plan, and it was eventually shelved. Ministerial promotion of an active monarchy, often against the stubborn refusal of Victoria and her unwillingness to let the Prince of Wales act for

---

[104] 'Topics of the Week. English Loyalty', *Spectator*, 14 Mar. 1863, 1712.
[105] BM Gladstone Papers Add. MS 44760/76.

her, exemplify the perceived importance of civic publicness. For ministers and newspapers alike, it had very much become the expected part of the role of the British royal family.

If, as relentless royal coverage seemed to prove, the activities of Victoria and Albert were invariably highly successful, what happened to radical critiques of the monarchy? There continued to be criticism of the mummery of pageantry, the cost of the court, and the Germanic influence of Prince Albert. *Punch*, for example, frequently deployed its satire against such mock dignitaries as Basting-Spoon-in-Waiting. In the early 1840s, there was also a brief continuation of the type of satire employed around Victoria's wedding. The idealization of her domesticity was turned against her as she continued to expand her public role beyond state occasions like the opening of parliament. A verse satire on the Queen's visit to Scotland attacked Victoria's abrogation of her maternal duties in leaving her children behind:

> Why does Victoria 'Lady of the Isles',
> Forsake her palace, and her children's smiles?
> (Those smiles that lowborn mothers ever prize;
> But far less dear in regal eyes.)[106]

A second satire on the birth of the Princess Royal in September 1840 makes it clear that this was a mode of criticism that sought to align Victoria with the long-standing trope of an unfeeling and dissolute aristocracy:

> Nor need our loyal bosoms feel alarm'd
> Lest by maternal cares out Queen be harm'd:
> Her constitution will be none the worse:
> Queen's suckle not—they leave it to their nurse!
> In common life, upon the mother's breast,
> The cherish'd babe finds nourishment and rest.[107]

During this period breast-feeding became one of the validating acts of a nurturing bourgeois femininity.[108] Nevertheless, despite the exploitation of Victoria's employment of a wet nurse, critiques of this sort were neutralized by the wholesome propriety of palace life. In journals like *Punch* and the *Penny Satirist*, Victoria's involvement with her ministers was reduced to a similar set of unthreatening household motifs. Cartoons like 'The New Servants', published in *Punch* upon the exit of the Earl of Derby's government in 1853, cast Victoria as the mistress of the house and the politicians as her servants.[109]

---

[106] HonBle ****, *The Queen's Voyage; or, the Follies of Scotland* (London: W. Gilling, 1842), 6.

[107] Hon. ****, *The Princess Royal; A Satire* (London: J. W. Southgate, 1841), 12.

[108] Sally Shuttleworth, 'Demonic Mothers: Ideologies of Bourgeois Motherhood in the Mid-Victorian Era', in Linda Shires (ed.), *Rewriting the Victorians* (London: Routledge, 1992), 31–51.

[109] 'The New Servants', *Punch*, 25 (1853), 5.

In attacking a morally dissipated, pampered, and financially self-serving monarchy, radicals employed a mode of critique that relied heavily on the enduring potency of Old Corruption. Similar attacks, especially against the more minor members of the British royal family, were to continue for the rest of the century. This period also saw the coming to prominence of critiques that focused on the relationship between Victoria and the press. The most prominent radical newspapers, the *Northern Star* and *Reynolds's Newspaper*, were heavily caught up in the new style of royalty inaugurated around Victoria's public activities. The *Northern Star*'s editorial upon Victoria's visit to Nottingham during her tour of the midlands in 1843 epitomizes the way in which the tropes of royal populism were simultaneously appropriated and assimilated:

The men will show their wives and children upon the auspicious occasion; and we have to request that her Majesty's managers will pray that her Majesty may be graciously pleased to put down the glass of the Royal carriage when passing the Town Common-side in order that her Majesty may see and judge the real condition of her loyal and loving subjects, who trust that they will be blessed and gratified with something more than a view of the blind that shuts out poverty from Royal Inspection . . . while she travels at our expense, we require to see and be seen. To see, in order that we may have the worth of our money—and to be seen in order that her Majesty may know from whence her Exchequer is filled.[110]

For the *Northern Star*, the working men should show no disrespect to Victoria, but, equally, they should make their hardship known. What is so fascinating about the editorial is that instead of the usual play upon Victoria showing herself transparently to her subjects, the *Northern Star* conceives of the visit as an opportunity for her loyal subjects to show their true condition to her. In a highly gendered process, the working men are to turn their wives and children into their own display. At one level, the *Northern Star*'s editorial illustrates that the stress upon the People could be appropriated into a very different type of collectivity. Equally though, the *Northern Star* is here akin to most metropolitan and provincial newspapers in that the focus of the royal tours did not rest with Victoria. The *Northern Star*'s belief in the process of seeing and being seen, both in Victoria seeing her subjects and being made to show herself, exemplifies the way in which the royal tours helped to mitigate criticism.

While the *Northern Star* was never a republican journal, the newspaper with the most consistently vociferous republican standpoint, *Reynolds's Newspaper*, devoted much of its energy to a struggle against what it cast as royal populism. It is not my intention in this book to examine

---

[110] 'The Queen at Nottingham', *Northern Star*, 3 Dec. 1843, 4.

nineteenth-century republicanism in detail. My concern is rather with the way in which anti-monarchism responded to, negotiated with, and was compromised by, the media making of Victoria. Nowhere is this condition more apparent than in the pages of *Reynolds's Newspaper*. *Reynolds's Newspaper* began publication in May 1850 at an initial price of 4*d*., a development from *Reynolds's Political Instructor*, which had started in November 1849. Its editor, George Reynolds, was already the author of the hugely successful series of cheap fiction, *The Mysteries of London* (1844–8) and *The Mysteries of the Court of London* (1848–56). He was also the instigator of *Reynolds's Miscellany* (1846–69). Along with the penny dreadfuls of Edward Lloyd, Reynolds was one of the major beneficiaries of the burgeoning popular print culture of the 1840s. Well known for his attacks upon the monarchy and the aristocracy in his fiction, Reynolds was also involved in the Chartist agitation of 1848, speaking on several mass platforms. His uniquely hybrid involvement in politics and popular publishing gave an added dimension to *Reynolds's Newspaper*'s attacks upon the monarchy. Through the sophisticated and ongoing attention it gave to Victoria's relationship with the press, *Reynolds's Newspaper* marks an evolution in critiques of the monarchy.

With *Lloyd's Newspaper*, the *News of the World*, and the *Weekly Times*, *Reynolds's Newspaper* was one of the four principal Sunday newspapers situated at the working-class end of the market. It emerged following the decline of Chartism and its attacks upon the royal family demonstrate both the shifts and the continuities within nineteenth-century anti-monarchism, its large circulation making it by far the most important anti-royalist publication. After the reduction in Stamp Duty, the price of *Reynolds's Newspaper* fell to 2*d*. in 1856, and it was selling at 1*d*. by 1865. Its circulation was approximately 100,000 in 1855, rising to 300,000 in 1865. The very extensiveness of *Reynolds's Newspaper* was a significant challenge to the royal populism promoted by the metropolitan daily press.

For *Reynolds's Newspaper*, scandal and sleaze were the preferred means of demonstrating the degenerate nature of the royal family. As such, critics have noted the continuities between *Reynolds's Newspaper* and scurrilous publications like the *Satirist*.[111] Much of its scorn, however, was also directed against the flunkeydom of the metropolitan press and the constitutional semantic they ascribed to the Queen's activities. In a typically vigorous protest against the coverage of the Queen's visit to Lancashire, *Reynolds's Newspaper* declared that it was absurd and false for newspapers to put forth that 'because Englishmen neither insult their Queen nor necessitate her travelling with

---

[111]   Rohan McWilliam, 'The Mysteries of G. W. M. Reynolds: Radicalism and Melodrama in Victorian Britain', in *Living and Learning: Essays in Honour of J. F. C. Harrison* (London: Scolar Press, 1996), 182–98.

regiments of cavalry to protect her, they are happy, prosperous, and contented under those much vaunted "constitutional institutions", so oppressive to the majority of the people'.[112] Most of the small republican journals of the late 1840s, like George Julian Harney's *Red Republican* and W. J. Linton's *English Republic*, looked to continental influences, particularly Mazzini, for their inspiration. It was principally *Reynolds's Newspaper* that directly engaged with the royalist support for Victoria.

Despite the artisan readership of *Reynolds's Newspaper*, it often attacked the deferential behaviour of the working class at large royal occasions. Royal populism had its counterpart in radicalism's frustration at the naivety of John Bull. *Reynolds's Newspaper's* disgusted commentary on the enthusiasm for the marriage of the Princess Royal emphasizes the difficulties faced by anti-monarchism in attempting to undermine support for Victoria:

there cannot be the least doubt that it is in the slime of idolatry which clothes and saturates the souls of the lower orders, those brilliant but poisonous and stinging reptiles, royalty and aristocracy, are generated. Nothing is truer, than there would be no tyrants, if there were no slaves—no obscene and cruel gods, if there were not beastly and idiotic worshippers. If the poor people who flock like sheep to do homage to their oppressors, upon the occasion of the birth, burial, or marriage, of a scion of royalty, knew the use to which their presence is perverted—the argument drawn from their shouts and grimaces—they would surely keep away. If the poor, hard working people of London, for instance, knew that their presence in such crowds along the line of the royal wedding procession, would be twisted into an expression of their indifference to reform, and of their approbation of Court robbery and extravagance, it is not surely too much to assume that they would have stayed at home . . . where no such political construction could be put on their presence.[113]

Reynolds's Newspaper challenges the overdetermined consensus founded on the seeming support of the People. Its approach betrays the difficulties for republicanism in the face of an exuberantly and broadly supported monarchy. In order to argue that these events were top-down impositions of an official culture, *Reynolds's Newspaper* has to deny working-class agency by claiming that the crowd's presence is mediated beyond its genuine wishes. The assertion is similar to that made by the letter from the Manchester Trades Council at the coronation in that their royalism is seen as a product of the newspaper press imposing an interpretation upon the event.

Against the adulatory reports provided by the majority of the newspapers, *Reynolds's Newspaper* provided its own narrative of royal occasions. In the previous decade, the *Northern Star* had frequently proffered its own

---

[112] 'The Public Press and the Queen's Progress', *Reynolds's Newspaper*, 12 Oct. 1851, 8.
[113] 'The Royal Wedding and the Working Classes', *Reynolds's Newspaper*, 31 Jan. 1858, 1.

interpretations of royal events. When Victoria visited Louis-Philippe, for example, the *Northern Star* discussed at length the political impetus behind the visit. It proudly declared that 'we struck our own course, while our contemporaries were luxuriating in large importations of "Cheshire cheese and bottled stout" for the entertainment of Britain's monarch'.[114] Much was made of the fact that Louis-Philippe had imported Cheshire cheese and bottled stout for Victoria's delectation, and the *Northern Star* is bemoaning the apolitical triviality of such narratives. The size and the success of *Reynolds's Newspaper* meant that it was able to extend the approach set by the *Northern Star*. It offered not just political commentaries upon Victoria's visits but used its own correspondents. On Victoria's visit to Napoleon III, its special correspondent gleefully drew attention to the lack of enthusiasm shown by the French crowds and their derogatory comments upon Albert's baldness and excessive paunch.[115] Whereas periodicals like the *Illustrated London News* sought to place Victoria at the heart of the imagined community of the nation by imagining her place in the hearts of the nation, *Reynolds's Newspaper* sought to factionalize and undermine her appeal.

The principal mode of criticism adopted by *Reynolds's Newspaper* foreshadows the royal role promoted by Bagehot. Again and again, it denounced the way in which the activities of Victoria dominate the public sphere. Attacks on sinecures and political interference were increasingly joined by a sustained critique of the diverting role of the Queen's public figuring. Here, we can see the emergence of the notion of monarchy as harmless entertainment. *Reynolds's Newspaper* attempts to engage with the triviality, the very lightness of Victoria's tours and visits. Whereas the *Northern Star* saw Victoria as a significant part of the political structure, *Reynolds's Newspaper* attacked the imaginative appeal that stemmed from her cultural prominence. This crucial shift took place because the latter often did not regard Victoria as powerful in herself. Monarchy was increasingly seen as a cipher disguising the operations of finance and commerce. Victoria functioned as nothing more than 'a gilded puppet, the passive tool of a rapacious oligarchy'.[116] Thus, *Reynolds's Newspaper* construed her visit to Napoleon III as both another episode of expensive court indulgence and a government-inspired attempt to divert attention from the reverses being suffered in the Crimea. An editorial claimed that it was with 'such ridiculous and insulting spectacles that they would fill the thoughts of the plundered classes of the two nations'.[117] Even more insidiously, a regular columnist who wrote under the name of Northumbrian claimed that

[114] 'The Congress of Monarchs', *Northern Star*, 16 Sept. 1843, 4.
[115] 'From our own Correspondent', *Reynolds's Newspaper*, 26 Aug. 1855, 4.
[116] 'Jenkins in Paris—Victoria's Visit to Louis-Napoleon', *Reynolds's Newspaper*, 26 Aug. 1855, 9.
[117] Ibid. 9.

Fig. 9. 'Queen Victoria Inspecting the Wounded at Buckingham Palace', *Illustrated London News*, 10 March 1855, 237

the visits of the Queen to the soldiers wounded in the Crimea had the nefarious effect of reconciling them to the degrading treatment and mismanagement they had suffered.[118] A brief examination of the differing interpretations of this one event exemplifies the way in which *Reynolds's Newspaper* challenged the deferential coverage of the monarchy.

Military reviews formed an important strand of Victoria's duties. Much was made of Victoria's personal concern for her troops at the time of the Crimean War and Indian Mutiny. When the casualties from the Crimea began to be shipped home, Victoria visited the military hospital at Chatham where the soldiers were being nursed. There was also an inspection at Buckingham Palace where Victoria distributed medals to the wounded and disabled (see Fig. 9). As the *Illustrated London News*'s engraving demonstrates, these were scenes charged with sentiment. Here was a compassionate and patriotic Queen, her feminine sympathy aroused by the heroism of her soldiers, all of whom were inspected while wearing the same uniforms in which they were injured. Not the formality of an official review for these men; they were accorded a personal audience in the grand hall of Buckingham Palace. *Lloyd's Weekly Newspaper*,

[118] Northumbrian, 'Soldiers and Civilians', *Reynolds's Newspaper*, 2 Sept. 1855, 7. See also Gracchus, 'Imperial Knaves and Royal Puppets', *Reynolds's Newspaper*, 2 Sept. 1855, 7.

then edited by Douglas Jerrold, described the ceremony distributing the medals as 'none so simply beautiful, so direct in the appeal to the heart'.[119] Conversely, in *Reynolds's Newspaper*, Northumbrian claimed that the demands for justice on behalf of the mismanaged soldiers had been 'swallowed in torrents of flunkey adulation, which has been evoked by what has been termed the kindness and condescension of the Queen in visiting the sick and wounded'.[120] The weight of supportive coverage given to Victoria meant that *Reynolds's Newspaper* recycled long-standing concerns about the politically corrupt nature of the press. There is a problem, however, with applying the language of Old Corruption on to a publishing industry driven by the commercial impetus of a popular readership. The power of Victoria's figure stemmed from the fact that it was not orchestrated by official political culture, and was rather the product of different groups projecting meaning on to the Queen.

Despite the anti-royalism of *Reynolds's Newspaper*, its specific attitude towards Victoria often betrays the same melodramatic melange as the street ballads commemorating her accession. Scathing towards the court and Prince Albert, only rarely does Victoria come in for any vitriolic personal criticism before 1861. This melodramatic separation between the feminine person of Victoria and the institution of monarchy is a key factor in understanding the scope and limits of anti-monarchism. In my view, it is also one of the reasons why *Reynolds's Newspaper* achieved such a large circulation while promoting a republican standpoint. Whether recruiting Victoria's feminine sympathy for a cause, or condemning one of her actions, the Queen portrayed by *Reynolds's Newspaper* was always intimately personal. In 1851, the newspaper claimed that the 'sex of the SOVEREIGN, more than her virtues, has closed many a quiver full of arrows that might have been discharged with fatal accuracy'.[121] The declaration establishes the paper's own chivalric credentials as much as it excuses the failure of republicanism. When it came to Victoria herself, *Reynolds's Newspaper*, like the *Northern Star*, often balanced its vitriolic critiques with an implicit acknowledgement of the widespread support she enjoyed. In 1858, in the very same article (quoted earlier) that it was splenetically complaining about working-class idolatry, *Reynolds's Newspaper* could still claim that the Queen was 'friendly to the extension of civil and political privileges to the toiling masses of the English people'.[122] The current state of affairs was blamed on the failure of the press and the government to draw Victoria's attention to the problem. *Reynolds's Newspaper* was never afraid to

[119] 'The Medal and the Reverse', *Lloyd's Weekly Newspaper*, 27 May 1855, 6.
[120] Northumbrian, 'Soldiers and Civilians', 7.
[121] 'French Imperialism and British Royalty', *Reynolds's Newspaper*, 2 Sept. 1855, 8.
[122] 'The Royal Wedding and the Working Classes', 1.

tap into sympathy for the innocent and feminine Victoria against the interest of a corrupt state.

The continued impact of the notion of a beneficent monarch upon both radicalism and liberalism during these decades should not be underestimated. During the campaign for the Second Reform Bill in 1866, John Bright made a series of speeches, all of which sought to appropriate Victoria and place her on the side of a reforming agitation. In the speeches at Birmingham Town Hall and St James's Hall, London, he accused Lord Derby of weakening the throne:

In our day the wearer of the Crown of England is in favour of freedom. For on many separate occasions, as you all know, the Queen has strongly, as strongly as become her station, urged upon parliament the extension of the franchise of the people. Parliament has been less liberal than the Crown, and time after time, these recommendations have been disregarded, and the offers of the monarch have been rejected or denied.[123]

Reynolds's Newspaper took very much the same standpoint as John Bright, a parallel suggesting that its contradictions were very much those of radicalism itself. Following the Hyde Park riot, it attacked the fact that a deputation of working men had not been allowed to see the sovereign. It declared that the Queen's promises of increasing the franchise for the working classes had been 'systematically falsified by her paid advisers and her favourite nobles'.[124] The politics of *Reynolds's Newspaper* was always fissured by the potent tradition of the benevolent sovereign who was, come what may, on the side of the People.

The contradictions in *Reynolds's Newspaper* stem, in part, from its position as part of the popular press. Despite its hostility to the monarchy, in 1851 even *Reynolds's Newspaper* was forced to admit that 'as public journalists we are more or less compelled to record the perambulations of royalty'.[125] Critics writing on *Reynolds's Newspaper* have tended to focus upon its anti-monarchist editorials. Ian Haywood has similarly argued that, through *The Mysteries of London*, Reynolds was able to radicalize the popular mode of serial publication.[126] The above admission nevertheless shows that Reynolds remained subject to the aesthetic and commercial demands of a successful newspaper. Readers had to be provided with news of the latest royal tour or visit. The one thing that Victoria could not be was ignored. In the course of at least one of its attacks upon the press, *Reynolds's Newspaper* felt it necessary to 'apologise to our readers for dwelling so long upon such sickening and

[123] John Bright, *Speeches on Parliamentary Reform* (London: Simpkin, Marshall & Co, 1867), 9.
[124] 'The Queen and the Working Classes', *Reynolds's Newspaper*, 26 Aug. 1866, 1.
[125] 'The Public Press and the Queen's Progress', *Reynolds's Newspaper*, 12 Oct. 1851, 8.
[126] Ian Haywood, 'George W. M. Reynolds and the Radicalisation of Victorian Serial Fiction', *Media History*, 4.2 (1998), 121–38.

transcendental trash', noting that 'the task has been forced upon us'.[127] Yet the impact of Victoria's civic visits lies precisely in the fact that even *Reynolds's Newspaper* provided its readers with a measure of such 'trash'. As Anne Humpherys has neatly stated, Reynolds's success stemmed from his unique ability 'to absorb the contradictory impulses and desires of the populace without making any "irritable" effort at resolution'.[128] The participation of *Reynolds's Newspaper* in the increasing scale of the newspaper press helped to produce its weekly engagement with the latest activities of the British royal family. Yet it also imposed a tension upon its republicanism.

It was only during the present reign, Walter Bagehot claimed, that the duties of a constitutional sovereign had ever been well performed. Bagehot's *The English Constitution*, first published in the *Fortnightly Review* in 1865–6, sought to explicate the working of the three estates of the realm, the Sovereign, the Lords, and the Commons. While acknowledging that the covert political influence of the Crown was often much greater than was commonly thought, Bagehot firmly set out the limited responsibilities of a constitutional monarch. His injunction against political interference—that it was the right of the monarch to be consulted, to encourage, and to warn—is the codification of much writing upon the Crown that took place in this period. Commentators have recently begun to unpick the undue sagacity and weightiness ascribed to *The English Constitution*, yet they have still tended to treat Bagehot's pronouncements within a narrow genealogy of high politics. They have consequently downplayed the extent to which his understanding of the monarch's position was profoundly influenced by the activities of Victoria and Albert.

Bagehot's pronouncements are premised as much on Victoria's media making as they are informed by a Whiggish grand narrative of constitutional progress. The duties of a constitutional monarch had only been performed well during the present reign because Bagehot's teleological model is founded on the high-profile public role adopted by Victoria and Albert. *The English Constitution*, both in its initial pronouncements and in the status it has enjoyed since its publication, is one culmination of royal populism. The different strands of the discourse are even enacted through the contradictions of Bagehot's thinking. Many reports of Victoria's visits appropriated the rhetoric of popular constitutionalism. Bagehot's book, however, marks an appropriation in the other direction in that he elevates Victoria's prominence into a set of political principles.

Bagehot's model of the constitution is divided into two parts, the *dignified*

[127] 'Jenkins in Paris', 9.
[128] Anne Humpherys, 'G. W. M. Reynolds: Popular Literature and Politics', in Joel Weiner (ed.), *Innovators and Preachers: The Role of the Editor in Victorian England* (Westport, Conn.: Greenwood Press, 1985), 13.

and the *efficient*. The dignified aspects are those which 'excite and preserve the reverence of the population'.[129] The efficient parts are those by which the state works and rules. Encompassing imaginative appeal, mystique, spectacle, and the affective hold of its venerable traditions, the Crown is the exemplar of the dignified aspect of the constitution. Bagehot condescendingly argues that the continued success of the monarchy stems from its intelligibility to the working class. He contrasts it with the enlightened understanding needed to follow the abstract intricacies of party politics. Monarchy is successful because the masses are governed not by the strength, but by the weakness of their imaginations. Constitutional monarchy 'has a comprehensible element for the vacant many, as well as complex laws and notions for the inquiring few'.[130] The Queen provided a concentrated focus of attention, fulfilling Bagehot's perceived need for the populace to have a central focus of imaginative and affective investment. The Crown consequently has a dignified triviality that permits the efficient parts of the constitution, the cabinet and the House of Commons, to govern in relative obscurity. As *Reynolds's Newspaper* demonstrates, Bagehot's dim view of the plebeian gullibility of John Bull was echoed by many sections of the radical press. Significantly, though, Bagehot's text is the antithesis of the libertarian constitutional narrative that was so important to radicals, Chartists, and republicans. Compared to the sophisticated anti-monarchist critiques expressed by *Reynolds's Newspaper* and the *Northern Star*, Bagehot drastically overestimates the naivety with which the royal media presence was consumed. For Bagehot, the deception of the royal culture industry supersedes the enlightening role of print culture; the doltish sentiments of subjects overwhelm the rational rights of citizens.

The English Constitution is keyed into a revivified royal populism and builds a schema around a national cultural presence now only achievable through the cumulative impact of the different media. The opening paragraph to Bagehot's chapter on the monarchy emphasizes the importance of Victoria's royal duties and their relationship with the publicity she received:

The use of the Queen, in a dignified capacity, is incalculable. Without her in England, the present English government would fail and pass away. Most people when they read that the Queen walked on the slopes at Windsor—that the Prince of Wales went to the Derby—have imagined that too much thought and prominence were given to little things. But they have been in error; and it is nice to trace how the actions of a retired widow and unemployed youth become of such importance.[131]

[129] Walter Bagehot, *The English Constitution*, introd. R. H. Crossman (London: Collins, 1963), 61.
[130] Ibid. 85.
[131] Ibid. 82.

Victoria's dignified role is very clearly identified with the prominent coverage that she is receiving from the newspaper and periodical press. It is Victoria's public and publicized position that is at the core of Bagehot's dignified role. Like the censure of *Reynolds's Newspaper*, like the commentary upon Victoria's visits by the metropolitan and provincial press, *The English Constitution* is part of the ongoing discourse regarding the status given to Victoria by print and visual media.

Bagehot gives the coverage of Victoria a constitutional significance corresponding to the importance that the press itself invests in her actions. Bagehot ascribes an importance to royal events because of the extent to which they absorbed popular attention. At the same time, though, he makes it absolutely clear that he sees such events as having a trivial and affective appeal that is far removed from the rational understanding required for a republic. As Bagehot reminds his readers: 'We smile at the *Court Circular*; but remember how many people read the *Court Circular*! its use is not in what it says, but in those to whom it speaks.'[132] Bagehot's comment encapsulates his conception of the cultural work achieved by Victoria's dignified role. The relationship it achieved with her subjects is as important as the discursive shape of her coverage. The constitutional position Bagehot envisages for the monarchy is premised on the weight of attention received by Victoria over the previous twenty years: Bagehot elevates the royal domination of the public sphere into a vital constitutional function.

Bagehot's description of the English constitution is clearly founded on the ostensible removal of the Crown from party politics. Nevertheless, his conception of the way in which the monarch's position actually functions is indebted to the media figuring of Victoria and Albert. While Bagehot never wholly reduces the monarchy to simply harmless entertainment and moral leadership, he argues that this is now a large part of its public function. As he notes, 'a royal family seasons politics by the seasonable addition of nice and pretty events'.[133] Given that Victoria had been in seclusion for four years and that dissatisfaction was slowly growing over precisely her refusal to undertake any public duties, Bagehot's writing uneasily combines an unabashed royalism with an implicit critique of Victoria's behaviour. On the one hand, he is able to state his belief that Britain is effectively a republic. This is a view that was intermittently reiterated by nineteenth-century radicals. On the other hand, Bagehot is able to perpetuate the all too familiar notion of the masses wholly and uncritically absorbed in the doings of the monarchy.

Throughout *The English Constitution* there is a revealing contradiction between the *lèse-majesté* of the dismissive tone with which Bagehot treats

---

[132] Walter Bagehot, 85–6.   [133] Ibid. 86.

Victoria's role and the political importance he actually ascribes to it. In irreverently assigning a high seriousness to royal triviality, an absorbing mystique to the incessant flow of banal royal news, Bagehot exemplifies the nature of Victoria's media making. *The English Constitution* dramatizes, often unconsciously, the discrepancy between the extent of the attention given to Victoria and the inconsequential nature of that attention. This split dynamic is part of a complex ideological slippage between the culture industry and constitutional politics. As *Reynolds's Newspaper* demonstrates, the contradictory nature of Victoria's figure was something the radical press found itself locked into when attempting to critique her role.

By the end of Victoria's reign, the civic publicness of the royal family had become the accepted model for the role of the monarch as a national figurehead. After the death of Albert in 1861, Victoria's own long seclusion only served to accentuate the importance of her previous industry. It is no coincidence that republicanism was at its strongest during the late 1860s and early 1870s when Victoria was perceived as receiving large amounts of money from the Civil List without performing any duties in return. Royal populism and the role of the crowd also continued as the dominant narrative at royal occasions. At the Thanksgiving Service for the recovery of the Prince of Wales from typhoid fever in 1872, *Lloyd's Weekly Newspaper* commented that the enthusiasm of the crowd demonstrated not a blind sycophancy but 'the wisdom, the moderation, and the sound heart'[134] which merited their enfranchisement. Whereas Victoria's creation as the Empress of India in 1876 added an imperial hauteur to her position, the subsequent decline of the British Empire and the slow fading of the Commonwealth has entailed the monarchy losing its imperial gloss. What has nevertheless remained is the round of public functions and philanthropic work. The value of each individual royal is now often measured according the number of engagements he or she carries out. Indeed, the recent casting of Diana, Princess of Wales, as the 'People's Princess' merely serves to underline the continuing hold of the rhetoric of royal populism. At the same time as the civic publicness of Victoria and Albert was an important part of the development of a constitutional monarchy, the attention they received was a reinvention of the monarchy's aristocratic prominence.

[134] Quoted in Williams, *Contentious Crown*, 48.

2

ROYAL PORTRAITURE

London, 28 June 1838: at Victoria's coronation fair in Hyde Park there was a printseller charging 6*d*. to enter his booth. Therein, you would have the privilege of witnessing the printing of your own engraved portrait of Victoria and a lithograph of the fair.[1] On the same day, 200 miles north in Preston, another enterprising printer was attaching his printing press to a horse-drawn carriage in order to join the local coronation procession. As the parade moved through the streets, he printed penny handbills that contained a short biography of Victoria and a narrative of the day's events.[2]

These two small episodes are exemplary in that the process of reproduction has been turned into a performance that is itself part of a larger royal spectacle. The printing presses were integral to the experience of the coronation. At the same time, they were the form through which that experience was expressed and disseminated. Both the symbolic and material importance of 'the Press' fed into the meaning of the occasion. These two incidents epitomize the way the experience of the monarchy was invariably an experience of the media through which it was communicated. It is a dynamic that is paradigmatic for understanding the way that a remarkable expansion in print and graphic culture shaped how Queen Victoria was thought of. This chapter traces the most significant publishing developments that created the figure of Victoria. It argues that their modernity engendered an extraordinary contemporary discourse upon the media making of the monarchy. Prints, periodicals, newspapers, and photographs: these produced the narrative of Victoria's reign and an acute reflexivity about the nature of that narrative. The figure of Victoria never existed in-itself. It was always for-itself, always aware of its own being. Necessarily so, given that the creation of a media monarchy could not but imply a self-consciousness towards its own representation.

---

[1] BM print no. 8826 (Chesleymore collection).

[2] 'Festivities in the Country', *Standard*, 31 June 1838, 3. Processions of printers and printing presses also took place to mark the passing of the Reform Bill. Louis James, *Print and the People 1819–1851* (London: Allen Lane, 1976), 17.

Whereas the previous chapter traced the populist discourse surrounding Victoria's tours and visits, this chapter focuses on the ubiquity of her cultural presence. Simply tracing the enormous number of artefacts that took the Queen as their subject, however, does not answer the question of why Victoria's presence was so pervasive, nor does it explain the enthusiastic nature of so many royal representations. While there are certain common factors at work, different media operated according to their own dictates. Developments in the publishing industry were also geographically and socially uneven in their impact. The influence of technological and regulatory changes was most evident upon the literate strata of London and other cities. There was certainly no national 'mass' media able to impose itself, although its slow development, and the consequent creation of a collective experience of Victoria, was a key element in the development of her iconic position.

The making of Victoria's figure was necessarily a multi-media phenomenon. It was a process involving different royal images from a variety of media, and the cumulative impact of their production, circulation, and consumption. The wealth of royal prints, ballads, and commemoratives demonstrates the shift towards more popular and large-scale forms of media. Changing technologies of graphic reproduction, for example, were diminishing the role of court portraiture. As a genre, court portraiture is especially important because of its traditionally privileged role in portraying the sovereign. The beginning of Victoria's reign both coincided with and exacerbated a long-term decline in its influence. The waning of court portraiture has to be seen as part of the creation of a more inclusive and less political style of monarchy.

My examination of court portraiture concentrates on the first years of Victoria's reign because this period was a crucial period of change. The focus on such a concentrated time-span means that it is also possible to capture the interaction between the various visual media. Different forms of graphic reproduction worked as relatively autonomous but interdependent fields of production. From fine art prints to engravings sold in the street, each type of publication had its own conventions, its own practices. Yet, equally, they were positioned by their hierarchical interrelationship. The dominance of Victoria's media figuring can therefore be shown through the changing structural relations between the competing visual media. The expanding market for prints and illustrated publications disrupted the existing hierarchy of the fine arts. Although Victoria's state portraits appear to be little different from those of her predecessors, well before the advent of photography their iconic function had been hollowed out from within. The dynamics at work in the overall field of graphic culture during the late 1830s and 1840s worked to privilege a portrayal of Victoria centred initially upon her beauty and glamour, and subsequently her domestic propriety. The marginalization of court portraiture therefore constitutes part of the movement away from pomp and circumstance that I traced in the previous chapter. In the same way that the increasing number of newspapers was keyed into Victoria's civic publicness, the changing modes of graphic reproduction assisted the emergence of a bourgeois royal family.

The accession of Queen Victoria engendered a rage for royal representations, a saturation coverage that was to typify the first two decades of her reign. *Cleave's London Gazette and Satirist of Variety*, which was started in 1836 by the radical John Cleave, declared that the press was suffering from an attack of 'Queenophobia'. It was reputedly afflicting all alike so that 'Tory, Whig and Radical, exhibit identically the same ludicrous extravagance whenever they approach the precincts of the Court'.[3] The *Spectator* bemoaned the malady of 'Reginamania' that continued to prevail to such an extent that the newspapers were under the necessity of 'dwelling constantly on the beauty not only of the Queen's face and features, but of her feet and even of her slippers'.[4] Lord Grey was certainly one admirer who was badly infected with the contagion. In the House of Lords, he cried with pleasure from the Queen's voice and speech.[5] Similarly, in his journal, the painter Charles Leslie described how he was moved to tears when Victoria entered Westminster Abbey for her coronation. He noted that many of the congregation were likewise affected.[6] How could 'Reginamania' exert such a widespread influence? Part of the frisson around the young Queen was fostered by the euphoric political aspirations discussed in the previous chapter. Significantly, though, the initial sentiment around Victoria was also seen as being driven by a commercially oriented print and visual culture. The discursive contours of Victoria's figure were constituted by the dominance of popular publications. I want to demonstrate the extent to which painters' portrayals of Victoria's innocence and beauty helped to create the nature of 'Reginamania'.

In the first years of Victoria's reign, the growth of the print trade meant that there were a phenomenal number of royal portraits. There was also a correspondingly large volume of prints depicting royal events. In February 1839, the *Art Union* commented that there were already above fifty portraits available.[7] Every publisher of note had at least one, whether cheap woodcut, expensive steel-engraving, or gaudily coloured lithograph. An examination of a well-known London publisher, Rudolf Ackermann & Co., demonstrates the

[3] 'Cleave's London Satirist', *Cleave's London Gazette and Satirist of Variety*, 28 Oct. 1837, 2.
[4] 'Postscript; the Reginamania', *Spectator*, 6 Jan. 1838, 8.
[5] Thomas Creevey, *The Creevey Papers*, ed. Sir Herbert Maxwell-Bart (London: John Murray, 1903), 664.
[6] Charles Robert Leslie, *Autobiographical Reflections*, ed. Tom Taylor (London: John Murray, 1860), ii. 239.
[7] 'Chit-chat about Art and Artists', *Art Union*, 15 Feb. 1839, 10.

Fig. 10. *The Royal Rose of England* (London: William Spooner, 1838)

eagerness and regularity with which these prints were released.[8] In addition
to the obligatory portrait, coronation, and wedding pictures, visits to Covent
Garden or appearances at Windsor were made into news events worthy of
commemoration. The engravings and lithographs sold by Ackermann & Co.
were for a predominantly well-to-do audience. Yet a portrait of Victoria published by William Spooner is a typical example of the inexpensive pictures
that were equally widely available (see Fig. 10). The *Art Union* claimed that

[8] *The Exterior and Interior of the Royal Chapel, St James's, February 10th, 1840* (Ackermann & Co.,
1840). *Her Majesty as she appeared on her visit to Covent Garden Theatre* (Ackermann and Co., 8 Dec.
1837). *Her Most Gracious Majesty Queen Victoria Crowned June 28th 1838* (Ackermann and Co., 3 July
1838). H. Jones, *Her Majesty as she appeared at Windsor Castle* (Ackermann & Co., 8 Dec. 1838). G. J.
Stewart, *Her Most Gracious Majesty Queen Victoria* (R. Ackermann, 12 Feb. 1838).

newspaper publishers had given thousands of royal portraits away. It tellingly noted that 'the said newspaper must be purchased, though not necessarily read'.[9] The extensive dissemination of Victoria's visual image meant that her media making was in no way confined to the relatively restricted social sphere of a literate print culture.

Printsellers' enthusiasm for Victoria was driven by the exceptional commercial success of their royal prints. They both capitalized on and exacerbated the flush of euphoria around the young Queen. What was created was a discursive momentum around Victoria, where the production of prints encouraged the release of yet more engravings. One publisher reputedly made £3,000 from a portrait released just after her accession.[10] Surviving records from a prominent London copper-plate engraving firm of the period, Dixon and Ross, include a Day Book which logs its daily sales transactions from 26 November 1838 to 15 December 1840. Despite being a somewhat scanty record from a single firm at the upper end of the market, Dixon and Ross's sales figures suggest that demand for portraits of Victoria far outstripped that of all other engravings. Demand for royal portraits was at its height between 26 November and 31 December 1838: 374 proofs and prints of Victoria were sold compared to a combined total of 165 other engravings. Astonishingly, just under 70 per cent of all the engravings sold by Dixon and Ross in that period were of Victoria.[11] Demand did wane throughout the first six months of 1839, yet engravings of the Queen remained by far the most popular.

Many printsellers composed only a rough likeness of Victoria, or even adapted a print from their existing stock. In contrast, fine art printsellers sought to reproduce one of the many oil paintings of Victoria. The success of the royal prints in the late 1830s and early 1840s helps to explain why there were so many different portraits of Victoria and so many different oil paintings of royal events. The number of large-scale canvases, in the volumes produced by recognized artists, was unprecedented. Sir George Hayter, Sir William Newton, Charles Robert Leslie, Edmund Parris, and John Martin all undertook pictures of the coronation (see Fig. 11). Indeed, Hayter went on to depict Victoria's marriage and the christening of the Prince of Wales, while Leslie was subsequently commissioned by Frances Moon, a premier London printseller, to produce a painting of the Princess Royal's christening. The well-established David Wilkie was also commissioned to produce a picture of Victoria's first Privy Council, a painting I will return to later in the chapter. The only notable forebears to this series of pictures were Sir William

---

[9] 'Chit-chat', 10.
[10] 'Fine Arts; Publishers and Printsellers', *Athenaeum*, 16 Jan. 1847, 71.
[11] Anthony Dyson, *Pictures to Print: The Nineteenth-Century Engraving Trade* (London: Farrand Press, 1984), 179–82.

Fig. 11. Engraving by Henry Ryall after Sir George Hayter, *The Coronation of Queen Victoria, 28 June, 1838* (London: Hodgson and Graves, 1840)

Hamilton's painting of the marriage of George IV and George Jones's *The Banquet at the Coronation of George IV.*

The objective behind many of the royal pictures was the execution of an oil painting that could be turned into a profitable engraving. When the *Art Union* reviewed Parris's painting of the coronation, it declared that it would 'make an effective and interesting engraving—the purpose for which it has been produced'.[12] Similarly, Wilkie noted in his diary in October 1838 that Moon had instantly arranged for an engraving of Alfred Chalon's portrait, and had paid a high copyright price.[13] An advertisement from Hodgson and Graves, another of the premier London printsellers of the period, also shows printsellers' reliance on the royal paintings that were produced by George Hayter, Richard Davis, and Thomas Sully (see Fig. 12). Many of the cheap prints of Victoria, invariably ephemeral in nature, have long disappeared into dust. Nevertheless, trade records and critical reviews of these quasi-official paintings by Hodgson and Graves survive. A detailed study of the life of these pictures as both paintings and prints reveals the influence of the print trade. Its dominance was such that, to paraphrase Walter Benjamin, the work of art reproduced was becoming the work of art designed for reproduction.

[12] 'Works in Progress', *Art Union*, 15 Apr. 1839, 47.
[13] A. Cunningham, *The Life of Sir David Wilkie* (London: John Murray: 1843), iii. 226.

BY COMMAND OF HER MAJESTY.

Messrs. HODGSON and GRAVES, HER MAJESTY's Printsellers and Publishers in Ordinary, have the honour to announce that they have *Nearly Ready* for publication

THE AUTHENTIC STATE PORTRAIT OF

HER MAJESTY IN THE IMPERIAL DALMATIC ROBES,

Painted for Buckingham Palace, by GEORGE HAYTER, Esq., her Majesty's Historical and Portrait Painter,
And engraving in Mezzotinto by SAMUEL COUSINS, Esq., A.R.A.

This whole-length Portrait of the QUEEN in her CORONATION ROBES, seated on her throne in Westminster Abbey, is acknowledged by the Court circle, and every one who has had the pleasure of seing the picture, to be the most correct Portrait of her Majesty yet produced, and altogether the most pleasing picture ever painted. The price to Subscribers for this splendid Portrait will be—

Prints . . 3*l*. 3*s*.   Proofs . . 5*l*. 5*s*.   Proofs before Letters . . 8*l*. 8*s*.

THE ROYAL CORTEGE IN WINDSOR PARK,

INCLUDING THE EQUESTRIAN PORTRAIT OF HER MAJESTY,

ATTENDED BY HER ILLUSTRIOUS VISITORS AND SUITE.

By Command of her Majesty, Painted by R. B. DAVIS, Esq., for Windsor Castle ; and engraving in the finest style of Mezzotinto by F. BROMLEY.
The Plate has been engraved on a scale proportionate to the great interest of the Picture. The Etching may be seen at the Publishers, and the Engraving will be shortly ready for Publication. Price to Subscribers :—

Prints . . 3*l*. 3*s*.   Proofs . . 5*l*. 5*s*.   Before Letters . . 6*l*. 6*s*.

THE ROYAL CORONATION PICTURE.

"Mr. Hayter had the honour of submitting to her Majesty his large oil sketch for the grand historical picture of the Coronation, with which her Majesty was graciously pleased to express the highest approval."—*Court Circular.*

"On Saturday her Majesty honoured Mr. Hayter by sitting to him in the Coronation robes ; and her Serene Highness the Princess of Hohenlohe also sat to him for his great picture of her Majesty's Coronation."—*Court Circular.*

"Her Royal Highness the Duchess of Kent honoured Mr. Hayter by sitting to him in the full Coronation robes, for his picture of that august ceremony."—*Court Circular.*

"Her Majesty was graciously pleased to do Mr. Hayter the honour to sit for him to paint her portrait into his great picture of the Coronation, and her Highness the Princess of Hohenlohe also sat for the same picture."—*Court Circular.*

"Her Royal Highness the Duchess of Cambridge did Mr. Hayter the honour to sit to him, to be painted into the grand picture of her Majesty's Coronation."—*Court Circular.*

"Her Royal Highness the Duchess of Gloucester did Mr. Hayter the honour to sit for the great Coronation picture."—*Court Circular.*

"His Royal Highness the Duke of Sussex honoured Mr. Hayter with a sitting for the historical picture of her Majesty's Coronation."—*Court Circular.*

MESSRS. HODGSON and GRAVES, Her Majesty's Printsellers and Publishers, have authority to announce that, by
HER MAJESTY'S SPECIAL PERMISSION,
they will shortly have the honour to exhibit, in their Gallery in Pall-Mall,
THE MAGNIFICENT PICTURE OF

THE CORONATION.

Painted by GEORGE HAYTER, Esq., her Majesty's Historical and Portrait Painter.

Any attempt at description of this Grand and Noble Picture must be very imperfect, but the Publishers trust that the SPLENDID ENGRAVING which they are to have the honour of publishing, will enable all the admiring Patrons of Art to possess this, the ONLY AUTHENTIC MEMORIAL of the most interesting event of her Majesty's Reign.

Subscribers' names for this National Engraving received by Messrs. HODGSON and GRAVES, her Majesty's Printsellers and Publishers, Pall-Mall, where the Subscription Book, containing the numerous Autographs of the Royal and Illustrious Subscribers, is now open, and the Impressions will be strictly delivered in the order of subscription.

LATELY PUBLISHED,

THE ADMIRABLE HALF-LENGTH PORTRAIT OF

HER MAJESTY THE QUEEN,

IN THE ROBES AND JEWELS OF STATE, ASCENDING THE THRONE OF THE HOUSE OF LORDS.
Painted by THOMAS SULLY, Esq., for the United States, and Engraved in Mezzotinto, by C. E. WAGSTAFFE.

"No one has been so successful in producing a correct likeness and so good a picture as Mr. Sully."—*Times.*
"The likeness is most striking, giving that pleasing appearance so much wanting in many of the previous portraits of her Majesty."—*Herald.*

Prints . . £1 1*s*.   Proofs . . . £2 2*s*.   India Proofs . . £3 3*s*.   Before Letters . . £4 4*s*.

London : HODGSON and GRAVES, Her Majesty's Printsellers and Publishers, 6, Pall-Mall.

Fig. 12. Hodgson and Graves, *Art Union*, 1 (1839), 125

Hodgson and Graves were very much at the upper end of the market. The royal prints they organized consequently illustrate the forces that would eventually spell the end of traditional court portraiture. The prints of Hodgson and Graves bear many of the hallmarks of royal portraiture in terms of their formal conventions and their production by officially recognized court painters.

Importantly, both Hayter and Wilkie held court positions. Victoria appointed Hayter as her historical and portrait painter in 1837. Wilkie was given the post of Principal Painter-In-Ordinary, a position that he had also held under William IV and George IV.

At one level, the reliance of Hodgson and Graves upon these paintings testifies to the continuing prominence and prestige of the official state portrait. This is particularly evident in the language of the advertisement. There is a repeated stress upon the assistance that Victoria and other aristocratic sitters had given to the paintings, and upon Hodgson and Graves's own privileged position as Printsellers-In-Ordinary. Yet it is important to emphasize that there was by no means a simple top-down aesthetic, whereby Victoria's official printsellers reproduced an authorized court portrait. In Hodgson and Graves's advertisement, the centrality of the Royal Arms and the liberal use of puffs from the *Court Circular* suggest that Victoria's assistance has already been reinvented as symbolic capital in the marketing of the prints for an aspiring and affluent bourgeoisie. Despite Victoria authorizing or at least sitting for the prints advertised by Hodgson and Graves, we have come a long way from the traditional model of royal patronage. The reproduction of the royal paintings reveals the extent to which they went beyond whatever patronage Victoria gave them. The number of prints was moving ever closer to the flow of engravings that would soon be produced by the illustrated press.

The coronation pictures had pretensions to be considered as national records, grand historical paintings belonging to the highest genre of the fine arts. Nevertheless, they were, as the *Athenaeum* bluntly put it, printsellers' prizes from their first conception.[14] In the run-up to Victoria's wedding, the *Spectator* mocked the number of wedding pictures that were anticipated. It derided the aesthetic façade that printsellers erected around what were essentially commercial undertakings:

LESLIE, we suppose, will be commissioned to paint the scene in the chapel, and PARRIS be started to distance him: CHALON, perhaps, as he has already been to Court, will be sketching the honeymoon drawing room, with HAYTER for his rival. The publishers, we should observe, always try to run down the game put up by another: thus, one no sooner announces the 'Waterloo Banquet', by the only artist who was permitted to paint the scene, then another advertises a second 'only artist'. The 'Coronation Plate' has already been a hard race, and the winner has been named before all those entered have run. The 'Matrimonial Sweepstakes' will be a close heat no doubt; and the 'First Appearance' handicap will have a numerous list of competitors. We have put the artists on the scent, and let those follow the trail who would be in at the death— 'Of my reputation' exclaims some impracticable painter who is bent on studying

---

[14] 'Our Weekly Gossip', *Athenaeum*, 14 May 1842, 430.

nature and the ideal, while he can keep on the safe side of starvation! We are talking not of reputation, but of profit![15]

In their zealous attempts to exploit the occasion, printsellers and artists undermined the very aesthetic distinction that they sought to invest in their wares. The *Spectator* satirizes the way in which these royal paintings were very much part of the vigorous market for individual prints.

The contractual arrangements between engravers, printsellers, and painters highlight the value placed upon the reproduction of the various royal paintings. Records from Hodgson and Graves reveal their efforts to maximize the lucrative opportunities provided by Victoria's accession. In December 1837, the firm paid 100 guineas to Edmund Parris for the copyright upon his portrait of Victoria. Parris's contract stipulated that he was not to undertake any other royal portrait during the next twelve months unless it was by the Queen's command.[16] Even then, he was bound to sell any further royal picture to Hodgson and Graves for 100 guineas. Aesthetic pretensions were no bar to commercial nous and a desire to corner the market. Negotiations by painters or their representatives could be equally prosaic, though. In September 1842, a London printseller, Thomas Boys, met Jacob Bell, the business manager of Edwin Landseer, to discuss the reproduction of a royal group portrait by Landseer. Bell subsequently wrote to the painter to inform him that Boys had 'consented to give our price for the copyright of the Royal mother and Brats'.[17] Bell's language is in marked contrast to the idealized maternity of Landseer's picture.

During 1838, the prints of the four royal pictures advertised in Fig. 12 were organized by Hodgson and Graves. Thomas Sully's and George Hayter's portraits cost the firm £200 and £300 respectively. Richard Davis was also paid £300 for the copyright upon his painting, while Hayter received the enormous sum of £2,000 for his coronation picture. Although Hayter's picture is now in the Royal Collection, the Lord Chamberlain only purchased it in 1892. It is important to emphasize that it was Hodgson and Graves who initially commissioned the work. Hayter and Sully's pictures only came into existence in order to be reproduced. Their anticipated success as prints was instrumental in setting their value. In 1842, when Hodgson and Graves paid £500 simply for the right to reproduce a small painting by Landseer of the Queen and her children, the *Art Union* proclaimed its astonishment because the picture itself was only worth £100–£150.[18]

Reviews of Victoria's coronation and wedding paintings tantalizingly

---

[15] 'Spring Fashions in Town Prints', *Spectator*, 1 Feb. 1840, 115.

[16] Graves Papers BM Add. MS 46140, fo. 82.

[17] Richard Ormond, *Sir Edwin Landseer* (London: Thames and Hudson: 1981), 12.

[18] 'The Queen and her Children', *Art Union*, 1 Dec. 1842, 283.

suggest that they were always already painted as reproductions. Their future existence as prints insinuated itself into their immanent form, testimony to the influence that the print market was able to exert. Printsellers had been active in commissioning paintings since the 1760s, but these reviews express a much more insidious order of influence.[19] When the *Athenaeum* reviewed Hayter's painting of Victoria's marriage, it noted that paintings of this sort were predominantly a series of portraits, a condition of their nature being 'that their lights and groupings are arranged for publication as prints'.[20] The painter's brush did not work to its own dictates but to those of the engraver's burin. Importantly, the *Athenaeum* was not alone in its comments. In its review of Hayter's coronation painting, *The Times* noted that 'This picture, from its peculiar treatment, is admirably adapted for the original of an engraving'.[21] Discussing Parris's coronation painting, the *Art Union* described how 'the general agroupment and composition seem to have been designed for yielding the very best effect in engraving'.[22] *The Times* similarly complimented Parris for his composition and his 'general outline, which, as the picture is about to be engraved, is certainly not among the least of its merits'.[23] In contrast to cheap prints of the coronation, which tend to concentrate on the overall spectacle of the Abbey, the paintings of Hayter and Leslie are notable for their focus on the central protagonists. They were essentially composed as a collection of portraits. Other adverts from Hodgson and Graves demonstrate that this was a principal selling point. The composition of the paintings was influenced by the method of sale by subscription traditionally employed by fine art printsellers. Hayter and Leslie's paintings were sold initially by subscription book. The aristocratic participants portrayed were expected to join the subscription list; the lustre of their names was then exploited as a means of attracting more subscribers. Paintings like those of Leslie and Hayter were conspicuously well attuned to the way in which fine art prints were sold.

The covert pressure exerted upon the coronation paintings reflects wider changes in the print market. The whole structure of the trade in fine art prints was unravelling because of a rapid expansion in demand. As Hodgson and Graves's advertisement shows, fine art prints were usually sold through a system of carefully graded impressions. These ranged from expensive artists' proofs to ordinary prints. Thus, prints of Sully's portrait were £1. 1s. and Proofs Before Letters were £4. 4s. The limited number of impressions that

[19] Timothy Clayton, *The English Print 1688–1803* (New Haven: Paul Mellon Centre and Yale University Press, 1997), 174.

[20] 'Our Weekly Gossip', *Athenaeum*, 14 May 1842, 430.

[21] 'Mr Hayter's Coronation Picture', *The Times*, 11 Apr. 1839, 3.

[22] 'The Coronation of Queen Victoria', *Art Union*, 1 June 1842, 144.

[23] 'Mr Parris's Picture of the Coronation', *The Times*, 2 Apr. 1839, 5.

could be reproduced from one copper plate guaranteed the value of each type of print. The introduction of the steel plate, however, threatened this system. Steel plates produced many multiples of the softer copper plates. Rarity was no longer rendered an element of value in many prints. Similarly, the advent of the electrotype process in 1839 meant that engraving plates could now be copied. In 1843, the London Art Union used the electrotype process to supply the annual engraving promised to its 12,000 members.[24] Printsellers feared the electrotype process as a dire threat to trade and their protests led to the formation of a government select committee in 1845.

The impact of the changes affecting printsellers is evident in an article published by the *Spectator* in 1841, which protested against the engraving trade being turned into an industry. The *Spectator* claimed that the number of impressions now taken from a copper plate 'would make an engraver of the Old School lift up eyes and hand in astonishment'.[25] The number of Proofs Before Letters was said to be equivalent to the number of common prints that had previously been taken. Retouching the plate, which used to be resorted to only in rare cases because it deteriorated the quality of the print, was now undertaken repeatedly in order to furnish the requisite number of impressions. According to the *Spectator* the difference between a common print and a first proof was now so great that it often seemed as if the two were not a product of the same plate.[26]

An article in the *Athenaeum* specifically singled out prints taken from paintings of coronations, royal marriages, and Waterloo banquets—whose value was estimated according to the number of aristocratic portraits they contained—as the last vestiges of the subscription system.[27] Hodgson and Graves might have been offering an exclusive set of coronation and royal wedding prints, but the very presence of their advertisement in the *Art Union* is symptomatic of the hollowing out of their aesthetic distinction. In the long-term shift from a relatively small number of cognoscenti to a much larger market, fine art printsellers were expanding because of the pressure upon them. At the same time, though, such growth was a threat to some printseller's traditional exclusivity. The influence of the fine art engraving trade upon the royal paintings is thus an index to the general expansion of graphic culture during the 1830s and 1840s. It stresses the modernity of the

[24] Lyndel Saunders King, *The Industrialisation of Taste: Victorian England and the Art Union of London* (Ann Arbor: UMI Research Press, 1982), 94.

[25] 'Fine Arts. Two Plans of Print Publishing', *Spectator*, 9 Oct. 1841, 980.

[26] Ibid. 980.

[27] 'New Publications', *Athenaeum*, 24 Aug. 1844, 781. The result of the pressure upon reproduction was the setting up in 1847 of a Printseller's Association, headed by Dominic Colnaghi. It was introduced after a particularly damaging affair involving a forged plate of a Van Dyck painting. Every proof was to be numbered and stamped by the Secretary of the Association. George Friend, *Alphabetical List of Engravings Declared at the Office of the Printsellers' Association since its Establishment in 1847 to the end of 1875* (London: 1876).

number of royal prints and their increasingly dominant role in Victoria's media making.

The new visual culture was a strong influence upon Victoria's representation. This is exemplified in her appropriation by one of the publishing phenomena of the 1830s: the Books of Beauty. The literary annuals, in vogue from the 1820s, and their offshoot, the Books of Beauty, which enjoyed a similar faddishness from the early 1830s, were two of the more prominent developments in the print market during this period. The Books of Beauty relied on steel-engraving for their appeal, and are one of the genres of publication that were marginalizing fine art printsellers. Their importance lies in their creation of Victoria as Beauty personified. Through their emphasis on glamour, desirability, and the language of feeling, the Books of Beauty played a significant role in causing the initial fervour around Victoria. They exemplify an important contention of this book: that Victoria's representation was not so much shaped as overdetermined by the Books of Beauty, and, later, by popular weekly newspapers and the illustrated press. Victoria was appropriated into the formal conventions and material constraints of the different media. The Books of Beauty portrayed a Victoria who is markedly different from the Victoria portrayed by the illustrated press and the first royal photographs. The aesthetics of the monarchy as a whole—the texture of the way it was experienced—was bound up with the dominance of specific modes of publication.

The Books of Beauty were fostered by the arrival of the steel-plate engraving and an aspirational bourgeois market. They combined high quality illustrations with verse from writers such as Laetitia Landon, Countess Blessington, Caroline Norton, and Mrs Samuel Carter Hall. They extended the audience of the woman's magazine and, in so doing, reinvented the role of the aristocracy as leaders of fashion for their growing middle-class readership. Expensive and ornately produced, the Books of Beauty usually sold for around ten or twelve shillings. They were luxury goods in their own right and were habitually given as Christmas or New Year gifts.

Published under such names as *The Keepsake*, *Heath's Book of Beauty*, *Affection's Keepsake*, and *Gems of Beauty*, the Books of Beauty were most notable for their glamorous promotion of a heavily idealized femininity. Engravings of 'Byron's Beauties'; exaggeratedly attractive personifications of various Virtues; portraits of renowned aristocratic women—these were their typical offerings. As Margaret Beetham has noted, the engravings produced Beauty 'as evidence of the viewer's taste, as the defining aspect of "the sex" and as the distinctive quality of particular individuals'.[28] Despite their fashionable status, the albums were frequently pilloried for the inanity of their

---

[28] Margaret Beetham, *A Magazine of Her Own?: Domesticity and Desire in the Woman's Magazine, 1800–1914* (London: Routledge, 1996), 40.

verse and illustrations. Thackeray memorably parodied the bathos of their poetry, with its 'lost affection, recollection, cut connexion, tears in torments, true-love token, spoken, broken, sighing, dying, girl of Florence, and so on'.[29] Many reviewers claimed that the success of the Books of Beauty derived from their exploitation of an excess of feminine sentimentality. Saturated by an aesthetic of ephemeral affect, their verse and illustrations were seen as pandering to a taste for the frivolous and superficially attractive.

Two articles, the first from the *Monthly Chronicle*, the second from *Fraser's Magazine* by Thackeray, exemplify the condescending ire aroused by the annuals. The *Monthly Chronicle* claimed that they debased the taste for art by encouraging only the talents of lushly sentimental artists like Edmund Parris and Alfred Chalon. The impact of the Books of Beauty on engraving was felt to be equally deleterious. The delicate finish characteristic of steel-engraving was exploited in order to manufacture a tinselled allure:

Effect is the one thing aimed at by superficial delicacy and smoothness, cleverly alternated with blackness so as to give the appearance of a vigorous and dashing style—a factitious attraction is produced that the eye glances over pleased with the vague impression, but deriving no particular satisfaction.[30]

The publishing success of the Books of Beauty meant the production of the illustrations was reputedly so mechanized that it was one engraver's responsibility to engrave all the backgrounds. Other individuals then added all of the foregrounds and the figures. Unsurprisingly, there was a high degree of similarity between the engravings published by the Books of Beauty. The standardization of production was mirrored in the uniform ideal of femininity they imposed. As the *Monthly Chronicle* put it, features deemed the perfection of beauty were 'caricatured into deformity, and wreathed into a sickly affectation of sentimentality, to which a healthy ugliness were far preferable'.[31] Thackeray's scorn was similarly aroused by the excessive and contrived sexuality pervading the illustrations—the pictures of women with enormous eyes in 'voluptuous attitudes and various stages of *deshabille*'.[32] The annuals certainly exhausted all possible identikit combinations of ringlets, tears, long eyelashes, naked shoulders, and impossibly slim waists.

The accusations levelled against the Books of Beauty conflated commercialism, affect, the feminine, and the ephemeral. These attacks position them very much within evolving debates upon the literary market-place. It also

---

[29] William Thackeray, *The Paris Sketch Book and Art Criticisms*, ed. George Saintsbury (London: Oxford University Press, n.d.), 338.

[30] 'Influence of the Annuals on Art', *The Monthly Chronicle, A National Journal of Politics, Literature, Science, and Art*, 3 (1839), 66.

[31] Ibid. 66.

[32] Thackeray, *Sketch Book*, 339.

highlights the rubric through which they created their figure of Victoria. With their aristocratic and feminine bent, the new 18-year-old Queen was their ideal subject. Paeans to Victoria punctuate the Books of Beauty during the late 1830s and early 1840s (see Appendix). The adulation around her was Janus-faced; it looked back to the courtly adoration of Elizabeth I and forward to the manufactured glamour of Hollywood stars. Lady Emmeline Stuart-Wortley proclaimed Victoria as virtue personified except that Virtue looked lovelier in Victoria's 'sweet form where all her Graces smile'.[33] In a similar vein, Laetitia Landon provides one example of the frequent use of a language of flowers to celebrate her beauty:

> Carnation, laced with many a streak
> of blooming red on its leaflets bright,
> May be a type of her mantling cheek,
> blent with a brow of pearly white.[34]

The homogenized femininity of the Beauty Books meant that their Victoria was characterized by her glamour, sexuality, and attractiveness. Importantly, though, given the widespread influence that the *Monthly Chronicle* bemoaned, many other royal portraits shared the same pictorial conventions and many other poems employed the same rhetoric. What Thackeray dismissed as sentimental slush and ephemeral glamour was a significant means of generating the attraction of Victoria's femininity. The Books of Beauty were consequently part of the apolitical realignment of the monarchy.

The portraits of Victoria disseminated by the Books of Beauty heavily fetishized her sexuality and desirability (see Fig. 13). Richard Lane's exquisite portrait, published in *Finden's Gallery of Beauty, Or Court of Queen Victoria*, is a typical example. Significantly, Lane exhibited two portraits and one profile of Victoria at the Royal Academy in 1838. He also held the position of Lithographer-In-Ordinary to the Queen. Lane's multiple activities are comparable to the influence of the engraving trade upon the coronation painters. Work for the Books of Beauty was highly lucrative for well-known artists. It fed back into the type and style of portraits exhibited at the Royal Academy. Lane's portrait promotes Victoria as nothing less than the principal Court Beauty. From the elongated neck and bare shoulders to the large eyes, the perfect ringlet, and the flowers decorating her elaborate hairbun, the portrait makes Victoria captivatingly attractive and glamorously fashionable. In contrast to the pictures that took their lead from traditional court portraiture, Victoria's regal position is symbolized only through her garter ribbon. As well

---

[33] Emmeline Stuart-Wortley, 'Sonnet to the Queen', *Sonnets, Written Chiefly during a Tour of Holland, Germany, Italy, Turkey and Hungary* (London: Joseph Rickerby, 1839), 141.

[34] Laetitia Landon, 'To Victoria', *Flowers of Loveliness* (London: Ackerman & Co., 1838), n.pag.

Fig. 13. Engraving by Edward Finden after drawing by R. J. Lane,
Queen Victoria (London, 1839)

as being reproduced in *Finden's Gallery of Beauty*, Lane's portrait was
released as an individual print in May 1839.

The influence of the Books of Beauty was such that they fed into a style
of portraiture that permeated the entire print market. A portrait by Alfred
Chalon epitomizes the doll-like quality of many prints of Victoria (see Fig.
14). Chalon was a fashionable artist whose style was notoriously well adapted
to the Books of Beauty. He was also appointed the official portrait painter to
Victoria in 1837. Exhibited at the Royal Academy in 1838, Chalon's portrait
has a formal hybridity in that it takes the traditional icons of court portraiture
and makes them more redolent of the frippery associated with the Beauty

Fig. 14. Engraving after Alfred Chalon, *Queen Victoria* (1838)

Books. Victoria's porcelain appearance is intensified by an extended train of regal robes that seem more decorative than majestic. The flowers strewn by her feet illustrate the painting's participation in the discourse of femininity promoted by the Books of Beauty.

Many less-finished prints mimicked the conventions of the annuals to promote an idealized and alluring Victoria. There was a complex process of diffusion into other graphic media. The type of aristocratic femininity promoted by the Books of Beauty—which had always already been reinvented and glamorized for a bourgeois readership—was itself copied by inexpensive wood-engraved prints. A cheap portrait reproduces all too blatantly the erotic

Fig. 15. *Queen Victoria* (London: A. Park, 1838)

desirability that is more tacitly expressed by Lane's steel-engraving (see Fig. 15). The print replicates many of the features used by Lane and Chalon. Flowers decorate the back and side of Victoria's head while her left hand grasps a rose. An expressionless face combines with an exaggerated neck, heaving bosom, and impossibly hourglass waist. Even the stylistics of the steel-engravings employed by *Finden's Gallery of Beauty* are crudely imitated. The delicately stippled effect of Victoria's face, neck, and shoulders metamorphose into a series of heavily shaded contrasts. Stippling is a style of engraving recognizable by a densely packed area of tiny dots, as opposed to the series of cross-hatched lines that identify a wood-engraving. Stippling was commonly used to add tone to the face, particularly in expensive steel and copper-plate engravings. Thus, when the cheap print adds stipple, even crudely, to the more quickly produced line-engraving used for the rest of the print, it is attempting to mimic more expensive forms of reproduction. Chalon's Royal Academy painting, Lane's refined steel-engraving, and the anonymously produced cheap print: the similarities between these three very different forms of reproduction demonstrate the impact of publishing phenomena like the Books of Beauty.

The diffusion of Victoria's glamorous portraits is matched by the way that poems, published in widely different journals, celebrated her beauty. Poems and prints fed off one another in a freely circulating royal mythology. The allure surrounding Victoria even led one overwhelmed poet in *Blackwood's* to refer to her as the 'Salome of the West'.[35] Tellingly, numerous poems explicitly addressed the way in which they implicated their readers in their admiration. As Charles Swain's 'Coronation Song' makes explicit, the use of Petrarchan conceits transforms all of those consuming her image into Petrarchan lovers:

> While thousand, thousand hearts are thine,
> And Britain's blessing rests on thee,
> Pure may thy crown Victoria shine—
> And all thy subjects *lovers* be.[36]

Matching the political fantasies of the street ballads was a swirl of sexualized affect enveloping Victoria. Prior to Victoria's marriage, the potency of her glamour and desirability owed much to her overtly sexual status as an eligible Virgin Queen. Even the *Penny Satirist* sardonically declared that she converted radicals by virtue of her beauty alone. The journal claimed to know 'to a certainty, that a great number of young and middle-aged men cannot obtain a comfortable night's rest on account of her'.[37] Victoria's creation as a Beauty was instrumental in helping to generate the type of idealized fervour around her.

The comments of the *Penny Satirist* are important in suggesting that the sentiments espoused by Landon and Stuart-Wortley were by no means confined to those writers associated with the annuals. The Victoria of the Beauty Books can be compared with Ebenezer Elliot's epithalamium on Victoria's marriage, versions of which appeared in the *Northern Star* and *Tait's Edinburgh Magazine*.[38] The annuals repeatedly stressed the benefits of queenly rule and Elliot's epithalamium portrays a Queen wholly identified with her subjects:

> But can the Queen be happy,
> If millions round her weep?

[35] 'Augusta Victrix', *Blackwood's Edinburgh Magazine*, 42 (1837), 815.

[36] Charles Swain, 'Coronation Song', *English Melodies* (London: Longman, Brown, Green & Longmans, 1849), 281.

[37] 'Penny Satirist Office', *Penny Satirist*, 22 July 1837, 2.

[38] Ebenezer Elliot, 'Epithalamium on the Marriage of Victoria the First', *Northern Star*, 15 Feb. 1840, 7.

> In love's elysium, while hope faints,
> Can Hope's Victoria sleep?
>
> No. Bringer of Redemption! thou,
> In love's elysium sleeping,
> Would'st wake, to grieve with starving men,
> And worth in dungeons deep.[39]

Victoria is so attuned to the privation of her poorest subjects that her own pleasure can only be achieved by the amelioration of their living conditions. Here, Elliot differs from the vacuous generalizations of many paeans in that Victoria's concern for her subjects is given a far more specifically political agenda. In the last two verses of the quotation, Victoria's identification with the radical cause is such that she is even grieving for the three imprisoned Monmouth Chartists. Elliot goes on to suggest that if Victoria knew their characters she would pardon them. Elliot's politics were far removed from those of the Books of Beauty. Significantly, though, his poem shares the same stress on the attractiveness of Victoria and the link between the Queen and her subjects. Despite the different appropriations of Victoria, the affinity between the multitude of poems and prints is testimony to their cumulative impact.

The Books of Beauty soon lost their charm and their circulation fell steeply from the beginning of the 1840s. The expanding and diverse market for women's periodicals nevertheless continued to encourage feminine sentiment towards Victoria. There were also several journals devoted to following the events of high society, such as the *Court Circular* (1856–1911) and the *Court Journal* (1829–1925). Fashion and high society news remained staple features of numerous women's periodicals. Their subject-matter reflects the continued influence of the aristocracy and the court. Margaret Beetham has argued that Victoria was also a key source of non-political news for a new genre of women's illustrated newspaper.[40] The two founding exponents of the genre, the *Lady's Newspaper and Pictorial Times* (1847–63) and *Queen* (1861–), are notable for the way that they involved their readers with the royal family. Both were 6*d.* publications, heavily illustrated with high production values, and aimed at a broadly middle-class readership. They were closely linked to publications like the *Illustrated London News* because they were centred upon news rather than simply romantic fiction and fashion. Contemporaries referred to them as 'class' papers. Beetham has argued that, at a time when news was usually connected with a masculine public political sphere, the presence of a female sovereign was crucial to inventing the category of women's news. Royal activities received widespread coverage.

---

[39] Ebenezer Elliot, 'Ode on the Marriage of Victoria the First', *More Verse and Prose. By the Corn-Law Rhymer* (London: Charles Fox, 1850), 19.
[40] Beetham, *A Magazine of Her Own?*, 98.

Many incidental articles were also devoted to Victoria's role; one typical piece in the *Lady's Newspaper* suggested that her feminine influence deserved its own female poet laureate.[41] Even after her retirement from public life, the health of the Queen and the romances of her children were given regular discussion.

Women's periodicals encouraged a personal and familiar relationship between Victoria and her female subjects. Upon royal occasions, the *Lady's Newspaper* and *Queen* enthusiastically promoted their female readers' loyal participation. At the wedding of the Prince of Wales, *Queen*, for example, provided its readers with a crochet pattern of a wreath of oak leaves surrounding the royal crest and the initials of Edward and Alexandra.[42] It was intended to ornament large flags, banners, and draperies. Similarly, in November 1862, *Queen* printed a pattern of 'The Queen's Shawl' for its readers to make.[43] They could enjoy the glow of being kept warm by a shawl that had supposedly been approved by Victoria herself. Women's periodicals created a bloc of articles upon the royal family that promoted the importance of the Queen's personal character. They domesticated the appeal of the monarchy and were far removed from any discussion of it as a political institution.

What was the effect of the seemingly omnipresent coverage of Victoria? One consequence was a bewildering contrast between her various manifestations. The *Art Union* wished that Victoria could find some way of punishing those who libelled her to her face. It declared that it was impossible not to be struck with the exceeding difference between one picture and another. Although both might profess to be true portraits 'one or both must be as like her as the Sovereign Lady of the Sandwich Islands'.[44] Similar comments can be found in the *Spectator*, the *Star*, and the *Athenaeum*.[45] Comparing the portraits so far examined underlines the extent of the contrast between the various Queens. Their discursive range emphasizes the fissures and instability of Victoria's representation.

It was the extensive circulation of royal portraits that placed contrasting representations of the Queen alongside one another. The ideological differences between them, however, were part of a more general condition. The novelty of a young female sovereign was matched by the bewildering diversity of paradigms attempting to depict her. There was a lack of appropriate forms for portraying Victoria's sovereign position. Comparisons to Britannia, Elizabeth I, and Princess Charlotte were common. Several poems and prints

---

[41] 'A Queen's Laureate', *Lady's Newspaper*, 18 May 1850, 269.
[42] 'The Royal Banner Screen', *Queen*, 21 Feb. 1863, 490.
[43] 'The Queen's Shawl', *Queen*, 22 Nov. 1862, 225.
[44] 'The Portraits of the Queen', *Art Union*, 15 May 1839, 64.
[45] 'Fine Arts', *Athenaeum*, 4 Aug. 1838, 556; 'Queen Victoria and her Illustrious Mother', *Star*, 7 Oct. 1837, 1.

even compared Victoria to Una from Spencer's *The Faerie Queene*.[46] The frequent stress on Victoria's femininity caused a tension between Victoria's state body and her private body. This tension, which reflects a fear of female power, is evident in numerous caricatures that either predicted a state of petticoat rule or showed Victoria wearing the breeches.

Court portraiture is a genre traditionally devoted to displaying the monarch's role as head of state. It was therefore particularly affected by the ideological tension around Victoria's sovereign position. Many prints continued to employ the traditional icons of majesty: the crown, sceptre, and regalia. Nevertheless, publications like the Books of Beauty created a style of monarchy that downplayed Victoria's sovereign position. The widespread dislike of royal ceremony also encouraged a reduction in any visible signs of formal pageantry. Court portraiture was a genre increasingly removed from the type of monarchy created through popular prints, newspapers, and illustrated periodicals. At the same time, though, Victoria's official portraits could not avoid the influence of these publications. This caused the disruption of a fine art hierarchy because, as Lynda Nead has pointed out, what was a suitable subject for a lithograph was not the same as what was acceptable in an oil painting.[47] Victoria's portraits were caught between the generic demands of court portraiture and the creation of a more informal style of monarchy.

A comparison between three paintings, David Wilkie's painting of Victoria's first Privy Council and portraits by George Hayter and Thomas Sully, exposes the contradictions embedded in court portraiture (see Fig. 16). The instability of the genre is evident in both the paintings themselves and their reviews in the periodical press. In Wilkie's painting, the first picture Victoria herself commissioned in the new reign, the influence of the melodramatic discourse around Victoria meant that Wilkie was felt to have contravened the conventions of the genre. Dressed in a white unadorned gown, Wilkie's Queen has none of the signs usually associated with a state portrait. Furthermore, the choice of dress could not have been further removed from what Victoria actually wore. Following the death of William IV only hours previously, Victoria was dressed in mourning black. Similarly, ninety-seven Privy Councillors actually took part in the council whereas Wilkie includes only a selection. Depicting them all would have ruined the contrast between Victoria and the Privy Councillors. Greville, the figure seated in the right foreground as Clerk of the Privy Council, called the painting 'a very unfaithful

[46] John Ord, 'Carmen Triumphale, the Royal Progress to the City', *The Bard and Minor Poems*, ed. John Lodge (London: Simpkin, Marshall & Co., 1841), 167; H.B., *The Political Sketches of H.B.*, vol. 6 (London: Thomas Maclean, 1841), no. 530.
[47] Lynda Nead, *Myths of Sexuality* (Oxford: Basil Blackwell, 1988), 62.

Fig. 16. Engraving by Charles Fox after David Wilkie, *Queen Victoria's First Council* (London: Francis Moon, 1846)

representation of what actually took place'.[48] Wilkie's painting was composed in accordance with a melodramatic narrative created through a large number of prints and newspaper reports.

The organization of space in Wilkie's painting conforms to an already existing mythology of the event. The contrast between Victoria and her Privy Councillors captured the public imagination in the days following her accession. Numerous reports dwelt on the melodrama of the ingénue Queen alone in the midst of the masculine powers of state. The *Examiner* adulated over the astonishing self-possession and modesty of Victoria when facing 'the sudden transition from the parent's side to the Privy council—the novel situation of appearing without any female attendants in the midst of a large assemblage of men'.[49] Greville declared there was 'never anything like the first impression she produced, or the chorus of praise and admiration which it raised about her manner and behaviour'.[50] Wilkie constructs a gendered contrast that is also a political contrast between Victoria and the patriarchal power of the Privy Councillors. Among the Privy Councillors depicted are the most powerful

[48] Charles Greville, *Greville's Memoir's of the Reign of Queen Victoria 1837–1852*, ed. Henry Reeve (London: Longmans, Green & Co., 1888), 104.

[49] 'The Queen', *Examiner*, 25 June 1837, 401.

[50] Greville, *Memoir's*, 3, 415.

men in the nation. They include Melbourne, Peel, Russell, Wellington, Lord Grey, and the Dukes of Sussex and Cumberland. They are grouped together as a distinct entity: their age and gravitas accentuate Victoria's youth and femininity. Significantly, the scene depicted by Wilkie is the moment immediately after the proclamation of Victoria's succession. The Privy Council, led by the Prime Minister, Lord Melbourne, are about to attach their signatures to the document officially declaring her reign. Wilkie's painting underlines the shift in the relationship between the Crown and parliament that was brought about by the Reform Bill. The painting is of a formal state occasion—the first of a new reign—yet political power clearly lies with the Councillors who are grouped en masse around the Queen. With echoes of 1688, it is the leading politicians who are just about to validate Victoria's succession. Wilkie's painting symbolically reinforces Victoria's position as a constitutional monarch. Her sovereignty is only possible by the validation of the Lords and Commons.

Despite the depiction of Victoria as a maiden monarch, there is no doubt as to the most important figure in the painting. Wilkie's composition belies Victoria's political weakness by giving her a spatial dominance. Wilkie noted in his journal that Victoria was positioned 'a little elevated to make her the presiding person'.[51] Thus, despite being seated and barely above 5 ft tall, Victoria is carefully placed on a level vertical plane with all of the standing Privy Councillors, thereby ensuring that they do not dominate the scene over her. The Privy Councillors are also obscured by their numbers and by the table across the right half of the painting. Victoria's strong position in the open left foreground makes her the undoubted focal point of the picture. These elements all ensure that the viewer's gaze, like that of the members of the Privy Council, focuses upon Victoria. The homology between these two gazes embodies a domain of patriarchal standpoints. Victoria's femininity is made the principal attraction in every sense of the word.

Contemporary reviews of Wilkie's painting reveal the tension between the conventions of court portraiture and the melodramatic discourses surrounding the event. When it was exhibited at the Royal Academy in 1838, the *Spectator* noted that it was the centre of attraction.[52] Reviewers gave more commentary to Wilkie's picture than to any other painting. Significantly, though, critical reaction was lukewarm. The reviews of Wilkie's picture can be usefully understood through Pierre Bourdieu's theory of symbolic capital. Bourdieu argues that practices of artistic display and reviewing are part of the production of the symbolic value of the work of art. They are thereby one of the means by which a fine art hierarchy is maintained. Reviews of Wilkie's paint-

---

[51] Cunningham, *Sir David Wilkie*, iii. 229.
[52] 'Fine Arts, Royal Academy Exhibition', *Spectator*, 12 May 1838, 445.

ing certainly attempted to uphold the traditional role of court portraiture in that they criticized it for failing to express the majesty of the Queen. They consequently worked to maintain the existing distinction between the different types of graphic media. The *Spectator* noted that the great fault of the picture lay in its lack of dignity: 'A stranger might take it to be a representation of an innocent girl under examination by a court martial, in the cabin of a ship, instead of a new-made Sovereign receiving the homage of recognition from the magnates of the land, in a palace.'[53] The *Spectator* feigns ignorance of an event that had already become part of the fabled narrative of Victoria's accession. In so doing, it calls attention to the generic expectations brought to the painting and to the power relations within it. The Queen herself was described as one of Wilkie's 'plump rustic simpletons with a doll-like air'.[54] Similar comments were made by the *Observer* and the *Athenaeum*. Wilkie was an artist renowned primarily for his genre painting and the *Athenaeum* suggested that he was unsuitable for such formal work. It claimed that Wilkie 'exceeded his mission when he passes the boundaries of the familiar and domestic'.[55] Anna Jameson, writing in the *Monthly Chronicle*, likewise complained that, while Wilkie need not have given Victoria the imperious airs of an Elizabeth, 'she sits on the edge of her chair like a timid country girl, and holds her "most gracious declaration" as if it were a petition for mercy'.[56] The criticisms of Wilkie's picture emphasize that what might have been appropriate for a lithograph or cheap melodramatic print was not acceptable for the formality that reviewers desired from an official state painting.

The reaction to Wilkie's painting can be compared with reviews of the royal portraits by Hayter and Sully (see Figs. 17 and 18). The latter's reception highlights the extent of the contradictory demands upon Victoria's portraits. Wilkie's Queen was inappropriate as a national painting of historical record. However, those portraits which employed the traditional icons of majesty found themselves equally out of step with the dominant perception of Victoria. The *Art Union* noted that 'most of the painters appear less ambitious to picture a fine young maiden than the British Queen; and as much importance seems to be attached to the Robes "Coronation" and "Dalmatic" and so forth, as to the form and features of the Royal Lady'.[57] Hayter's two portraits betray the tension of the field of court portraiture in that they overstress the signs of Victoria's maturity and sovereignty. Hayter's first portrait was a

[53] Ibid.

[54] Ibid.

[55] 'Fine Arts; Royal Academy', *Athenaeum*, 12 May 1838, 347; 'Royal Academy', *Observer*, 13 May 1838, 3.

[56] Anna Jameson, 'The Exhibition of the Royal Academy: English Art and Artists', in John Olmsted (ed.), *Victorian Painting: Essays and Reviews* (London: Garland, 1980), i. 227.

[57] 'The Portraits of the Queen', 64.

Fig. 17. Sir George Hayter, *Queen Victoria* (1838), now in the
National Portrait Gallery

commission from the London Corporation and his second was the result of a
request from Victoria. Writing in *Bentley's Miscellany* in 1837, Richard
Hengist-Horne declared that Hayter's Guildhall portrait portrayed a Victoria
who was at least twenty years too old. He wondered whether it would not better
pass as one of Victoria's royal aunts.[58] Oliver Millar has recently drawn attention to the unusual conventions employed by Hayter's second portrait. It was

---

[58] Richard Hengist-Horne, 'Her Majesty's Portrait's—the Great State Secret', *Bentley's Miscellany*, 4
(1838), 243.

Fig. 18. Mezzotint by Charles Edward Wagstaff after Thomas Sully, *Queen Victoria* (1838)

not customary for the monarch to be seated. In painting, as opposed to engraving, since Van Somner painted James I, the sovereign had seldom been shown actually wearing the crown and holding the sceptre and orb.[59] The regalia was normally set to one side and the monarch shown in the Robes of State. Whereas it was once court portraiture that engravings copied, Hayter may well have unwittingly reflected the cheap prints in circulation.

The reviews of Hayter's portraits reveal that they too were considered to be poor likenesses. The *Examiner* claimed that the portrait that showed Victoria enthroned in the House of Lords, was 'too grave, formal and determined in the assumed expression to do justice to that open, lively and gregarious character, which is more frequent with the illustrious original'.[60] In its review of the Guildhall portrait, the *Athenaeum* likewise noted that Victoria had a more

[59] Oliver Millar (ed.), *The Victorian Pictures in the Collection of Her Majesty the Queen* (Cambridge: Cambridge University Press, 1992), i, p. xix.
[60] 'Fine Arts', *Examiner*, 26 Feb. 1838, 118.

serious air than other portraits. However, in 'rendering this expression of dignity to the full, something of likeness has, perhaps, been sacrificed'.[61] Artists were caught between the mutually exclusive demands of state portraiture and the dominant perception of Victoria. Critics have rightly noted that the long-term trend of court portraiture was to present a domesticated rather than a divine monarch. At Victoria's accession, however, her lack of regality resulted in a series of portraits that were perceived to overstress the majesty of the monarch.

Hayter's portraits of an excessively mature and regal Victoria can be usefully compared to Thomas Sully's highly praised portrait. Sully was an American painter commissioned to undertake a portrait by the Society of the Sons of St George in Philadelphia. As well as fulfilling his initial commission, he produced a three-quarter length version for Hodgson and Graves. Sully's painting portrays a youthful and attractive Queen, who yet retains some of the stately dignity that Hayter was attempting to convey. In a highly revealing review, the *Art Union* declared that it was both simple and dignified, 'the picture of a fine young maiden, and, yet, of a crowned Queen'.[62] Sully's portrait is far more successful than Hayter's in combining the ideological contraries of Victoria's majesty and femininity. Victoria is not swamped or obscured with swathes of ceremonial robes and velvet hangings. The *Art Union* specifically praised that fact that her robes were not heavy or overlaid with ornament. There was 'no object to attract the eye from her gracious bearing and generous countenance. Her state is more in her person than in any accessories by which she is surrounded.'[63] The latter sentence sums up the difference between the portraits by Wilkie and Sully and those by Hayter: the former stress her femininity while the latter mitigate it. Sully's picture employs the generic conventions of court painting, but does so within a context of fashionable portraiture influenced by the Books of Beauty. Hence it was successful in bridging across the conflicting demands upon Victoria's representation. Taken together, the contrary reviews of these paintings express the way in which the weight of Victoria's media making was being taken up by newspapers, the Books of Beauty, illustrated periodicals, and, later, photography. In so doing, they emphasize that the changing character of the monarchy cannot be separated off from Victoria's reproduction through the expanding range of graphic media.

Individual portraits and prints continued to be released with impressive regularity throughout the 1840s and 1850s. These decades are nevertheless most notable for the development of an illustrated press. The employment of wood-engraving for graphic reportage came into its own with periodicals like

---

[61] 'Our Weekly Gossip', *Athenaeum*, 17 Feb. 1838, 125.
[62] 'Engravings', *Art Union*, 16 Apr. 1839, 52.   [63] Ibid. 52.

the *Illustrated London News*, the *Illustrated Times* (1855–62), the *Pictorial Times* (1843–8), and the *Illustrated News of the World* (1858–63). Of the new swathe of illustrated periodicals, *Punch* and the *Illustrated London News* were by far the most long lasting and influential, commencing publication in July 1841 and May 1842 respectively. The graphic coverage of Victoria's tours examined in the previous chapter does not fully capture the important epistemological shift in the character of the monarchy that was created by the illustrated press. Tracing its development emphasizes the difference between the illustrated press and the individual prints of the 1830s. At one level, there is a very discernible formal shift. Even when compared with the portraits by Sully and Lane, the royal coverage of the *Illustrated London News* obviously has a much less traditional or aristocratic aesthetic.

In a conjunction that had far-reaching effects, Victoria's accession coincided with the emergence of an illustrated press. Many provincial and metropolitan newspapers sought to provide illustrations of the coronation, competing with the large number of individual prints and lithographs produced. In a ground-breaking study of graphic journalism, Celina Fox has argued that the 1830s were a crucial period of equipoise between the decline of individual prints and the technical and societal changes that precipitated the success of *Punch*, the *Illustrated London News*, and their host of imitators:

> In 1830, such a generic term [graphic journalism] is almost too portentous to describe what amounted to an unpredictable flow of political and personal satirical prints in London, sporadic outbursts of visual propaganda in the provinces and an irregular supply of topographical illustrations in newspapers and broadsides. By 1850, the vehicles for such material had been developed and streamlined into a continuous, large-scale production of illustrated newspapers and magazines, distributed throughout the country.[64]

During the 1820s and 1830s, few newspapers gave illustrations of contemporary events. The *Observer, Bell's Life in London*, and the *Weekly Chronicle* were the most prominent newspapers who occasionally did so.[65] The *Observer* started publishing visual news in the early 1820s, although only of very exceptional events such as the Cato Street conspiracy, the trial of Queen Caroline, the coronation of George IV, and the notorious Weare murder of 1823.

The scarcity of events considered worthy of illustration underlines the novelty of the numerous commemorative coronation newspapers (see Fig. 19). The *Observer* produced an illustrated edition that was sold as a

---

[64] Celina Fox, *Graphic Journalism In England during the 1830s and 1840s* (New York: Garland, 1988), 21–2.
[65] The same proprietor owned the *Observer* and *Bell's Life in London*.

Fig. 19. Henry Vizetelly, 'Victoria', *Observer*, 28 June 1838, 2

double-number costing 10*d*. Many provincial newspapers were also able to produce an illustrated edition. In Devon, for example, *Woolmer's Exeter and Plymouth Gazette* and the *Western Times* printed portraits of Victoria and a view of the interior inside Westminster Abbey. Both were four-page weekly newspapers selling for 4½*d*. Significantly, the *Leeds Mercury* also used the illustrations printed by the *Western Times*. This duplication would have been achieved through stereotyped engraving plates and reflects both the use of new technology and the inability of individual newspapers to resource their own illustrations. All of the special editions were works of major effort and expense. The *Observer* produced its largest-ever illustrations, yet its engravings still only consisted of three portrayals of the coronation service and a panorama of the procession. It was only the high level of interest in Victoria's coronation that was able to supply the necessary commercial impetus to produce the numerous commemorative newspapers. The circulation of the *Weekly Chronicle* reportedly doubled for its illustrated coronation edition.

By far the most innovative of the coronation newspapers was the *Sun*. Its front page was printed entirely in gold typeface with a large medallion engraving of the Queen in its centre.[66] With no type on its reverse, the illustration was explicitly designed to function as a removable portrait. Quickly gaining the name of the 'Golden *Sun*', its publication became an event in itself; understandably so considering its striking quality. The *Western Times* claimed that it was as 'elegant and beautiful as it is unrivalled in the annals of a newspaper'.[67] The *Cork Standard* exhibited the copy that reached the town in its office window as a public attraction because it was considered so extraordinary.[68] The complexity of its publication reputedly required the labour of three large establishments, comprising between 200 and 300 workers. At the same time as large numbers of pages had to be printed with the gold typeface and the engraving, paper of sufficient quality able to hold the ink also had to be specially made. Demand for the 'Golden *Sun*' was enormous, with the paper going through twenty editions by 20 July. Rival newspapers estimated that 250,000 copies were sold, testimony to the popularity of the Queen and to the novelty of its printing techniques.[69] Indeed, the extra number of coronation newspapers that were sent by post to the provinces, 175,000 at one count, was such that the Post Office had to organize extra carriages to transport them from London.[70] One of the more telling indexes to the amplified impact of newspapers and prints upon the monarchy—their role as part of a ritualistic and national coming together—is that circulation figures were invariably far higher for those editions reporting large royal occasions.

[66] The 'gold' was in fact dusted bronze mixed with varnish.
[67] 'The *Sun* in Gold', *Sun*, 2 July 1838, 2.   [68] 'The Golden *Sun*', *Sun*, 5 July 1838, 2.
[69] 'The Golden Sun', *Sun*, 6 July 1838, 4.   [70] 'The Metropolis', *Spectator*, 7 July 1838, 625.

Despite the effort that went into graphic reportage of Victoria's coronation, newspapers' achievements were soon surpassed by the impressive modernity of both *Punch* and the *Illustrated London News*. The large cuts of *Punch* far outstrip the small single cut provided by *Figaro in London*. Published weekly, the *Illustrated London News* was equally innovative in providing a constant and extensive supply of visual news. In contrast to the single sheet of engravings provided by the *Observer* in 1838, from 1842 the *Illustrated London News* supplied over two dozen illustrations each week. The standardized regularity of the illustrated press was at the core of a crucial difference between the constant supply of visual news and the various portraits released as individual prints. Chris Brooks has argued that, whereas formal portraits are iconic, fixed in both convention and action, the illustrated press was concerned, above all, with the flow of events.[71] In a defining shift, Victoria and Albert's relationship to their visual image moved from the iconic to the dynamic, from the portrait to the image. Rather than events producing a spate of prints, the illustrated press had itself to produce a constant series of events. The succession of royal civic engagements traced in the preceding chapter was the perfect foil for the new illustrated press. Victoria and Albert's ongoing public duties were ideal for being created in the form of regular graphic news. They exemplify the way in which the character of the monarchy was defined by the emergence of modes of publication like the illustrated press. The attention that the *Illustrated London News* gave to the monarchy established the ubiquitous presence of Victoria on a week to week basis.

The illustrated press provided a distinctly modern experience of the monarchy. Writing in *Blackwood's Magazine* in 1844, the novelist Catherine Gore declared that the new art of illustration belonged to the quickness of the modern age. She predicted that the world of letters would be replaced by the world of emblems. Illustration would replace written matter because it allowed greater speed of comprehension. It was the ideal media to be 'available to those sons of the century always on the run'.[72] Gore predicted that MPs' portraits would soon be daguerreotyped for the morning papers; the best artists would delineate Victoria's drawing-rooms for general consumption; and close-up engravings of boxing-matches would avoid the need for vivid description of the injuries received. Gore's prophesies, many remarkably prescient, reflect the excitement caused by the potential of the illustrated press. They demonstrate the way that publishing developments could create a novel yet immediate interaction with Victoria.

The *Illustrated London News* was the industrialization of wood-engraving in

[71] Chris Brooks, 'Representing Albert', in Chris Brooks (ed.), *The Albert Memorial* (New Haven: Yale University Press, 2000), 42.

[72] Catherine Gore, 'The New Art of Printing', *Blackwood's Magazine*, 55 (1844), 47.

its ambitious production of visual news. It was also, however, its aestheticiza-
tion. The initial address of the *Illustrated London News* was keen to stress that
its engravings were far removed from the crudeness associated with the woodcuts accompanying Catnach's street ballads or the scurrility of the various
satirical journals:

To the wonderful march of periodical literature [wood-engraving] it has given an
impetus and rapidity almost coequal with the gigantic power of steam. It has converted blocks into wisdom, and given wings and spirit to ponderous and senseless
wood . . . Art—as now fostered and redundant in the peculiar and facile department
of wood-engraving—has, in fact, become the bride of literature; genius has taken her
as its handmaid; and popularity has crowned her with laurels that only seem to grow
the greener the longer they are grown.[73]

Integral to this self-promotion is the association of wood-engraving with both
the march of progress and the widespread belief in the edifying influence of
art. Whereas the style of the satirical engravings of Charles Grant in the
Penny Satirist owed much to the ideographic woodcut tradition, full of thick
heavy lines, uniform tones, and coarsely rendered detail, the engravings of the
Illustrated London News are notable for their finely hatched lines and more
delicate tonalities. The formal quality of the *Illustrated London News*'s
engravings functioned as a mark of aesthetic distinction and a sign of its
realist aesthetic. The style of its engravings was instrumental in dissociating
the periodical from the disreputable practices and low regard with which
woodcuts were associated.

  The respectability that informed the whole tone of the *Illustrated London
News* is particularly evident in its approach to the fractious political issues
of the 1840s and 1850s. It is crucial to emphasize that the *Illustrated
London News* was far removed from the partisanship of the daily metropolitan
newspapers, which were invariably heavily focused on events at Westminster.
The *Illustrated London News* decried any party political alignment. Its
first issue declared that it would be 'less deeply political than earnestly
domestic'.[74] Ruled by the household gods of the English people, the *Illustrated
London News* would devote itself to depicting the 'beautiful chain, which
should be fastened at one end to the cottage, at the other to the palace, and
be electric with the happiness that is carried into both'.[75] This ideology
of communal harmony underpins the nature and the ubiquity of the
Illustrated London News's soft-focus coverage of Victoria. During the 1840s
and 1850s the *Illustrated London News* enacted its holistic views through
its regular coverage of Victoria's activities. The periodical's own widespread

[73] 'Our Address', *ILN* 14 May 1842, 1.   [74] 'Our Principles', *ILN* 21 May 1842, 17.
[75] Ibid. 17.

dissemination consequently helped to build a link between the royal family and its readers.

From its inception royal events loomed large in the news values of the *Illustrated London News*. The very first edition of the periodical was timed to coincide with a lavish historical costume ball hosted by Victoria. The majority of the first issue's engravings consisted of drawings of the participants in period dress. Five months after its initial publication was the Queen's first tour of Scotland, an episode to which the *Illustrated London News* responded with commercial relish and royalist gusto. After despatching two artists to shadow the royal party, the *Illustrated London News* devoted most of its resources during the following five weeks to illustrating every aspect of Victoria's journey. Sixty-three engravings of the tour were eventually published, an exceptional number. Ranging from small vignettes to large ceremonial set-pieces, they depicted subjects as various as their sizes, from Victoria's marine arrival to Romantic highland landscapes.

Compared to events that took place unexpectedly, Victoria's tours and visits provided a guaranteed source of coverage in that they followed an itinerary that was well broadcast in advance. Through recording the number of front pages on which the *Illustrated London News* and its principal competitors included either an engraving or an article devoted to Victoria and Albert, it is possible to quantify the weight of attention devoted to the monarchy.[76] The royal media coverage of the latter part of the twentieth century is more than matched by the sustained attention given to Victoria and Albert over a twenty-year period from the commencement of the *Illustrated London News*. Figure 20 shows the number of royal front pages of the *Illustrated London News*, the *Pictorial Times*, and the *Illustrated Times*. I have chosen the latter two papers to demonstrate the extent to which the agenda of the *Illustrated London News* was imitated by its chief rivals amongst the illustrated press. Between 1842 and 1847, the royal coverage of the illustrated press was exceptional. The percentage of royal front pages of the *Illustrated London News* over that period was 18.5 per cent. For the *Pictorial Times* it was 18.3 per cent between 1843 and 1847. These figures stem from the number of engagements undertaken by Victoria in the early years of her reign, and to the initiative of the *Illustrated London News* in turning them into graphic news. The *Illustrated London News*'s royal coverage was at its lowest in 1848, but throughout the 1850s there continued to be substantial if rather formulaic coverage. As the 1850s progressed, more and more attention was paid to the younger members of the

[76] While newspapers had advertisements on their front pages, the illustrated press led with a combination of engraving and article. The most sumptuous illustrations were rarely on the front page, but the engraving and article were usually of the most important news items.

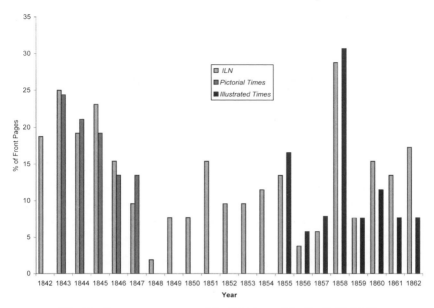

Fig. 20. Front-page coverage of the British royal family, 1842–1862

royal family. It is the shift to the next generation that accounts for the overall rise in coverage in the late 1850s that is shown in Fig. 20.

Royal civic events not only dominated Victoria's coverage; they set the agenda for the overall coverage of the illustrated press. It was more than the front pages that Victoria and Albert monopolized. The attention given to Victoria's visit to Napoleon III in 1855, a year in which the *Illustrated London News* was claiming weekly circulation figures of 130,000, is symptomatic of its wall-to-wall coverage. The event was certainly one of the largest royal occasions of the 1850s. Nevertheless, quantifying the illustrations of the visit of the *Illustrated London News*, in relation to the space taken up by engravings devoted to other subjects, reveals an illustrated press in thrall to the monarchy:[77]

18 August 1855	43 per cent engraving space devoted to royal visit
25 August 1855	100 per cent engraving space devoted to royal visit
1 September 1855	97 per cent engraving space devoted to royal visit
8 September 1855	64 per cent engraving space devoted to royal visit
15 September 1855	43 per cent engraving space devoted to royal visit

[77] Each engraving in the five-week period was graded according to its approximate size, 1 point for A4 or just under, 2 for a full-page A3, and 3 for double-page A2. Incidental vignettes were not included.

Over a five-week period, an average of just over 70 per cent of the visual space of the *Illustrated London News* was devoted to the royal visit to Paris. The extent of the *Illustrated London News*'s coverage is the material embodiment of the royal populism examined in the previous chapter. Constituting a ubiquitous royal narrative that was modern in both deed and the way it was experienced, the *Illustrated London News* did its level best to ensure that Victoria really was the popular figurehead it so desired her to be.

The momentum surrounding Victoria was nevertheless only possible because of the breadth of artefacts through which she was expressed. The vibrant aural culture of the London streets was equally as important as fine art prints and newspapers, especially at the beginning of the reign. One commentator writing at the time of Victoria's marriage expresses wonderfully the experience of being constantly bombarded with the presence of the royal couple to be:

our ears were stunned in walking the streets by jangling ballad-mongers, chaunting the praises of the royal couple, likenesses of whom stared us in the face at every corner. Here you had a ragged vagabond who howled through his nose a choice ditty about the Prince, to the tune of 'Welcome Charlie' . . . Further on, you were accosted by a man with shaggy hair, who bawled loud enough to be heard over half the metropolis, 'Vill you buy the *poortreat* of the wonderful furriner vot's to have our beautiful Queen for his loving and confectionary wife'. You hurried off, stealing a glance in passing at a print shop, hoping to regale your eyesight with some fine picture, when lo! You saw a very small lady, sitting upright in a chair, with an infinite litter of flowers at her feet, and a little crown on her head . . . You peevishly pursue your way, and in your haste narrowly escape upsetting an image-board and its bearer. You *must* look up. Heaven grant the beautiful group of the Graces be there. Silly delusion. Who can blame the absence of beauty when royalty fetches so high a price. Well, a host of Albert and Victorias occupy the whole board, of all sizes and dimensions—some of them, in truth, of such babyish proportions, that, in the vagueness of wanton fancy, you might imagine that the royal pair had already multiplied sweet images to an alarming extent.[78]

Victoria and Albert were one of the most frequently worked subjects of the ballad sellers and street patterers. One ballad singer told Henry Mayhew that he worked twenty-three different songs regarding the marriage of Queen Victoria.[79]

As well as the numerous ballads marking the latest royal occasion, the street patterers were notable for the cocks and squibs they cried in the London thoroughfares. Typically, these were fictional stories of murders, elopements,

---

[78] Rigdum Funnidos, *The Royal Wedding Jester; or Nuptial Interlude* (London: J. Duncombe, 1840), 7–8.
[79] Charles Hindley, *The Life and Times of James Catnach* (London: Reeves and Turner, 1878), 327.

suicides, and affairs in high society. Included amongst the patterers' reper-
toire were accounts of pretended marital jealousies between Victoria and
Albert. Significantly, though, when Mayhew was conducting his interviews for
London Labour and the London Poor, he was told that these patters were now
never worked. One patterer, who had no compulsion over crying the death of
Wellington or a broken limb for Prince Albert in a hunting accident, stated he
could find nothing sensational or salacious to say about the Queen.[80] A second
patterer declared of Victoria that 'nothing can be said against her, and nothing
ought to; that's true enough'.[81] The last time she was confined, however, he had
cried the birth of triplets because 'Lord love you, sir, it would have been no use
crying *one*, people's so used to that'.[82] The patterers' comments are evidence
of Victoria's ability to escape most of the sleaze that had afflicted William IV
and George IV. It is also a telling sign of the stability of the royal family that,
by the early 1850s, Victoria's maternity had become so unshakeably matter of
fact that it could only be made newsworthy by the birth of triplets. The most
profitable royal stories for the street sellers were domestic tiffs; attempted
assassinations; intruders inside Buckingham Palace like the 'Boy Jones'; the
latest royal visit. These narratives, although sensationalized, were premissed
on the same domestic propriety and civic publicness perpetuated by the
newspapers and illustrated press.

   Complementing the sales of ballads was an equally vigorous street trade in
prints. Usually sold from upturned umbrellas for either 1*d*. or ½*d*., the engravings traded in this fashion were part of the protean nature of popular culture.
Many had started off as frontispieces to sixpenny works or as illustrations for
the annuals. Mayhew explicitly notes that individual prints sold in the streets
included portraits from waste *Flowers of Loveliness* and *Forget-Me-Nots*. They
were said to 'go off very fair', particularly the coloured versions.[83] Individual
engravings circulated well beyond their original milieu because of the thriving print trade. The multiple readership of rented and second-hand newspapers is a well-known phenomenon, yet the afterlife of the engravings from the
albums suggests a similar circulation of prints. In the transmission of the royal
portraits we can see the beginning of the creation of a communal experience
of the same visual image.

   When Mayhew interviewed the street sellers of prints, he was told that sales
of 'Queens', 'Alberts', and 'Wales's' were notably reduced from what they once
were. One street seller complained to him that 'There's so many "fine portraits
of Her Majesty," or the others, given away with the first number of this or that,
that people's overstocked. If a working man can buy a newspaper or a number

---

[80] Henry Mayhew, *London Labour and the London Poor* (1861; New York: Dover, 1968), i. 228.
[81] Ibid. 228.   [82] Ibid. 228.   [83] Ibid. 303.

why, of course, he may as well have a picture with it.'[84] As well as being more evidence of the oversupply of royal prints, the comment suggests that aural ballads and cheap woodcuts were being passed over in favour of the attractions of new reading matter: weekly newspapers, miscellanies, penny fiction, and sensational police gazettes.

Alongside the aural culture of the streets, there was a flourishing trade in shows, spectacles, and commemoratives. Victoria and Albert found their names appended to a bizarre variety of goods. Their wedding immediately produced what the *Sunday Times* called the 'Albert Mania'. The 'Victoria wax-wicks' gave way to the 'Albert Lucifer' firebox and the 'Albert rush-light'. It was even rumoured that the 'Widow Welch's Pills' were to be newly christened the 'Saxe-Gotha Boluses'.[85] Such practices were highly enduring. At the marriage of the Prince of Wales, *Punch* complained about the exploitation of the Alexandra corset, hair-waver, and dentifrice.[86] Commemorative artefacts were matched by the number of shows that broadcast the occasion. At the time of the coronation, London theatres put on tableaux of the event for the majority unable to get inside Westminster Abbey. At Astley's Royal Amphitheatre, performances were being advertised even before the coronation itself had taken place. Astley's show was a pageant 'including England, Ireland, and Scotland, and Wales, with all the attributes of the nations, paying homage to our beloved Queen'.[87] The coronation fair in Hyde Park included a similar display.[88] Provincial cities such as Exeter and Plymouth also received touring shows. At the end of July 1838, Exeter's Theatre Royal put on a spectacle consisting of three coronation tableaux.[89] Similarly, Howe's Exeter Bazaar proudly advertised that it had engaged a top London artist to supply its Gothic Gallery with pictures of the coronation procession and the interior of Westminster Abbey, along with portraits of Victoria and the principal personages.[90]

Closely related to the theatrical tableaux were the panoramas, cosmoramas, and dioramas commemorating royal occasions (see Fig. 21). These spectacles functioned as both entertainment and reportage. Panoramas, like the illustrated press, were ideal for conveying the spectacle of royal occasions. Several large panoramas of the Queen's first visit to the City were produced and coronation panoramas 20 ft and 40 ft long were being advertised soon

---

[84] Henry Mayhew, 303.

[85] 'The Albert Mania', *Sunday Times*, 2 Feb. 1840, 5.

[86] 'The Prince and the Puffers', *Punch*, 43 (1863), 155.

[87] 'Astley's Royal Amphitheatre', *Sunday Times*, 24 June 1838, 4. See also BM Add. MS 27729, James Planché, 'The Fortunate Isles', a masque performed at Covent Garden in honour of Victoria's marriage.

[88] Agnes Strickland, *Queen Victoria: From her Birth to her Bridal* (London: Henry Colbourn, 1840), ii. 68.

[89] 'Exeter Theatre', *Trewman's Exeter Flying Post*, 3 Aug. 1838, 3.

[90] 'Howe's Exeter Bazaar', *Western Times*, 16 June 1838, 1.

Fig. 21. *Tableau of the Procession at the Queen's Coronation* (London and Edinburgh: R. Tyas, 1838)

after the event.[91] Much smaller hand-held panoramas designed for home consumption were also widely available. In April 1839, the Diorama in Regent's Park opened for its new season with a show of the coronation service.[92] Cosmoramas, which were elaborate forms of peepshow, also frequently included scenes of the latest royal event. In 1848, the Thames Tunnel was still offering cosmoramic views of the Queen's wedding for a penny.[93] Complementing the range of entertainment were various waxwork exhibitions that often included domestic royal tableaux. At Madame Tussaud's, there was soon a new group of waxworks in a coronation tableau (it was replaced by a marriage group in 1840 and changed thereafter as events dictated).[94] The various newspapers, prints, and entertainment demonstrate the cumulative effect of Victoria's media making. Through the vigour and variety of the way in which Victoria was materialized, in provincial cities such as Exeter as well as London, we can see the scale of resources mobilized around the monarchy.

What did all the different portrayals of Victoria add up to? What sort of monarchy did they denote? These questions were as pressing for writers in the late 1830s and 1840s as they are for this book. A comic article in *Bentley's Miscellany* by Richard Hengist-Horne in 1838 devoted itself to examining the uncanny number of portraits. Horne, a poet best known for his *New Spirit of*

[91] 'Mr Robin's Coronation Panorama', *Sunday Times*, 1 July 1838, 1; 'Messrs Fores Coronation Panorama', *Sunday Times*, 22 July 1838, 1.

[92] 'Our Weekly Gossip', *Athenaeum*, 27 Apr. 1839, 316.

[93] Richard Altick, *The Shows of London* (Cambridge: Belknapp Press of Harvard University Press, 1978), 374.

[94] 'Madame Tussaud's', *Art Union*, 15 July 1839, 110.

the Age (1844), was then involved in the radical metropolitan circle of the unitarian preacher William Johnson Fox. This circle included Robert Browning, Harriet Taylor, and John Stuart Mill. In this essay Hengist-Horne, an occasional writer on art for the periodical press, captures the impact of the unprecedented number of portraits upon the way that Victoria was experienced. His article is extraordinary because it enacts an epistemological shift from the fixity of the portrait to the fluidity of the image. Through the expansion of the print market that I have just been tracing, the royal portraits ceased to be portraits. There was no change in their material form but they were now living and meaning within a different order of things. For Hengist-Horne, the portraits created Victoria as a media monarch because their volume, and the differences between them, meant that they foreground the nature of their own mediation.

Hengist-Horne's article, entitled 'Her Majesty's Portraits—the Great State Secret', declared that there was an extraordinary hallucination in the minds of artists painting Victoria. None of the portraits was alike. Moreover, printers and proof-takers shared the hallucination because 'the very copies of the same picture or plate differ from one another'.[95] Like a game of Chinese Whispers, the original portrait became increasingly unrecognizable as it was reproduced. For Hengist-Horne, the authenticity of Victoria's portraits had disappeared beneath the weight of their own reproduction. The excessive volume of portraits meant that they lost any notion of Victoria's presence behind or within the pictures. His claim that dissimilar versions of the same image were in circulation stems from the transmission of Victoria's portraits into different graphic media. The same portrait was often available in versions ranging from steel-engravings and etchings to lithographs.[96] Each was not simply a copy but, as Ruskin would later emphasize in *Ariadne Florentina*, a translation into another media. Commemorative pottery and pirated versions of more expensive prints also tended to produce crude copies of Victoria's portraits, as did the expansion in the number of impressions being taken from the plates engraved for the fine art printsellers.

The contrast between reproductions of the same portrait was matched by the contrast between the number of different representations of Victoria. Tongue in cheek, Hengist-Horne warns that such differentiation threatens a national calamity. Each portrait should be treated as a treasonable offence he declares. He recounts an anecdote of a Cornish farmer complaining about the expense of financing seven Queens after having seen seven very different

---

[95] Hengist-Horne, 'Her Majesty's Portrait's', 241.

[96] Chalon's portrait, for example, was published as a print by Moon & Co. on 1 May 1839, with a smaller version released to coincide with Victoria's coronation on 28 June 1838. A coloured etching had also been published as early as 1 Feb. 1838. See BM Oversize Portfolio 82 [Queen Victoria and Prince Albert].

'likenesses'. After all, Hengist-Horne asks, what else can an honest country-
man think: 'he sees a quantity of portraits, some fat, some slim, some short of
stature, some full ten heads high, some very pale, some very rosy, many
brunette, and with features and expressions of all sorts of different and
opposite characters;—what *can* honest folks think but that there are as
many Queens as portraits?'[97] Playing with the notion that there has to be a
physical referent for each image, Hengist-Horne uses the rustic's response to
express the alien modernity of such a degree of mediation. Significantly,
though, the comedy of the article is premissed on a knowing metropolitan
standpoint that is shared by both author and reader. In its dialectic between
the familiar and the uncanny, Hengist-Horne's essay catches media culture in
a moment of becoming. He parades the seemingly incomprehensible differences between the portraits of Victoria. Yet, at the same time, his argument
assumes an assured birds-eye comprehension of the range of royal prints in
circulation.

To prevent the unrestrained reproduction of her image, *Bentley's Miscellany* wished Victoria would follow the example of Elizabeth I. She should
decree the existence of one authentic Patron Portrait. All other likenesses
would be banned. Every portrait would have to adhere to the likeness of the
Patron Portrait or the artist would face punishment according to the degree of
deformity produced. Without one picture depicting one officially sanctioned
likeness, Hengist-Horne prophesied that a host of disasters would follow. The
article argued that the recent rebellion in Canada could be directly ascribed
to forty-three portraits that were shipped to St John's, Brunswick, with nine of
them finding their way into Upper Canada. The Canadians could not be convinced that the nine were treasonable imitations because the Patron Portrait
had yet to be produced. Consequently, the people of Toronto took up arms
directly. When foreign suitors came to court the Queen after having seen
Victoria's portrait, the result would be 'each foreign prince dying over a different queen, and no foreign prince falling in love with the real one because
there is no Patron Portrait'.[98] Hengist-Horne's concern over the loss of a
uniquely authentic image is keyed into contemporary anxieties over the
control and copyright of texts (a new Copyright Act was passed in 1842 after
several years of agitation). These concerns were themselves caused by the
increasing market for cheap fiction and the consequent multiple piracy of
novels like *The Pickwick Papers*. Hengist-Horne's article can also easily be
compared with Walter Benjamin's work on mechanical reproduction.
However, it is the case with Hengist-Horne, and perhaps with Benjamin's
aura too, that the Patron Portrait is not what has been lost because of the welter

<hr>

[97] Hengist-Horne, 'Her Majesty's Portrait's', 247.   [98] Ibid. 248.

of reproductions. Rather, it is something that has taken on a fetishized value precisely because of that process.

Hengist-Horne's article is crucial because it dramatizes the loss of portraiture's ability to fix an iconic, ideal, stable depiction. His article is premissed on treating the pictures of Victoria as images rather than as portraits: they were portraits that had come loose from their material moorings. Victoria's pictures existed within long-standing conventions of portraiture but because of their very multiplicity they were now functioning as media images. The article's principal conceit can be usefully compared to the way Andy Warhol's work plays with the image of iconic figures like Marilyn Munroe and Elizabeth Taylor. Warhol's *Marilyn Diptych*, for example, depicts fifty images of Marilyn Munroe. All of them are different screen prints with each face having very slight variations in detail, colour, and features. However, Warhol's choice of such a fetishized icon means that all of the reproductions are instantly recognizable, despite their differences, in exactly the way that those of Victoria were claimed not to be. Richard Brilliant has argued that the subject of Warhol's *Marilyn* is 'image-making rather than portraiture because the work so clearly emphasises the mechanism of popular representation in the modern age but not the person represented'.[99] Warhol's screen prints and Hengist-Horne's article are responses to the same process of image making. Whereas *Bentley's Miscellany*'s concern is for maintaining the physical referentiality of Victoria through her Patron Portrait, Warhol concentrates on the way in which the images refer only to each other. The difference in approach shows that Hengist-Horne stands at the beginning of the conceptual and historical spectrum that would culminate with Warhol.

Hengist-Horne did not have to concern himself for long as a Patron Portrait was soon in circulation. It was, of course, the Penny Black postage stamp. The ubiquity of Victoria's presence in the first three years of her reign, and the concern over the copyrighting and authenticity of graphic images, come together revealingly in the circumstances that led to its publication. A brief examination of the Penny Black, a coda to Hengist-Horne's call for a stamp (*sic*) of authenticity, situates the stamp within the expanding graphic culture of the 1830s. Through her circulation on the Penny Black, Victoria very literally helped to bring the nation together. The subsequent status of the Royal Mail makes it second only to the coinage in terms of circulating the royal image. The Penny Black was one of the most successful developments to emerge out of the graphic culture of the late 1830s.

The Penny Black was first released on 6 May 1840. Its issue was the result of long-standing abuse of the existing postal system. Following the passing of

[99] Richard Brilliant, *Portraiture* (London: Reaktion Books, 1991), 49.

the parliamentary bill legislating for prepaid penny postage, a Treasury competition was announced on 6 September 1839 for the design of the stamps and postal stationery. At this stage there was no definite plan to use the Queen's head as the icon for the new stamp. Of the four prize-winning entries, only that of Benjamin Cheverton used the Queen's head. Out of the 2,600 overall entries, only Cheverton's and an entry by William Wyon, a prominent medallist of the period, are known to have centred their designs on Victoria. Most entries relied on intricate geometrical or heraldic designs. The Treasury was deeply concerned about the forgery of the new stamps and one of the principal reasons for the use of Victoria's head was the need to identify forgeries easily. Cheverton thought that using the head of Victoria would be the best guarantee against counterfeiting: '[the eye being] educated to the perception of differences in the features of the face, the detection of any deviation in the forgery would be more easy—the difference of effect would strike an observer more radically than in the case of letters or any mere mechanical or instrumental device.'[100] Rowland Hill recommended Cheverton's suggestion in his competition report to the Treasury. He noted that the Queen's head was 'the essential part of the stamp and that which presents the most difficulty to the forger'.[101] After all, what face could be more recognizable than Victoria's? Moreover, as Hengist-Horne's article demonstrates, the difference between her portraits was all too identifiable. Victoria's initial popularity and the vigorous trade in royal portraits cannot be directly linked to the choice of icon for the first stamps. Yet they are indubitably part of the same configuration. Ironically, it was only the recognition value of Victoria's profile achieved by the extensive circulation of the Penny Black that would prevent it being counterfeited. Here was a Queen who was forged, in every sense, by her representation.

[100] Douglas Muir, *Postal Reform and the Penny Black* (London: National Postal Museum, 1990), 87.
[101] Quoted ibid. 102.

3

OF HYPE AND TYPE

We are not to be deceived by the lip and the pen, for the lip of the courtier and the pen of the snob have no relationship to the character of Englishmen.

(*Reynolds's Newspaper*)[1]

The variety of images and artefacts concerning Victoria was unprecedented. Nevertheless, on its own, such plenitude constitutes only one-half of Victoria's media making. The monarchy was not just the product of an extensive procession of graphic and written news. There was an ongoing epistemological endeavour to interpret the modernity of Victoria's publicness, to understand the forms through which she was experienced. Hengist-Horne's article is merely one example of the way in which the ensemble of prints and poems was actually conceptualized as a specifically media aesthetic. Numerous commentaries testify to a pervasive self-consciousness towards Victoria's figure. The language of royal reportage; the nature of Victoria-as-celebrity; the intimate bond that the press achieved between the Queen and the People; these were all subjects engaged with by a variety of radical and satirical periodicals, especially *Punch*, the *Penny Satirist*, and *Reynolds's Newspaper*. The numerous commentaries of these journals add up to one of the defining features in the media making of Victoria: namely, her contemporaries' own conception of it as such.

The extent of the attention given to Victoria caused a corresponding shift in anti-monarchist critiques. In a fashion akin to Bagehot's *The English Constitution*, public fascination with the monarchy was such that writers often ascribed to it an overwrought political agency. Antony Taylor has recently argued that British anti-monarchism is largely dependent on a long-standing stock of images of corrupt political practices. These imply that the 'aristocratic and kingly lifestyle is irredeemably flawed by the sloth, intrigue and

---

[1] 'The Great Epidemic of Typhoid Loyalty', *Reynolds's Newspaper*, 17 Dec. 1871, 1.

dissoluteness of a leisured and pampered life'.[2] While Taylor is right to stress the continuities of anti-royalist writing, I think he thereby downplays a shift in the nature of its critiques. Responses to Queen Victoria exemplify the way that the Crown reinvented its imaginative prominence in the aftermath of the 1832 Reform Bill. Traditional radical tropes regarding the beguiling effects of aristocratic mummery were applied to the burgeoning supply of royal prints, ballads, and newspaper stories. Critiques of the absorbing spectacle of royal pageantry metamorphosed into protests regarding the diverting role of the royal culture industry. Similarly, the pretension of royal journalism was claimed to falsify the gloss of the monarchy in the same way that its true nature had formerly been accused of being hidden by the tawdry splendour of the court.

Concern over the relationship between the monarchy and the press was hardly a novel phenomenon. In a famous case in 1812, Leigh and John Hunt were sentenced to two years imprisonment for libelling the Prince of Wales in the *Examiner*. The *Examiner's* prosecution came about through its response to an article in the *Morning Post* that had rhapsodically celebrated the Prince's virtues, describing him as an 'Exciter of Desire' and an 'Adonis of Loveliness'. The *Morning Post* was notorious for its fulsome coverage of high-society events and its devotion to the aristocracy. The *Examiner* castigated it as a byword for cant. It was a purveyor of absolutist adulation that 'none but the most prostituted pens would consent to use,—the paper, in short, of the STU-ARTS, the BENJAFIELDS, the BRYNES, and the ROSA MATILDAS'.[3] Importantly, Leigh Hunt's offending article can be contrasted with the critiques made during Victoria's reign in that it derived directly from the strong political influence of the Crown. Hunt's anger was motivated by newspapers' attempts to curry party favour with the newly appointed Regent. His piece in the *Examiner* was the culmination of a series of articles attacking the sycophantic language used by Tory and Whig newspapers.[4]

The *Examiner's* prosecution was part of the widespread self-consciousness towards print culture that characterized Regency radicalism. Marcus Wood has argued that this dynamic is particularly evident in the satirical work of George Cruikshank and William Hone.[5] Their pamphlets, including *The Political House that Jack Built*, *Non Mi Ricordo! The Man in the Moon*, and *The Queen's Matrimonial Ladder*, were among the most widely circulated and

---

[2] Antony Taylor, *'Down with the Crown': British Anti-Monarchism and Debates about Royalty since 1790* (London: Reaktion, 1999), 55.

[3] 'The Prince on St Patrick's Day', *Examiner*, 22 Mar. 1812, 179.

[4] Other articles include Charles Lamb, 'The Triumph of the Whale', *Examiner*, 15 Mar. 1812, 173; 'Ministerial Movements and Regal Flatterers', *Examiner*, 1 Mar. 1812, 129; 'Princely Qualities', *Examiner*, 8 Mar. 1812, 144–5; 'The Regent's First Levee', *Examiner*, 15 Mar. 1812, 161–2.

[5] Marcus Wood, *Radical Satire and Print Culture 1790–1822* (Oxford: Clarendon Press, 1994).

influential anti-government satires between 1815 and 1822. In 1817, Hone's notoriety was enhanced through three trials where he was prosecuted for blasphemous and seditious libel. The charges were bought against three of his pamphlets, *The Late John Wilkes's Catechism*, *The Political Litany*, and *The Sinecurist's Creed*. In these pamphlets, Hone used the form of sacred texts to attack the government. For Wood, the work of Hone and Cruikshank is marked by its appropriation of the language and graphic forms of an expanding print media; that of advertising, chapbooks, children's literature, almanacs, and showman's bills. *A Slap at Slop* (1821) parodied the form of a four-page folio daily newspaper, while *Non mi Recordo!* (1820) ended with three pages of mock handbill advertisements. *The Political House that Jack Built* (1819), published after the Peterloo massacre, famously used the language of a children's nursery-rhyme book. It typifies the method of Hone and Cruikshank in that its satiric impact owes much to the extensive publishing of cheap chapbooks, ballads, and catechisms between 1795 and 1815. These pamphlets often sought to educate morally the poor and their children, and, in so doing, encourage their loyalty to King and Country. The political potency of *The Political House that Jack Built* stems from its imitation of these heavily ideological tracts.

In addition to parodying the official forms of the judiciary and the Church, Hone and Cruikshank also imitated rituals connected with the court.[6] One typical example of this latter type of political appropriation is a pamphlet published in 1820 after the trial of Queen Caroline. Its title piously declared that it was a set of prayers '*to be used daily by all devout People throughout the Realm, for the Happy Deliverance of Her Majesty, Queen Caroline From the late most Traitorous conspiracy*'. The pamphlet provided psalms and prayers for the protection of Caroline against those who would besmirch her. They were supposedly to be read at the beginning of the morning and evening service. Hone plays upon the practice of releasing an official form of prayer to commemorate a royal birth or wedding. In parodying court conventions, the pamphlet celebrates Queen Caroline and attacks the institutional forces ranged against her.

Hone and Cruikshank's appropriation of new developments in popular publishing, along with their parodies of official forms of language, help to explain the later self-consciousness towards Queen Victoria's figure. Although Wood places their publications within a tradition that goes back to the 1790s, he argues that their work marked a final flowering of radical satire. Yet, the dynamic he identifies infuses periodicals of the 1830s and 1840s such as *Figaro in London*, the *Penny Satirist*, and *Punch*. The use of parodic

---

[6] Marcus Wood, 14.

versions of the Queen's speech to parliament occurs frequently in these jour-nals, and was certainly still in use by *Punch* as late as 1870. The lampoons of the *Court Circular* and the court newsman also exist firmly within this gen-ealogy. They are part of a long-standing concern with official ritual and langu-age. The *Penny Satirist*, for example, regularly printed its own domesticated version of the *Court Circular* between 1838 and 1843. In the mock versions published after Victoria's wedding, Victoria and Albert are often portrayed discussing the latest political event at the breakfast table. Similarly, the attacks upon royal reportage by *Reynolds's Newspaper*, while certainly not satiric, owe much to the way deferential language was perceived to aid the monarchy. The self-consciousness towards Victoria's figure was not an iso-lated dynamic; it constituted part of an ongoing radical engagement with the impact of print media and the imaginative appeal of the monarchy.

The first responses to Victoria's figure emerge out of the phenomenon of 'Reginamania' that surrounded her accession. One recurring expression of the affect around Victoria was the belief that a widespread revival in monar-chical loyalty was taking place. A series of articles yoked together constitu-tional paradigms with a belief in the almost totemic influence of the press. These commentaries interpreted Victoria's prominence as a reversion to an older form of sovereignty. Significantly, there were two very different histori-cal models used to describe what was happening to the monarchy. The first saw a revivified personal allegiance to Victoria in terms of a resurgence in her governing role. The popular emotion aroused by Victoria's accession seemed to threaten a return to the type of unquestioning loyalty received by divinely appointed monarchs. Alternatively, though, the second model had a far more progressive slant, one which was akin to the discourse around Victoria's civic tours. An important element of the Gothic Revival—then coming into its full force—was a constitutional mythology that looked back to the pre-Conquest Saxon kings. The Gothic Revival promoted a medieval golden age of Saxon liberty where assemblies of the People elected monarchs to limited powers. The Saxon period provided the starting-point for a mythic narrative of popu-lar freedom that went on to encompass the Magna Carta and the Glorious Revolution. This model of the monarch as a communal figurehead was used by Benjamin Disraeli to turn Victoria's accession into the latest chapter in a national Gothic genealogy. In *Coningsby* (1844) and *Sybil* (1845), Disraeli creates a loaded political contrast between the type of elected 'representa-tiveness' associated with the Reform Bill, and the popular 'representative-ness' that Victoria seemed to embody. Instead of representation achieved through the extension of the franchise, Disraeli suggests that the emotional and political investment in Victoria made her equally able to carry out the popular political will.

In Disraeli's Young England trilogy, both *Coningsby* and *Sybil* are notable for the idiosyncratic version of constitutional history they espouse. It was a subject of ongoing importance for Disraeli. As early as 1835, he published *A Vindication of the English Constitution*. This was two years prior to becoming a Tory MP in the election following Victoria's accession. Fundamental to *Coningsby* and *Sybil* is their dramatization of the past, present, and future condition of the British monarchy. The primary target of both novels is what Disraeli frequently described as the Whig oligarchy. For Disraeli, this was a movement that had its first inception under John Hampden and its most successful fulfilment in 1688. The Whigs had allegedly established what the young Coningsby calls a 'high aristocratic republic in the model of the Venetian'.[7] State power was subsequently confined to an aristocratic coterie consisting of a few prominent Whig grandees. Throughout *Coningsby*, post-1688 political history is unflatteringly referred to as the reign of the Venetian constitution. The position of the British monarch is correspondingly portrayed as being degraded to that of a Venetian Doge. This is a role that was essentially that of chief magistrate. In Disraeli's view, when William IV was forced to give his assent to the Reform Bill, he furthered the erosion of the monarch into a mere Doge.

At the same time as Disraeli attacks the Whig oligarchy, he accuses the contemporary Tory party of being manifestly untrue to the spirit of conservatism. It is described as a party which wishes to conserve 'the prerogatives of the Crown as long as they are not exercised; the independence of the House of Lords, provided it is not asserted; the Ecclesiastical estate, provided it is regulated by a commission of laymen.'[8] *Coningsby* derides the Tory party for the succession of arbitrary lines it had drawn in the sand over constitutional issues. Each line had invariably been washed away by the passage of reform because the party held no abiding creed over what specifically should be conserved. In its policy of exclusiveness in the constitution and protectionism in trade, *Coningsby* claims that current Toryism has nothing in common with the 'ancient character of our political settlement, or the manners and customs of the English people'.[9] Only the heroes of Young England, in the form of the Etonian youths Coningsby and Millbank, can restore genuine Tory principles. The most conspicuous of these is a rejuvenation of the monarchy and the freely given loyalty that it once naturally enjoyed.

In *Coningsby* and *Sybil*, the early enthusiasm around Victoria is opportunistically appropriated into a Tory version of the English Gothic constitu-

---

[7]   Benjamin Disraeli, *Coningsby, or the New Generation*, ed. Sheila Smith (1844; Oxford: Oxford University Press, 1982), 232.

[8]   Ibid. 86.

[9]   Ibid. 66.

tion. The Young England movement can be accused of simply attempting to preserve feudal social structures from the encroachment of industrial capitalism. Disraeli none the less suggests that the nation is on the verge of a new monarchism. In *Coningsby*, the Reform Bill does not pave the way for a further diminution in the Crown's influence. Rather, it is the necessary prerequisite for its populist restoration. Coningsby's mentor, Sidonia, a man who has reputedly been an adviser to every ministerial or royal council in Europe, declares that England is moving ever closer to a truly monarchical system:

> The tendency of advanced civilisation is in truth to pure Monarchy. Monarchy is indeed a government which requires a high degree of civilisation for its full development . . . An educated nation recoils from the imperfect vicariate of what is called representative government. Your House of Commons, that has absorbed all other powers in the State, will, in all probability, fall more rapidly than it rose. Public opinion has a more direct, a more comprehensive, a more efficient organ for its utterance, than a body of men sectionally chosen. The Printing-press is an element unknown to classical or feudal times. It absorbs in a great degree the duties of the Sovereign, the Priest, the Parliament; it controls, it educates, it discusses. That public opinion, when it acts, would appear in the guise of one who has no class-interests. In an enlightened age the Monarch on the throne, free from the vulgar prejudices and the corrupt interests of the subject, becomes again divine![10]

A revived monarchy that will supersede electoral government is central to the reactionary conservatism advocated by *Coningsby* and *Sybil*. Moreover, according to Sidonia, it is a royalist revival that stems directly from the growth of the representative agency of the printing press.

Given the looming presence of Victoria, Disraeli's political schema in *Coningsby* is fascinating because it is conceived around the way in which different forms of mediation shape the individual roles of parliament, monarchy, and the press. *Coningsby* is deeply opposed to the kind of representative government advocated by Chartism. Discussing the parliamentary debate of the Reform Bill, Coningsby comments that 'nothing is more remarkable than the perplexities into which the speakers of both sides are thrown when they touch upon the nature of the representative principle'.[11] He casts the debate in terms of an opposition between Tory claims that the majority of citizens were virtually represented under the old parliamentary system, and the argument of their radical opponents that if the principle of representation was conceded, 'the people should not be virtually, but actually represented'.[12] According to Coningsby both standpoints misinterpret the central issue. This is because neither party examined the original character of the popular assemblies that had always prevailed among the 'Northern' nations.[13] These

---

[10] Ibid. 266.   [11] Ibid. 31.   [12] Ibid.   [13] Ibid. 32.

Gothic assemblies included all of the estates of the realm. Thus, in Norman England there were the Clergy, the Barons, and the Community. The first two appeared personally, while the third, comprising small landowners, appeared by representation purely because of their number. Coningsby argues that the Reform Bill debate mistakenly treated the House of Commons as the House of the People rather than the House occupied by the privileged class of the third estate. In so doing, the parliament of 1831 conceded the principle of universal suffrage. The £10 property qualification was merely an arbitrary restriction on the franchise because parliament had already made the fallacious admission of the People as an estate of the realm. Hence, for Coningsby, parliament had conceded a right to mass electoral representation when, but for its own misconception, 'the bewildering phrase "the People" would have remained what it really is, a term of natural philosophy and not of political science'.[14] The latter comment emphasizes the degree to which *Coningsby* was part of the larger contest over the meanings ascribed to the People. As part of his attempt to deny the historical legitimacy of the desire for widespread enfranchisement, Disraeli attempts to empty the term of any political connotations.

Despite Disraeli's hostility to the franchise, his new conservatism is premissed on incorporating the principle of 'representation'. *Coningsby* disavows a specifically electoral version of representation, yet instead proclaims a new political arena established upon the representative properties of the printing press. Following the views of Sidonia, Coningsby explicitly declares that Public Opinion transmitted through the press now counts for more, because it is more genuinely representative than the opinions expressed in parliament. In the future, Public Opinion would be communicated to the sovereign via the press. Such transmission would remove the need for that other intermediary, a parliament that justified itself upon its ability to metonymically represent the views of all of the different estates of the realm. The press would not only literally become the fourth estate, it would replace the second and third estates of the Lords and Commons. It is an all-encompassing schema that can be compared to Habermas's conception of the ideal bourgeois public-sphere. Disraeli promotes a similarly critical and enlightened space, whose autonomy is unmarked by any inherent social or political bias. *Coningsby* is typical of the period in ascribing a totemic agency to the press as a fourth estate. However, the model of transparent mediation via the printing press it promotes is obviously one that bears little resemblance to the suppression of large numbers of unstamped newspapers between 1830 and 1836.

The new role taken on by the press is the precondition for the transition of

---

[14] Benjamin Disraeli, 32.

the sovereign from an Italian Doge to an archetypal English Gothic monarch. *Coningsby* prophesies the forging of a new relationship between Victoria and her subjects. Through the press, Public Opinion would be communicated into the mind of the sovereign by an unexplained form of osmosis. The monarch would consequently be able to identify with those interests and inspire a rejuvenated loyalty. In contrast to the factionalism of the House of Commons, Disraeli depicts the monarch becoming a 'representative' sovereign. The monarch would both be the cathexis of Public Opinion and act as its figure-head. The utopian dream of Coningsby, and of the entire New Generation of Young England, is 'the idea of a free monarchy, established on fundamental laws, itself the apex of a vast pile of municipal and local government, ruling an educated people, represented by a free and intellectual press'.[15] For Disraeli, the class tensions of Chartism and the 'two-nations' could not but disappear with such a monarchy. Like Bagehot, Disraeli builds an entire constitutional framework around the ability of the sovereign both to embody and connect with the interests of the People.

In Disraeli's convoluted and specious rewriting of constitutional history it is the Whig oligarchy that has come between the monarchy and the People. Far from moving slowly away from autocratic sovereignty towards a democratic enfranchisement, *Coningsby* claims that the erosion of the sovereign's power under the Venetian constitution has been a chimera obscuring the operation of the Whig oligarchy:

Sovereignty has been the title of something that has had no dominion, while absolute power has been wielded by those who profess themselves the servants of the People. In the selfish strife of factions, two great existences have been blotted out of the history of England, the Monarch and the Multitude; as the power of the Crown has diminished, the privileges of the People have disappeared; till at length the sceptre has become a pageant, and its subject has degenerated again into a surf.[16]

With the press now functioning as a fourth estate and a reformed parliament marred by an inherent factionalism, Young England sees the downfall of the Venetian constitution as nigh. Its fall is the opportunity to reconfigure the original umbilical relationship between the majority and the monarch. The Charter is not the answer to the clamour for reform. *Coningsby* and *Sybil* imply that, as the monarch is rescued from being a mere Doge, the People will be restored to their original political rights.

The presence of Victoria stands behind both *Coningsby* and *Sybil*. Both novels are set amidst the political events of the 1830s and 1840s. This gives

---

[15] Ibid. 313.
[16] Benjamin Disraeli, *Sybil, or the Two Nations*, ed. Sheila Smith (1845; Oxford: Oxford University Press, 1981), 421.

an immediacy to the prophecies of the New Generation that they may soon see 'England once more possess a free Monarchy, and a privileged and prosperous People'.[17] At one level, the claims of Young England could legitimately be seen as mere fantasy given the contradictions within Disraeli's novels, and the contrast between his work and the radical criticism directed towards William IV and Victoria. Nevertheless, the narrative of a royal revival that would reconnect the monarchy and the People is wholly implausible without the looming presence of Victoria. Disraeli exploits Victoria's appeal to criticize the type of representativeness furthered by the Reform Bill. The contrast between the two types of representation is another expression of the utopian political energies creating the figure of Victoria. Disraeli comes close to the street ballads that portray Victoria as a reforming Queen working against the political system. His political project is so significant because the restoration of the monarch's role as a figurehead is directly linked to the press. *Coningsby* is another version of the way that Victoria's media making was believed to have engendered a new type of monarchy.

Victoria's influence on *Coningsby* and *Sybil* is particularly evident in the way Disraeli's constitutional history reaches its inevitable fulfilment in her accession. In *Sybil*, Victoria is explicitly promoted as the Queen who would revive the Gothic constitution. Victoria was the first monarch since Queen Anne who did not jointly hold the British and Hanoverian thrones, a fact used to signify the end of the Hanoverian Dogeship. Thus, in *Sybil*, Disraeli celebrates the appearance of Victoria at her first council by declaring that 'Fair and serene, she has the blood and beauty of the Saxon'.[18] It was Victoria who would 'break the last links in the chain of Saxon thraldom'.[19] Through a severe warping of Victoria's genealogy—which ignores the fact that she was a granddaughter of George III—her accession is mythologized as a return to the true English Gothic constitution. *Coningsby* and *Sybil* are reflective commentaries upon Victoria's populism, wherein Disraeli's constitutional schema is remarkable for both disavowing and appropriating the modernity of her mediated position. Simultaneously, though, in the inordinate agency that both novels ascribe to Victoria, they participate in the very royal revival that they are claiming objectively to describe.

The Young England movement was far from being the only expressed belief that monarchism was resurgent. In its first issue following the celebrations for the Queen's wedding, the *Spectator* bemoaned the rise of royalism in an editorial entitled 'Hue and Cry—What has become of Old Whiggery?'.[20] Old Whiggery, as Disraeli rightly claimed, conventionally saw the monarch as

---

[17] Benjamin Disraeli, *Sybil*.   [18] Ibid. 41.   [19] Ibid.
[20] 'Topics of the Day', *Spectator*, 15 Feb. 1840, 156.

more than the chief magistrate. For the *Spectator*, Whigs might respect the Crown but they ought to know nothing of 'what a Tory terms loyalty—love for the Sovereign in virtue of the Kingly character'.[21] The *Spectator* quoted an extract from the Whig-supporting *Morning Chronicle* to warn that a Whiggish royalism was coming back into prominence with Victoria's accession:

> In the brief space since the commencement of her reign, she has done more to revive the feelings of *popular loyalty* than has been done to damage it through successive generations. The effect has been working slowly, but surely, in the popular breast; and is *ripening into a love for Monarchy stronger than has been felt since the epoch of the Great Rebellion.*[22]

Like Disraeli, the *Morning Chronicle* turned to a pre-1688 paradigm in an attempt to explain the place of Victoria. Although the *Morning Chronicle* and Disraeli are coming from opposite ends of the political spectrum, they both share an endeavour to describe a 'democratic' royalism. In so doing, it is notable that they cut across conventional Whig and Tory discourses. Disraeli's prophesied royal revival appropriated a Gothic narrative beloved of radicals and Whiggish parliamentarians. Likewise, when the *Morning Chronicle* described its support for a Queen, even a Whiggish Queen, in terms of a Tory-style loyalty, it threatened one of Whiggery's most traditional tenets.

Many of the contradictions evident in the *Morning Chronicle's* article and Disraeli's novels stem from the pervasive nature of constitutionalism. The inconsistencies in their claims also throw into relief the unprecedented nature of Victoria's position in the late 1830s and early 1840s. In the same way that there was a bewildering variety of different representations of Victoria, there was a lack of appropriate paradigms through which her mediated position could be understood. Disraeli and the *Morning Chronicle* arguably misconceive the character of the monarchy in that they attempt to understand the enthusiasm for Victoria through a historical narrative that equated loyalty with sovereign power. Nevertheless, it is precisely because this dominant rubric was used to conceptualize Victoria's position that there was an interface between a constitutional and a media monarchy. Indeed, the link between representation and representativeness was a crucial feature of Victoria's reign. As the bourgeois mother of the nation or as the Great White Empress, Victoria both represented the nation and was representative of it. The connection between these two processes, where Victoria was both a subject inspiring imaginative investment and an object created through that investment, helps to explain how she was so closely identified with her age. As

[21] Ibid.   [22] Ibid. 157.

the period became Victorian, her agency seemed to facilitate everything from the march of progress to the moral condition of the nation.

Another major strand in the discourse upon Victoria's media making is a critical engagement with the way in which her life was turned into and consumed as a spectacle of personality. Twentieth-century Hollywood stars are often characterized as performative figures created by an industry of dreams. They express what Christine Gledhill has called 'the intimacies of individual personality, inviting desire and identification'.[23] The attempt to describe a strikingly comparable mixture of identification, intimacy, and performance characterizes many of the responses to Victoria. There was a dialectical relationship between the identification with Victoria and the perceived authenticity of her figure. The degree of collective imaginative investment in Victoria promoted a sense of intimate connection and empathy. Yet the greater the degree of investment, the greater the risk of Victoria being turned into a wholly fabricated figure. Publications like the Books of Beauty helped to produce a sophisticated commentary upon Victoria-as-celebrity, particularly in the first years of her reign as satirical journals played with the novelty of the phenomenon.

Figaro in London was one periodical concerned with exposing what it saw as the performative quality of Victoria's persona. The language of theatricality had long been used to satirize royal events. George Cruikshank famously dubbed George IV as the 'Great Entertainer', while the *Poor Man's Guardian* was one of numerous periodicals to describe William IV's coronation as a theatrical farce.[24] This discourse was now extended to describe the way Victoria herself functioned as a type of popular entertainment. Upon Victoria's first opening of parliament, *Figaro in London* furthered the shift from a notion of royal show, conceived of in terms of pageantry, to the conception of Victoria herself as a celebrity show: 'If it be true that "all the world's a stage", we suppose that Kings and Queens must be tip-top performers; stars engaged at heavy salaries, to play the leading business of this terrestrial hemisphere, Victoria has come out, in the character not only of a lady actress, but as a manageress on her own account.'[25] *Figaro in London* observed that Victoria had long been a favourite in her role as the juvenile princess but she had now appeared in the arduous character of the 'Youthful Queen' (see Fig. 22). It was a role that 'established her at once on the pinnacle of public admiration'.[26] Victoria's role as an actress obviously refers to a sense of her theatricality. The comment is also significant, however, because of the dominance of a star

[23] Christine Gledhill, Introduction, in *Stardom: Industry of Desire* (London: Routledge, 1991), p. xiii.
[24] 'Friends. Brethren and Fellow Countrymen,' *Poor Man's Guardian*, 16 July 1831, 5.
[25] 'The Royal Actresses Debut', *Figaro in London*, 25 Nov. 1837, 185.
[26] Ibid.

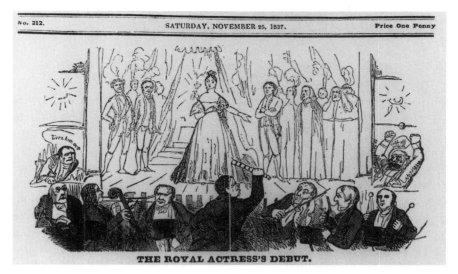

Fig. 22. 'The Royal Actress's Debut', *Figaro in London*, 25 November 1837, 187

system of actors in the nineteenth-century theatre. *Figaro in London* is thus responding to the way in which the monarchy was becoming both a public and a publicized spectacle.

The pressure upon Victoria actively to exploit the impact of print media is reflected in a series of commentaries published by the *Penny Satirist*. It suggested that the Queen should correspond more with her subjects to inform them of her activities, and that, if she was unable to accomplish this personally, it could be achieved through the newspapers. In what could be seen as the precursor to the royal press conference, or even to the monarch's annual Christmas television broadcast, the *Penny Satirist* had its own suggestion as to how Victoria should broadcast herself to her subjects:

Were your Majesty to write a letter occasionally to a morning-paper, or start a paper of your own, you might be of great use in inspiring both the morals and manners of your people. Your Majesty's subjects have at present no opportunity of knowing your Majesty's mind. They only hear of you through flatterers. They hear that you possess every excellence, but they have no opportunity of seeing this excellence.[27]

Despite its facetiousness, the *Penny Satirist* is typical in its desire to replace ersatz flattery with a form of royal communication that is personally guaranteed. Demanding an unmitigated publicness fifty years before the advent of the New Journalism and the celebrity interview, these various suggestions

---

[27] 'Mr Crow to the Queen', *Penny Satirist*, 24 Aug. 1845, 2.

capture perfectly the self-interested pressure that the press was exerting upon Victoria. The monarch's role was not just to submit to his or her appropriation by newspapers, periodicals, and artists. She or he now had to participate actively in the creation of themselves as media beings.

Significantly, the *Penny Satirist's* suggestion was not an isolated one. Following the succession of royal visits and tours, the *Penny Satirist*, the *Family Herald*, and the *Spectator* prophetically advised the Queen to publish an account of her travels.[28] The *Penny Satirist* claimed that all of her female subjects would read it and even proffered its own editorial advice. It recommended that if she entered into particulars respecting her dress and boudoir arrangements 'they would study it like a prayer-book, a book of Queen Elizabeth's homilies'.[29] The making of courtly fashion statements was to be combined with Victoria's creation as an exemplar of domestic propriety. Her private life was to be appropriated for the greater good of public instruction and entertainment. The demands upon Victoria's representation *qua* representation were increasingly collapsing back into material demands upon Victoria herself. As the *Penny Satirist* declared, 'we want a queen who will speak to the nation, who will show us her mind by the expression of her thoughts, which can only be done through the medium of the press'.[30] The demands of the *Penny Satirist* illustrate the way that the expansion in print and graphic media furthered the aim for a greater interaction between Victoria and her subjects. This desire was an act of self-promotion by the press because of its own envisaged role. Yet political demands upon Victoria did stem from the fact that her subjects were increasingly becoming active consumers of her image.

The connection between the intimacy towards Victoria created by the pervasive media coverage and the affect surrounding her is embodied in a whole set of images portraying her as the Queen of Hearts. It was a trope used on numerous occasions to describe the emotional relationship between Victoria and her subjects in the first years of her reign. The 'Golden *Sun*'s' coronation poem and Ebenezer Elliot's epithalamium both referred to Victoria as the Queen of Hearts.[31] In November 1837, *Figaro in London* published a cartoon of Victoria's face embossed on to a playing card (see Fig. 23). A poem in *Blackwood's Magazine* employed the same image when celebrating Victoria's visit to the Guildhall in November 1837:

---

[28] 'News of the Week', *Spectator*, 23 Sept. 1843, 889. 'A Law of Manners—How the Queen Might Be Usefully employed as a Writer for the Press', *Family Herald*, 7 Oct. 1843, 344.
[29] 'Royal Visits', *Penny Satirist*, 28 Sept. 1844, 2.
[30] Ibid.
[31] Murdo Young, 'Coronation Day', *Sun*, 28 June 1838, 1.

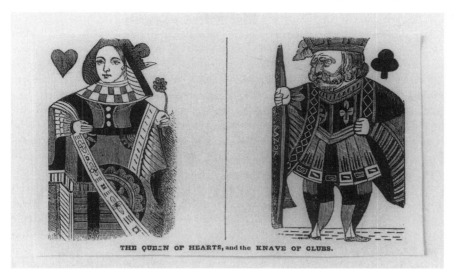

Fig. 23. 'The Queen of Hearts and the Knave of Clubs', *Figaro in London*, 18 November 1837, 181

Sweet as the blushing rose, as lily fair,
She twines the laurel round her golden hair,
And aims at conquest: fearing not to lose,
A Nation's love she smilingly subdues;
Her natural graces all her arms and arts,
Loved soon as seen, she reigns the Queen of Hearts.[32]

The poem moves from a series of overblown Petrarchan conceits to a description of Victoria as the Queen of Hearts. In so doing, it exemplifies the way that the trope was a product of her overall idealization. For example, Victoria never had the golden tresses that the poem suggests. The figure of the Queen of Hearts has to seen as an expression of Victoria's affective connection with her subjects. Curiously, though, in being turned into the Queen of Hearts, Victoria was actually effaced by the media dynamic around her. It was a role that defined her solely through the relationship between her and her subjects.

Victoria's royal celebrity presupposed and constituted an intimate connection with her subjects. The nature of this celebrity was the subject of a letter from Elizabeth Barrett-Browning to her close friend and long-time correspondent, Mary Russell Mitford. Written in June 1844, Barrett-Browning's letter tellingly compares literary celebrity to the recognition enjoyed by the Queen:

[32] 'Augusta Victrix', *Blackwood's Edinburgh Magazine*, 42 (1837), 814.

The inconvenience of celebrity, my dearest friend . . . which is the interest taken in you by the whole world . . . is a noble tax to pay after all,—& it is hard for me to understand how you can have the heart to complain of it. When we are beloved in private life, our very headaches, our very smiles & the choosings of our ribbons are matters of interest to the persons who love us. Do we complain of the tax of this attention to minute things?—Then enlarge the circle of interests, & see if we sh.d. complain any more. Let the writer who has endeared himself to numberless persons & has thus created an interest in them for his person, his habits, his manner of life—complain of the 'tax' when they demand from others, a description of his person, habits and manner of life—& does he not object to the very love and its essential interest which he has created?—Can you look at the matter in another light? Is this tax not a love-tax? If it is an over-worn tax sometimes sh.d. the objection strike against the existence of it? Consider, my dearest friend!—Take the vulgar sovereignty of Victoria, has *she* a right to complain because the newspapers say she 'walked on the slopes'?—And is not the true royalty, after all, (ask Carlyle) *that* ruling by Grace of genius.[33]

In Barrett-Browning's love-tax, an interest in a celebrity's life flows naturally from their admirers' attachment. The letter provides one way of understanding the link between the narratives detailing the minutiae of Victoria's activities and the intimacy felt towards her. Barrett-Browning certainly throws into relief the type of attention surrounding Victoria when she condescendingly refers to her 'vulgar sovereignty'. Victoria's holidays in Scotland provoked numerous complaints of press harassment. Yet, for Barrett-Browning, she has no right to protest given the fact that it was a sign of her subjects' attachment to her. Like Peel's new income-tax, the love-tax was something that Victoria had to pay. It was the necessary price exacted from the Queen for the loyalty she received from those consuming her image.

The intimacy described by Barrett-Browning testifies to an emotional space in which a whole series of identifications and desires were played out. The ballads depicting Victoria as a radical Queen were the projection of hopes and desires that gave her agency and yet, simultaneously, robbed her of any self-agency. Satirical articles on the plethora of prints and news stories were complemented by a discourse that sought to understand Victoria's complicity in their circulation. Sophisticated commentaries emphasized Victoria's personal impotence in the face of her own media creation. The Queen was shown as the puppet of her subjects as they invested her with charismatic qualities. One complaint from the *Penny Satirist* takes the form of an imaginary conversation between the Queen and her mother. Victoria complains about her puppet status and its undermining effect upon her self-identity:

[33] Elizabeth Barrett-Browning, *The Letters of Elizabeth Barrett-Browning to Mary Russell Mitford*, ed. Meredith B. Raymond and Mary Rose Sullivan (Waco, Tex.: Armstrong Browning Library of Baylor University, The Browning Institute, and Wellesley College, 1983), ii. 375.

I am an artificial thing—a puppet that goes by strings without any self-determining power. Everything I say is repeated. Everything I do is imitated and recorded. If I smile they find and suspect a reason for it; if I do not smile, another reason is forthcoming; and the consciousness of this so affects my nerves, that I lose self-possession, and raise the suspicions which I strive to prevent. I wish I were a milk-maid or a shepherdess, or any blythe country lass, whom nobody knows or cares for but her own dear lad . . . Every lady in the country has a private home but myself. The palace is a public house into which everyone claims a right to peep, and whose domestic arrangements everyone claims a right to judge.[34]

It seems that the hothouse atmosphere of celebrity was not an exclusively twentieth-century phenomenon. The *Penny Satirist* acutely dramatizes the psychic split caused by Victoria's awareness of her multiple identities. Not only does she have to face up constantly to the artificiality of her independently created public self; her status as Queen threatens to overwhelm any alternative private self. The puppet metaphor empathises with Victoria's subjection to forces over which she had no command. An unfortunate extension of the justification of Victoria's civic engagements—that she was placing herself before the People—was that she was regarded as very much general property.

A second complaint suggests the degree to which the excess of signification invested in Victoria was a gendered phenomenon. Faced with yet another suitor, upon this occasion the French duc de Nemours, an exasperated Victoria declares that she will be a free woman forever. She states, 'I don't care about the nation. I tell you I am nothing but a spectacle, a Judy without a Punch.'[35] The *Penny Satirist* employs the familiar puppetry trope to link Victoria's femininity with the extent to which she is signified upon. This is partly because her visibility is neither subsumed into the role of a wife, where she would be represented as one of a couple, nor the role of a mother, where she would be seen in relation to her children. Victoria would soon be depicted in both of these guises and it is noticeable that she never again enjoyed the same frisson of prominence as she did in the period before her marriage. Marina Warner has called attention to the frequency with which women are used to symbolize ideals such as Justice, Liberty, and Nationhood. This is exemplified by figures like Britannia, Columbia, and La Liberté.[36] Warner argues that the gender of these monumental figures stems from the fact that it is far easier for women to be invested with such idealized meanings. A comparable process helped to turn Victoria into the type of spectacle that the

[34] 'From the Queen to her Mother', *Penny Satirist*, 20 July 1839, 2.
[35] 'The Penny Satirist', *Penny Satirist*, 8 Dec. 1838, 2.
[36] Marina Warner, *Monuments and Maidens: The Allegory of the Female Form* (London: Weidenfeld and Nicolson, 1985), 1–60.

Penny Satirist's queens chafe against. There is nevertheless a severe irony in Victoria's actions and motives being thus dramatized by the *Penny Satirist*. It imagines Victoria's personal reaction to her coverage in order to criticize her appropriation by the press. Yet, in so doing, it reproduces the very tendency that it is criticizing.

Such commentaries stem, in part, from an inevitable disappointment over the initial hopes raised by her accession. Whereas the first years of Victoria's reign provoked discussions about the unparalleled phenomenon of 'Reginamania', reaction to subsequent royal events betrays a far greater scepticism towards the plethora of prints and commemoratives. This reaction is particularly evident amongst radicals who had held out impassioned hopes for Victoria's accession. When street ballads portrayed Victoria enacting reform or simply providing a bountiful dinner table, they aspirated popular aspirations through her. The use of her name during the campaign for the Second Reform Bill makes manifest the degree to which she continually became the overdetermined vessel of contemporary anxieties and wishes. The growth of disenchantment with Victoria also included a sceptical reaction against the emotional relationship between her and her subjects. There was a coming-to-awareness of the degree to which the aspirations present at Victoria's accession had been exploited and exacerbated.

A letter published in the *Northern Star* in December 1840 typifies the reaction against an excessive identification with Victoria. Written by an anonymous columnist, Junius Rustiqus, the letter movingly traces the shift from the bright optimism of Victoria's accession to the current bitterness of self-delusion:

Joy had paved in advance for all the blessings which hope contemplated for your reign; but the people soon found out that they had been the dupes of their own vain imagination. They felt it would be unjust to blame you, and they could scarcely bear to blame themselves. In the bitterness of their self-accusation and self-condemnation, they almost welcomed the added miseries as proper punishment for their self-deception. They now saw, and acknowledged their own folly, in supposing that you would have the power, even if you possessed the inclination, to better their condition.[37]

Rustiqus's letter expresses a loss of innocence in relation to the hopes imbued in Victoria. There is a realization of the extent to which the public were part of a loop responsible for circulating and amplifying the overstated claims made around Victoria. Rustiqus's letter emphasizes the way that consumers of Victoria's image were responsible for buying into a creation that was the projection and exploitation of their own imaginings.

---

[37] Junius Rustiqus, 'To your Queen's most excellent Majesty', *Northern Star*, 12 Dec. 1840, 6.

Rustiqus hoped his readers would realize that they now had to rely on themselves to achieve political change. No longer would they put their trust in idols, whether of wood and stone or of flesh and blood. In supporting a monarch who they believed was going to represent their interests, they had actually been alienated from a belief in their own political agency:

> Your Ministers virtually abolish your office by making it a sinecure. England is now not under a monarchy but an oligarchy. We are a nation of star-gazers. Our attention is drawn from ourselves, and, fixed upon shows that, in the meanwhile, we may be robbed of all that is substantial. Your reign has hitherto been one of delusion and mockery.[38]

Rustiqus's critique betrays an acute awareness of the ideological processes at work in the making of the Queen's figure. It is based on the continuing prominence of the monarchy in national life in spite of the loss of its power. Like Bagehot's dignified role, there is an overriding sense of the beguiling simulacrum of Victoria's diffuse yet intimate presence. For Rustiqus, when radicals looked up to Victoria their attention was diverted from a self-fashioned reforming agenda. Their reforming aspirations were projected into the Queen herself. The affective and imaginative labour invested in Victoria become an independent property possessed by her.

Unsurprisingly, given the news values of the illustrated press, many responses to Victoria's media making were concerned with the ubiquity of the royal news coverage. The impact of news—as a specific cultural form—was conceived of as an integral part of the monarchy's changing character. While 'news' was invariably given a political agency, there was a significant spectrum of responses to the impact of Victoria's coverage. On the one hand, *Punch* and *Reynolds's Newspaper* frequently criticized the frivolous and inconsequential weight of attention that the royal family received. These critiques, however, existed alongside a much more liberal view of the press. In this model, news was celebrated as a reforming and revelatory force, able to strip away the last vestiges of aristocratic mummery. Such faith in the totemic power of the press was, in part, a legacy of its political oppression during the 1820s and 1830s. In *The House the Jack Built*, Hone exemplifies this in that he portrays the printing press as a reforming weapon:

> This is,
> THE THING
> that, in spite of new Acts,
> And attempts to restrain it,
> by Soldiers or Tax,

---

[38] Ibid.

> Will *poison* that Vermin,
> That plunder the Wealth
> That lay in the House,
> That Jack Built.[39]

The trial of Queen Caroline, characterized by its wealth of satirical pamphlets and prints, demonstrated the power of anti-monarchist reportage. Although Victoria mostly escaped similar tribulations, *Reynolds's Newspaper* did its best to use its position to expose the personal foibles of the royal family.

As early as July 1839, the *Spectator* devoted a leading article to the news coverage of the monarchy. Provoked by the indignities of the Flora Hastings affair, the journal argued that news of court scandal was a powerful revolutionary agent. In the past, it did not matter if the barons knew the king for a weak fool as long as the majority acknowledged him as a hero or a demigod. Now, 'news' was a dangerous influence:

But when first the panoply of forms and ceremonies that had veiled the moral proportions of kings and their knights began to give place, like the armour that magnified their persons, to lighter fashions and more transparent wear—that was an evil day for the great genius of *counterfeit*! *News* was the first general enemy of courts—the first revolutionizer. (Who can wonder at the upholders of *counterfeit* regarding cheap postage with antipathy?) *News* came—that kings were not Gods, nor courts heavens; and the faith of the multitude received its first shock. *Court Gazettes* have more lately proved their claims as Radical incendiaries: the twenty-four hours of Royalty are chronicled, and all the world is let in to see 'quam parva sapientâ regitur mundus'![40]

Under the constant spotlight of news, the mummery of ceremonial could no longer hide the 'true' characteristics of kings and queens. While Barrett-Browning's letter stresses how Victoria's own life became part of the lives of her subjects, the extension of this process meant that they became involved in events which the court would prefer to keep to itself. The monarchy had previously inspired respect or fear. Yet the advent of news meant that it was now open to the critical appraisal of an ever-increasing audience. To survive it had to be respected, but 'to be respected, it must absolutely be *respectable*'.[41] Victoria's much vaunted propriety was, in part, a necessary product of the unprecedented focus on her life.

For the *Spectator*, news was a revelatory force because it was able to strip away royal mystique. Such a belief testifies to the way that the intimate coverage of Victoria helped to create a perception of her true self. Victoria's

---

[39] Edgell Rickword, *Radical Squibs and Loyal Ripostes: Satirical Pamphlets of the Regency Period, 1819–21* (Bath: Adams and Dart, 1971), 41.
[40] 'The Throne', *Spectator*, 20 July 1839, 681.
[41] Ibid.

civic visits were celebrated because they seemed to eschew layers of aristocratic ceremony. Accordingly, royal news was promoted because it revealed a bourgeois ordinariness. The political potency of Victoria's natural character can be seen in a *Punch* article from 1844. In response to a letter that had been printed in the *Sun*, which had complained of the Queen's overly plain dressing in a straw bonnet and shawl, *Punch* printed a fictional letter from the Marquis of Londonderry. As discussed in the previous chapter, the reactionary Marquis had been one of the most vociferous Tory complainants about the revised organization of the coronation ceremony. His mock letter in *Punch* is a pastiche of the Tory attachment to formality and ceremony. It is exaggerated to the extent that even Victoria's clothing takes on radical connotations:

The people, may it please your Majesty, confound simplicity with want of power. Use them to nothing but the bonnet and the shawl, and the diadem and the imperial robes will be to them a fiction of the law. In a brief time they will cease to believe even in the existence of such things; and then—but I tremble to speak of the revolutionary consequences. The people are a vulgar sight-seeing mob; their eyes are, in fact, their greatest part of them. The late lamented GEORGE THE FOURTH knew this, and fed their eyes, and nothing but their eyes.[42]

This letter is a relentlessly ironic critique of both Tory and radical conceptions of the ideological nature of royal display. At one level, *Punch* is satirizing the Tory belief in the need to impress John Bull with large servings of pomp and circumstance. Only within the parameters of this discourse could portrayals of a domestic or bourgeois Queen take on radical or progressive connotations. However, *Punch* is not simply parodying Tory attachment to pageantry. Its satire is equally a critique of the belief that stripping Victoria of her mystique—leaving her with bonnet and shawl—could be any type of threat. Far from being a revolutionary peeling away of layers of mystique in order to reveal a 'real' Victoria, royal news was instrumental in creating an ordinary depiction that was equally mediated.

In the first decade of Victoria's reign, satirical journals frequently attacked the language of royal reportage and the voluminous accounts of the penny-a-liners following Victoria. In one typical comment in 1837, *Figaro in London* sarcastically noted: 'If she blows her nose, the penny-a-liners must blow their trumpets with a most sweet echo and swear they never heard anything so musical as the lower orders of the Queen's nasal organ.'[43] *Figaro in London* even introduced its own regular column of 'Queeniania', consisting of bathetic anecdotes satirizing the published accounts of Victoria's virtue and

---

[42] 'Her Majesty's Straw Bonnet and Shawl', *Punch*, 7 (1844), 166.
[43] 'The Queen's Flatterers', *Figaro in London*, 15 July 1837, 10.

charity. During the 1840s, when *Punch's* satire was at its most acerbic, similar burlesques emphasize the way in which the attention given to Victoria made her into something very close to Max Weber's definition of a charismatic figure. For Weber, charisma was a quality of personality that distinguished an individual as exceptional. Significantly, he also argued that monarchy was an institutionalized form of charisma. The attention given to Victoria constituted her as an exceptional figure. Sovereigns were no longer divinely ordained. Yet they could still be made extraordinary by an incessant focus on their character and daily activities. The coverage given to the Queen performed what it claimed to represent—that Victoria was a figure whose charisma meant that even the trivia of her life was noteworthy.

Nowhere is the charismatic construction of Victoria more apparent than in the example of the *Court Circular*. *Punch* and similar journals like *Pasquin* regularly lampooned its bland descriptions.[44] The *Court Circular* was the focus of satire because its official status and daily publication suggested that the monarchy was actively encouraging public interest in its affairs. In its presumption that the Queen's subjects were thirsting for information of her activities, it symbolized the whole communicative overload surrounding Victoria. In *The Book of Snobs*, first published in *Punch*, Thackeray promised to take out a year's subscription to any newspaper that refused to print the *Court Circular*. He argued that its pretentious language helped to encourage a sense of deference towards those whose activities it catalogued.[45] Another of *Punch's* favourite ploys was to publish bathetic versions of the *Court Circular*. One typical burlesque appeared just after the birth of the Prince of Wales. Detailing the Prince's actions at 12.30, 1.15, 2.00, 2.30, and 3.00, *Punch* recorded such auspicious actions as a smile at 12.30 and a touch of colic at 2.30.[46] Newspapers that imitated the pretension of the *Court Circular* were also criticized. In September 1844, *Punch* printed a royal proclamation by Victoria that was addressed to the press:

Henceforth, all Vain, Silly, and Sycophantic verbiage shall cease, and good, Straightforward, Simple English be used in all Descriptions of all Progresses made by Ourself, Our Royal Consort, and Our Dearly Beloved Children. And furthermore, it shall be permitted to our Royal Self to wear a white shawl, or a black shawl, without any idle talk being passed upon the same.[47]

[44] 'The Royal Visit to Scotland', *Punch*, 3 (1842), 121; 'Royal Wit on the Royal Tour', *Punch*, 2 (1842), 135; 'Punch's Court Circular', *Punch*, 3 (1842), 182; 'Beauties of the Court Newsman', *Punch*, 8 (1845), 169; 'The Queen's Visit to Scotland', *Pasquin*, 1 (1847), 27; 'The Queen in Scotland', *Pasquin*, 1 (1847), 33.
[45] William Thackeray, *The Book of Snobs and Sketches and Travels in London* (London, Smith Elder and Co., 1879), 20.
[46] 'The Royal Bulletins', *Punch*, 1 (1841), 226.
[47] 'Royal Proclamation', *Punch*, 7 (1844), 138.

The undue attention given to minutiae encouraged a news language that maintained traditional obsequiousness towards the monarchy. Throughout its spoof *Court Circulars*, *Punch* continually undermined the elevation of the mundane into charismatic acts.

While *Punch* was usually content with deflating the bombast of the *Court Circular*, similar criticisms were given a far more political edge in *Reynolds's Newspaper*. Like *Punch*, *Reynolds's Newspaper* vigorously derided the deferential news values of the press. Royal journalism even acquired its own figurehead in 'Jenkins' of the *Morning Post*. The *Morning Post* was notorious for its coverage of events in aristocratic high life. *Punch* aptly christened it the 'Fawning Post'. Its 'Society' reporter par excellence was an individual by the name of Rumsey Forster, who acquired the mocking label of Jenkins. The pen of Jenkins was a byword for purple prose and one of *Punch*'s stock targets in the 1840s. Richard Altick has traced over thirty anti-Jenkins/*Morning Post* jokes in 1843 alone.[48] Jenkins provoked one delightful caricature after the reporter had been awarded a dubious French title. *Punch* attacked Jenkins's social and linguistic pretensions by kitting him out in new ducal regalia that incorporated another of its favourite targets, the Albert Hat (see Fig. 24). Personally designed by Prince Albert for Jenkins, the accompanying article noted that 'Ven de hat grow old (or vat you call zeedy), Brinz Albert has arranged so dat it will make a beauwdiful and ornamental flower-bot'.[49] *Punch*'s targeting of the *Morning Post* and the *Court Circular* highlights a clear continuity with Regency satire and the prosecution of the *Examiner*. Their language was parodied in the same way that Hone and Cruikshank parodied official ritual and discourse in the 1820s.

Reynolds's Newspaper, like *Punch*, frequently defined itself against the sycophancy of Jenkins. He symbolized an œuvre of society journalism that *Reynolds's Newspaper* despised. The correspondence with *Punch* demonstrates the cumulative prominence of Victoria's media making in popular culture. It situates *Reynolds's Newspaper* within a current of anti-royalist critique that was far broader than its own dedicated espousal of republicanism. An editorial upon Victoria's visit to Napoleon III in 1855 serves as a typical example of its ongoing frustration with the values Jenkins symbolized:

to dwell upon all the miracles related by JENKINS to have attested the divine sanction for the Queen's visit is beyond our power. Art has been exhausted, and nature, it is clear, has been rather violently exerted to celebrate the unparalleled event which is to astonish Europe, besides having plunged the inestimable JENKINS into a series of ecstatic fits . . . From Boulogne to Paris, from St. Cloud to the Exhibition and Elysee,

[48] Richard Altick, *Punch: The Lively Youth of a British Institution 1841–1851* (Columbus, Oh.: Ohio University Press, 1997), 79.

[49] 'The Ducal Hat for Jenkins', *Punch*, 6 (1844), 32.

Fig. 24. 'The Ducal Hat for Jenkins', *Punch*, 6 (1844), 3

the faithful creature has seen everything through the unctuous medium of his own sublime toadyism. JENKINS eye, in flunkey-frenzy rolling doth glance from heaven to earth, from earth to heaven, and as imagination bodies forth the form of things unknown, JENKINS'S pen turns them to shape . . .[50]

Reynolds's Newspaper expressed similar sentiments in an editorial printed before the wedding of the Prince of Wales. Suitably entitled, 'Jenkins in his Glory—Toadyism Triumphant', the editorial suggested that, since the editors of the London journals were so in thrall to the monarchy, it would be fitting if they pulled Princess Alexandra's carriage through the streets.[51]

For *Reynolds's Newspaper*, the newspaper press was instrumental in maintaining the imaginative prominence of the monarchy. Its reaction to the Prince of Wales's illness with typhoid fever in 1871 is typical. Several editorials attacked 'the miserable lackeys of the press'.[52] Journalists were accused of fanning public concern and spreading a great epidemic of typhoid loyalty. It argued that the attention given to the Prince of Wales, and the concomitant depth of public reaction, created a misrecognition of national belonging:

[50] 'Jenkins in Paris—Victoria's Visit to Louis Napoleon', *Reynolds's Newspaper*, 26 Aug. 1855, 9.
[51] 'Jenkins in his Glory—Toadyism Triumphant', *Reynolds's Newspaper*, 1 Mar. 1863, 3.
[52] 'The Prince of Wales', *Reynolds's Newspaper*, 2 Dec. 1871, 5.

What is a nation? Is it the mere head that rules, or the body that primarily composes it? Is it the monarch, the president, or the people? Are geometrical laws sometimes reversed, and does the lesser include the greater? Can delusion act so potently on the human mind as to prevent it causing all things to be looked at from a false standpoint? A monk once remarked about the pictures in his convent, that he occasionally considered the painted figures the realities and the living tenants the mere shadows. The people of England—or, at least, a goodly portion of them, would seem to labour under a similar hallucination.[53]

For *Reynolds's Newspaper* the royal family was wholly illusory and yet overly present. Its members were painted figures and yet imaginatively concrete. The newspaper sought to understand, through its dialectic of the spectral and the material, the type of influence enjoyed by Victoria and the Prince of Wales, and the royalist subjects that this identification produced.

Elsewhere in his publishing activities, Reynolds was equally alive to the personal appeal of Victoria. His interest, however, was conducted for very different ends. The attraction of Victoria and Albert's family life meant that there was a widespread desire for an intimate insight into their domestic pastimes. Reynolds's *The Mysteries of London* is one notable example of the way publishers took advantage of the fascination exerted by the royal private sphere. From its commencement in October 1844, Reynolds's weekly penny numbers were enormously popular. Sales of 30,000 to 40,000 were soon reported.[54] Nowhere are the contradictions in Reynolds's treatment of Victoria more evident than in *The Mysteries of London*. Three chapters from the first series and, in the repetition of an obviously successful formula, four similar chapters from the second series focus on Victoria and Albert.[55]

Reynolds's depiction of the royal couple underlines his debt to the inordinate aural, print, and visual coverage of royalty in the early and mid-1840s. His narrative is very much part of the spectacle of a domestic monarchy. The *Mysteries of London* combines a through-the-keyhole account of Buckingham Palace—a titillating revelation of the most intimate conversations of Victoria and Albert—with a condemnation of the luxury enjoyed by the court and an attempted Regicide. The narrative is simultaneously an exotic exposé of aristocratic high life and an idealization of royal domesticity. The chapters encourage a strong sympathy towards Victoria by showing her relationship with Albert stifled by the court formality to which they are forced to conform. Reynolds denounces aristocratic etiquette because 'even the best and most tender feelings of the heart are to a certain extent subdued and oppressed by

---

[53] 'The Late Public's Panic', *Reynolds's Newspaper*, 2 Dec. 1871, 4.

[54] Trefor Thomas, Introduction, in George W. M. Reynolds, *The Mysteries of London*, ed. Trefor Thomas (Keele: Keele University Press, 1996), p. vii.

[55] *The Mysteries of the Court of London* also deals with royalty, although this series is set back in the Regency period and details the debauchery of the Prince of Wales.

[its] chilling influence'.[56] *The Mysteries of London* saturates radical politics with royal melodrama and romance. Reynolds attacks the court and the inequities of aristocratic wealth. Yet he does so through encouraging his readers' sympathy for, and empathy with, Victoria. The contrary political directions of Reynolds's melodramatic tropes are similar to prints and pamphlets produced around the Queen Caroline trial.[57] Although Reynolds uses the popular sentiment around Victoria for radical ends, she is treated as the innocent victim of the court rather than the fount of its very existence.

The central protagonist of Reynolds's chapters is neither Victoria nor Albert, but one Henry Holford, a potboy cum burglar. Holford begins by breaking into Buckingham Palace and ends by committing Regicide after he has been ejected from its splendours. Reynolds's narrative draws upon five or six actual incidents where intruders entered Buckingham Palace in the late 1830s and early 1840s. The most notorious of these was the 'Boy Jones' affair. A young street lad, Edward Jones, was caught inside Buckingham Palace. When questioned, he claimed to have lived there unobserved for several weeks. The Boy Jones gained his reputation through claiming to have repeatedly entered the palace and to have overheard the conversations of all the royal servants. *The Mysteries of London* similarly revels in following Holford around the palace. The principal attraction of the royal chapters is the thrill of being a voyeur on the intimacies of Victoria and her household. Through Holford, the reader overhears courtiers discussing the licentiousness of George IV; the injustice towards Queen Caroline; the Duke of Cumberland's alleged murder of his manservant; and Victoria's own increasing tendency to bouts of melancholy concerning the anticipated onset of the hereditary madness that afflicted George III. All of the most widely circulated episodes of recent royal scandal are uninhibitedly ranged over. Without any irony towards his role in communicating such gossip to his readers, the narrator declares that nowhere are 'scandal and tittle-tattle more extensively indulged in than amongst the members of that circle of courtiers who crowd about the sovereign'.[58] Reynolds disapproves of the court gossip of a prurient aristocracy. Yet, at the same time, the narrative offers a full account of the self-same scandal. Like *Reynolds's Newspaper*, *The Mysteries of London* provides details of Victoria's court for the reader both to consume and condemn.

---

[56] George Reynolds, *The Mysteries of London* (London: George Vickers, 1846), ii. 198.

[57] Thomas Laqueur has argued that the use of melodramatic tropes reduced the trial to a form of popular entertainment, 'The Queen Caroline Affair: Politics as Art in the Reign of George IV', *Journal of Modern History*, 54 (1982), 417–66. Anna Clark has disputed Lacquer's claims, arguing that the melodramatic representation of Queen Caroline was necessary to make a radical mass movement possible. Anna Clark, 'Queen Caroline and the Sexual Politics of Popular Culture in London, 1820', *Representations*, 31 (Summer 1990), 47–68.

[58] Reynolds, *The Mysteries of London*, ii. 196.

Holford's exploits include a visit to the throne room and a brief but symbolic occupancy of the throne itself. None the less, what he sees inside the palace is experienced with unbounded wonder and delight. He is enchanted by several covert encounters with Victoria, including a premarital tête-à-tête between Victoria and Prince Albert. His royal voyeurism is said to be 'as necessary to Holford's mental happiness as tobacco, opium, snuff, or strong liquors are to many millions of people'.[59] Holford is eventually discovered by none other than Albert himself, but is ejected from the Palace without arrest due to the magnanimity of the Prince. Albert's actions drive Holford to despair and hatred and he subsequently attempts Regicide. His actions, though, do not stem from republican principles. His assassination attempt is caused by his expulsion from the charms of royalty. *The Mysteries of London* is thus both predicated on, and a representation of, the potency of Victoria's domesticity. It is reflexive in that it depicts both Victoria's private life and its attraction. Holford's obsession exemplifies the interest it aroused and the prominent role it played in the construction of Victoria for a popular readership.

The sensation around Victoria in the early 1840s meant that the metaphor of an individual and collective madness was used to describe the unrestrained adulation of an enchanted public. With the sexualized glamour of the Beauty Book Queen existing alongside the constitutional prophecies of the street ballads, the cumulative affect around Victoria was tremendous. In June 1837, Mrs Stevenson, the wife of the American ambassador, wrote that everybody was 'run mad with loyalty to the young Queen. Even the Americans here are infected. In all societies, nothing is talked about but her beauty, her wisdom, her goodness & self-possession.'[60] Likewise, at the time of Victoria's wedding, the *Satirist* complained that Bedlam was let loose: 'We are all going stark staring mad. Nothing is heard or thought of but doves and Cupids, triumphal arches and white favours.'[61] The portrayal of excessive affect as madness stems from the common use of Enlightenment values to deride the lack of rationality in popular politics. Responses to the sentiment Victoria aroused are significant, moreover, because its excesses were often believed to stem from the influence of the large number of royal prints and news stories.

The feelings around Victoria are bound up with her creation as a fetishized figure. The remarkable cathexis of desire around Victoria in the first years of her reign, which ranged from the sexual to the political, can best be seen through a group that became collectively known as 'the Queen's lovers'. Until her marriage, Victoria was frequently stalked, physically intruded upon, and bombarded with letters from subjects, whose sole intent was seemingly to gain

[59] Ibid. 247.

[60] Edward Bodgkin (ed.), *Victoria, Albert and Mrs Stevenson* (London: Frederick Miller, 1937), 74.

[61] 'London, February 9, 1840', *Satirist*, 9 Feb. 1840, 44.

her hand in marriage. Acting under the conviction that they were destined to be the chosen Consort, their criminal behaviour was widely reported. It usually resulted in their subsequent committals to Bedlam or similar institutions. In an inversion of the Medusa's gaze, they had seemingly been overwhelmed by the extravagant idolatry of their own looking upon Victoria.

Foremost amongst the Queen's lovers was the case of one Captain Goode. He began to follow Victoria when she was a Princess at Kensington. As well as making daily calls at Kensington, he followed her to Ramsgate and Hastings when she holidayed there prior to her accession. Every evening Goode used to wait for the Princess's carriage to emerge from her private road in Kensington Gardens. He would then follow her wherever she went. Captain Goode believed himself to be a son of George IV and rightful heir to the throne. It was an honour he would forgo as long as Victoria consented to be his wife. After being imprisoned several times for his harassing behaviour, he was eventually examined and committed in November 1837.[62] Goode was far from alone, however. Another suitor managed to obtain admission to the Chapel Royal, where he began to bow and kiss his hand to Victoria.[63] Then there was Tom Flower, who was arrested after trying to gain entrance to Westminster Abbey during the coronation.[64] Flower was well known for his attempts to gain Victoria's hand. He had been twice bound over to keep the peace after similar incidents, including an attempt to enter the Queen's box at the opera. Tom Flower was removed to Tothill Fields House of Correction for his troubles. Ned Hayward, another unfortunate, was also committed for stopping the Queen's horse in Hyde Park in order to give her a letter. He had previously written numerous letters to the Home Office wondering whether Victoria would consent to be his wife.[65] Next, in October 1839, came a Scottish admirer. Having persuaded himself that he was the object of Victoria's affections, he made a pilgrimage to see her. At one of the Queen's appearances on the Windsor terrace, the extravagance of his behaviour rendered the interference of the police necessary. In January 1840, there was the case of Thomas Richard Evans. He declared his undying passion for Victoria in numerous letters written to Lord John Russell, begging him to intercede on his behalf and stop the marriage to Prince Albert.[66] The most famous case of all, however, was the Boy Jones. As *The Mysteries of London* demonstrates, he embodied the general fascination with Victoria's life.

I have given only the bare facts of these somewhat bizarre individual cases.

[62] *The Times*, 13 Nov. 1837, 5; *The Times*, 7 Nov. 1837, 3; *The Times*, 24 Nov. 1838, 2.

[63] Agnes Strickland, *Queen Victoria: From Her Birth to Her Bridal* (London: Henry Colburn, 1840), ii. 84.

[64] 'Police', *The Times*, 29 June 1838, 8; 'Police', *The Times*, 5 June 1838, 7.

[65] 'Edmund Hayward', *The Times*, 10 Aug. 1839, 7; 21 Aug. 1839, 7.

[66] 'Another Suitor to Her Majesty', *Sun*, 8 Jan. 1840, 2.

None the less, it is important to register their frequency and the fascination that they provided for the culture at large. In its early years, *Punch* regaled its readers with mock reports from the Boy Jones. Dickens, too, borrowed their behaviour. A joke with John Forster and Daniel Maclise involved the trio pretending that they were all hopelessly in love with the Queen. In a letter written three days after Victoria's wedding, Dickens imagined a journey down to Windsor on the day after the event:

On Tuesday we sallied down to Windsor, prowled about the Castle, saw the corridor and their private rooms—nay, the very bedchamber (which we know from having been there twice) lighted up with such a ruddy, homely, brilliant glow—bespeaking so much bliss and happiness—that I, your humble servant, lay down in the mud at the top of the long walk, and refused all comfort—to the immeasurable astonishment of a few straggling passengers who had survived the drunkenness of the previous night. After perpetrating sundry other extravagances we returned home at Midnight in a Post Chaise and now we wear marriage medals next to our hearts and go about with pockets full of portraits which we weep over in secret.[67]

Dickens's letter clearly plays upon the behaviour of the Queen's lovers. He links their devotion with the affect invested in the commemoratives of the occasion. In Dickens's somewhat risqué excursion to the Queen's honeymoon bedchamber, Victoria's attraction creates an obsessive following of her every action.

The Queen's lovers are significant because of the way they were transformed into a discursive entity. As individuals they were profitable news stories. However, as the Queen's lovers, they were used as a group psychological case study to comprehend the collective ardour concerning Victoria. Those who were literally mad became symptomatic of a general condition of mania through excessive loyalty. In the first years of her reign, the Queen's lovers were an important part of the discourse upon the monarchy. They were part of a fascination with trying to understand how she was thought of, and why she seemed to dominate the imagined and imaginary lives of her subjects.

Over a period of six months, starting in July 1839, the *Penny Satirist* printed a series of fictional letters under the heading 'The Queen's Lover'. The periodical claimed that for several months it had been receiving letters filled with rapturous poetry:

I find it hard to love a Queen. I see her lovely features so often in picture shops, and her name is too often mentioned to effect a speedy cure. I must find some retreat, where no journals come, where no picture-shops are, and where her name is never, or seldom, heard. I must find some Cave, and live like a hermit, and write about her till

[67] Charles Dickens, *The Letters of Charles Dickens 1840–41*, ed. M. House and G. Storey (Oxford: Clarendon Press, 1969), 25.

I die, or make a perfect cure . . . Could I only respect her as my Queen, then I should do; but her sweet lips, her pure bosom, and her lovely eyes, are eternally before me, and I speak to her as if she were my equal.[68]

The Queen's lover is infatuated with Victoria to the extent that she dominates his everyday experience. His inability to regard Victoria as the Queen, with all the corresponding implications of social and personal distance, is intrinsic to his fetishizing. The proximity between them has been compressed into an affective and sensual intimacy, and this is explicitly linked to the impact of the various royal prints, newspaper stories, and ballads. The Queen's lover is not a subject of Victoria. Rather, he is a consumer of her image. In the close but wholly one-sided relationship between Victoria and the Queen's lover, the letter is comparable to the intimacy of celebrity expressed by Barrett-Browning. It is also an eroticized version of Disraeli's promotion of a monarch who was close to the People.

Dickens and the *Penny Satirist* see the interest in Victoria as having a specifically sexual dimension. Yet it is clearly part of the larger concern over the connection between her and her subjects. The importance of prints, newspapers, and photography in creating an immediate relationship is something that recurs throughout the commentaries upon Victoria. It is a key part of the press's mythologizing of its own importance. The constantly deployed icon of Victoria as mother of the nation is not simply, as many critics have rightly noted, a reflection of the hegemony of bourgeois domesticity. It is also an expression of the affective connection many of her subjects felt they had with her. At the birth of the Prince of Wales, the *Spectator* suggested that the poet laureate commemorate the occasion by running a parallel between a Queen who was mother to her subjects and a mother who was a queen of her subjects.[69] The *Spectator* demarcates two strands usually run together in the symbolization of Victoria as the mother of the nation. In the first, there is a Victoria who occupies a queenly position because she is a literal paragon of domestic propriety. In the second, there is a Queen who stands as a mother to her subjects. The former addresses Victoria's literal motherhood. The latter uses her motherhood as a metonymy for the emotional relationship her subjects experienced towards her. Victoria's national motherhood was a position given to her rather than simply a description of her maternal feelings towards her subjects. Familiarity bred familiality. Prior to Victoria's marriage, this relationship was expressed through the invasive desire of the Queen's lovers. However, the birth of her children soon offered a far less threatening symbol for the bond between Victoria and her subjects.

[68] 'The Queen's Lover', *Penny Satirist*, 6 July 1839, 2.
[69] 'Hints for a Birth-Day Ode', *Spectator*, 13 Nov. 1841, 1094.

The Queen's lovers were also taken up as part of a wider attack on the newspapers and journals that were most exuberant in their support for the monarchy. Individual acts of obsessive loyalty in the style of the Queen's lovers were equated with the fawning language that often characterized news accounts of royal occasions. In a mocking exposé in *Punch*, Douglas Jerrold pounced on a comment made by the editor of the *Athenaeum* over the birth of the Prince of Wales. The editor had claimed that at least half the day he was in his fancy at the palace taking his turn of loyal watch by the royal cradle.[70] Jerrold gleefully took the editor at his word. He dramatized the results of his imagining himself to be besides the cradle for at least twelve hours of the day. Taken literally, his absorption is quickly turned into fanatical delusion. The editor's housemaid is dandled up and down like a baby; the printer's devil is force-fed with the ink for the presses; the tax-gatherer is treated to a rendition of ride a cock horse to Banbury Cross when he knocks at the editor's door. Jerrold questions whether the editor should be prevented from carrying on his working activities by such 'beautiful evidences of an absorbing loyalty'.[71] In its most solemn tone, a tongue-in-cheek *Punch* declares the question to be one of great importance. An end to all individual liberty is threatened if the enthusiasm of loyalty is to be rendered as madness. Jerrold claimed to believe fully the editor's profession of his loyalty in that it was comparable to similar statements made by other public figures. Nevertheless, harking back to the Queen's lovers, he warns that many men had been deprived of their freedom for much less fanciful feelings towards the Queen.

Jerrold warns that there is an arbitrary line between royal fantasy and rational loyalty. He recounts the case of a Greenwich man who was declared insane, losing a fortune of £120,000, because he declared that he intended to marry Victoria. What is this but loyalty *in excess* Jerrold argues. Through eliding the distinction between the extravagant pronouncements that newspapers made about Victoria and the actions of the Queen's lovers, *Punch* questioned why only the latter were placed outside the bounds of reason. Jerrold did not want to inspire sympathy for those committed to asylums; he was seeking to attack the unrestrained avowals of loyalty that were being amplified by the press. *Punch* desired forbearance in the mania surrounding Victoria; otherwise, like the editor of the *Athenaeum*, the public risked progressing from a metaphorical insanity to being very literally mad about Victoria:

If, however, he and other influential wizards of the broad-sheet, succeed in making loyalty not a rational principle, but a mania—if, day by day, and week by week, they insist on deifying poor, infirm humanity, exalting themselves in their own conceit, in their very self-abasement—they may escape an individual accusation in the general

---

[70] Douglas Jerrold, 'Loyalty and Insanity', *Punch*, 1 (1841), 258.   [71] Ibid.

folly. When we are all mad alike—when we all, with the editor of the *Athenaeum*, take our half-day's watch at the side of the little Prince's cradle—when every man and woman throughout her empire believe themselves making royal pap and airing royal baby-linen—then, whatever fortune we may have, we may be safe from the fate of Poor Weekes . . . who, we repeat, is most unjustly confined for his notions of royalty, seeing that many of our contemporaries are still at liberty to write and publish.[72]

Jerrold acerbically evokes the prominence that Victoria had been forced to occupy in the lives of her subjects. For Jerrold, like Dickens and the letter-writer in the *Penny Satirist*, such absorption was directly linked to an extensive royal presence. Jerrold's commentary, however, is far more targeted than the playfulness of Dickens and the *Penny Satirist*. He is attacking the sustaining of the monarchy through a kind of flunkeydom of the imagination.

Most of the commentaries examined so far have dealt with the newspaper and periodical press's understandably narcissistic conception of their own role. The circumstances of the publication of *Leaves from the Journal of Our Life in the Highlands* in 1868 provide an alternative perspective. They demonstrate the royal household's understanding of the press milieu in which Victoria existed. Its reviews correspondingly emphasize the political agency that continued to be ascribed to the dissemination of Victoria's figure through popular print media. The journal presents Victoria's own account of the numerous journeys of Albert and herself amongst the Scottish highlands. It includes details of the couple's innocent delight in their several incognito expeditions, when they took on the identities of Lord and Lady Churchill and revelled in the supposed simplicity of their anonymity as private citizens. As the editor, Arthur Helps, notes in his introduction, all reference to political questions had been studiously omitted. The journal was confined to 'throwing itself, with a delight rendered keener by the rarity of its opportunities, into the enjoyment of a life removed, for the moment, from the pressure of public cares'.[73] Its publication was an immense success. The 2*s*. 6*d*. version sold 103,000 copies in 1868 alone.[74]

Victoria's highland journal presents an idealized version of her married life. It was highly praised for its artlessness and for offering up the type of intimacy that Holford had to break into Buckingham Palace to glimpse. As the *Daily Telegraph* put it, 'the charm of the happy fireside is the veil that hides it from the public gaze'.[75] Yet the publication of the highland journal is more complex than a simple desire by Victoria to make her journal available. Its

[72] Douglas Jerrold, 258.

[73] Queen Victoria, *Leaves from the Journal of Our Life in the Highlands*, ed. Arthur Helps (London: Smith Elder, 1868), p. x.

[74] Richard Altick, *The English Common Reader: A Social History of the Mass Reading Public, 1800–1900* (1957; Columbus, Oh.: Ohio University Press, 1998), 388.

[75] 'London, Friday, January 10', *Daily Telegraph*, 10 Jan. 1868, 6.

release stemmed from the pressure that the press was able to exert and the consciousness of this on the part of the royal household. Helps notes that Victoria initially intended to have extracts of her journal printed only for the other members of the royal family and her closest friends. But Helps pointed out to her that, however limited the number of impressions, portions of the journal— perhaps garbled or embellished versions—would be sure to find their way into the press. Therefore, it would be prudent for Victoria to provide gratification for her subjects by making the journal generally available. Helps's argument both acknowledges and disavows an awareness of the role of the press. It assumes that the newspaper and periodical press has a powerful influence, to the extent that Victoria has to prevent it taking advantage of her privately printed journal by publishing it herself. Conversely, by giving the press such a motivating force, Helps circumvents any potential accusation that Victoria was knowingly exploiting the appeal of her journals to bolster her reputation. The publication of the highland journal therefore embodies both the benefits and drawbacks of Victoria's relationship with the press.

The impact of *Leaves from the Journal of Our Life in the Highlands* makes it part of the symbiosis between a constitutional and a media monarchy. This is especially evident in a review by Charles Kingsley in *Fraser's Magazine*. Kingsley linked the highland journal with the publication of Theodore's Martin's *The Early Years of the Prince Consort*. His review valued the books in the same way that Victoria's civic visits were valued: they were signs of her willingness to show herself to her subjects. Kingsley opened his review by declaring that *The Early Years of the Prince Consort* had a political effect of which the authors (Victoria and Martin) could not have dreamt. In setting forth the virtuous history of the Prince, they also unknowingly set forth the history of the Queen.[76] For Kingsley, the potency of *The Early Years of the Prince Consort* and the highland journals stemmed from their unaffectedness and transparency. By telling her own story 'simply, earnestly, confidently', Kingsley believed that Victoria had appealed to 'women's suffrage, of a most subtle and potent sort'.[77] She employed a private language of sentiment that promoted an empathetic and immediate relationship with her subjects.

Kingsley stresses the importance of Victoria's highland journal by making it part of the genealogy of the English Gothic constitution. In a fashion comparable to Disraeli, Kingsley's constitutional genealogy argues that the personal experience of royalty constituted through the highland journal was

---

[76] See Margaret Homans, *Royal Representations* (Chicago: Chicago University Press, 1998), 115–34, for the way in which *The Early Years of the Prince Consort* was construed as Victoria's book because of the official assistance Martin received.

[77] Charles Kingsley, 'Leaves from the Journal of Our Life in the Highlands', *Fraser's Magazine*, 77 (1868), 154.

actually the long-standing historical norm for European monarchs. It was the foundation of their 'democratic' existence. For Kingsley, the association between ceremony and an excessive reverence for royalty was an aberration. Its antecedents lay with the Pharaohs and the Incas rather than Europe, where the monarch had always 'been more or less the elected ideal of his people'.[78] By virtue of his intimate familiarity with his subjects, and his consequent knowledge of their collective will, the monarch ruled by a 'rough kind of universal suffrage'.[79] Kingsley's model draws heavily upon the free Saxon polity celebrated by the Gothic Revival. He used the medieval court as an example to claim that the popular existence of the monarchy was founded on the king and queen mixing freely with their subjects. In this tradition the king 'ate, chatted, joked, hunted, came to blows, got wet, weary, and worse, with men of all ranks'.[80] According to Kingsley, it was only with Louis XIV that European monarchies began to be enveloped in a sacred cloud of ceremonial etiquette. Such ceremony removed the intimacy of the link between Crown and subject. In contrast to the French monarchy, *Fraser's Magazine* congratulated itself that ceremony had never really taken hold upon the English Crown. The first three Georges were, if nothing else, honest German country gentlemen. Whatever political power the British monarchy had lost had been superseded by the moral power it derived from this still pervasive ideal. And nobody had utilized this more effectively than Victoria and Albert at Balmoral.

In Kingsley's genealogy, Victoria's highland journal aligns her with the original English Gothic constitution. Through a large amount of historical myopia, *Leaves from the Journal of Our Life in the Highlands* is metamorphosed into the culmination of the interactive relationship that should always pertain between monarch and subject. In promoting the relationship as the foundation upon which the English monarchy has survived, Kingsley's review exemplifies the importance ascribed to Victoria's dissemination through print media. Rather than Victoria's relationship with parliament, personal immediacy is the essential aspect of both a constitutional and popular monarchy. Nevertheless, Kingsley's genealogy only works through eliding the difference between the literal presence of Victoria and the work of her representations. The face-to-face bond characteristic of the medieval court bears little resemblance to the type of communication achieved through the large-scale circulation of *Leaves from the Journal of Our Life in the Highlands*. Kingsley's idealized relationship between monarch and subject disavows the mediated conditions upon which that bond was now based.

Many of the critical and celebratory commentaries in this chapter have been from the first decade of Victoria's reign. They are testimony to both the

---

[78] Charles Kingsley, 155.   [79] Ibid.   [80] Ibid.

novelty of her role and the modernity of the publishing developments during the 1830s and 1840s. Aside from *Reynolds's Newspaper*, there is not the same degree of self-consciousness during the 1850s. It was not until the release of the first royal photographs in the early 1860s that there was a similar burst of commentary. The 1850s were more notable for the working out of the precedents introduced by the dynamism of periodicals like the *Illustrated London News*. Victoria's coverage became both established and, in consequence, slightly formulaic. Satirical critiques also acquired a certain familiarity, a working over of an easily available stock target. They are not characterized by the type of rhetorical excess and theatricality derided by *Punch*, *Figaro in London*, and the *Penny Satirist*. The layers of meaning around Victoria built up into an increasingly discursive solidity. As *Punch* astutely commented in 1848, the difficulty in filling the vacant job of poet laureate was that there was nothing to do. The Queen's virtues were 'of too everyday occurrence, to be the subject of holiday odes, or, indeed, of fiction of any shape'.[81] If there is one thing that this chapter has indicated it is precisely the everydayness of Victoria. She was interpolated into people's lives through being the subject of a letter, of a ballad heard in the street, of an article in the latest copy of the newspaper. Prints, newspapers, and periodicals can be grouped together under the homogenous rubric of 'the media'. Yet Victoria's being was as much about gossip, empathy, affect, reverence, habit, and—above all else—her indubitable thereness.

[81] 'A Poetical Interregnum', *Punch*, 14 (1848), 55.

4

PHOTOGRAPHY AND
THE ROYAL FAMILY

if we have lost something in artists, we have gained something in gratifi-
cations. If our curiosity be excited by daring deeds or prominent actions,
the lens and chemical paper present the doer and the place to our eyes,
and we see what manner of man he is and where the events took place.
Our kings, queens, and princes, our statesmen, our scholars, our pretty
women and our mountebanks, may be brought for eighteen pence
apiece—genuine likenesses; for the lower priced articles may or may not
be such. Is there a Royal marriage, instantly a Mayall produces carte-
de-visite of the Prince, his bride, and all the bridesmaids . . . Or their
artists follow our future King to his private retreat, and send amongst his
people's homes thousands of views of Sandringham.

(*London Review*, August 1863)[1]

In August 1860, the royal image became photographic. John Edwin Mayall, a
leading Regent Street photographer, was permitted to publish his *Royal
Album*. Consisting of fourteen *carte-de-visite* portraits of Victoria, Albert, and
their children, Mayall's venture was a phenomenal success. A general mania
for celebrity *cartes*, with the *Royal Album* at its forefront, heralded the beginning of a turbulent relationship between mass culture, photography, and the
royal family. The development of photography initiated a dynamic that has
been responsible for much subsequent media coverage of the British monarchy. The *carte* was instrumental in exacerbating the expectation that the royal
family would have a publicized existence. Susan Sontag has described the
camera as a promiscuous form of seeing and, from the early 1860s, it began to
live up to that description.[2] Not only were numerous portrait *cartes* placed in
circulation, the camera was quickly utilized for journalistic purposes. In

---

[1] 'Photography as Industry', *London Review*, 22 Aug. 1863, 213–14.
[2] Susan Sontag, *On Photography* (1977; Harmondsworth: Penguin, 1979), 129.

March 1863, the marriage of the Prince of Wales became the first major royal occasion where photographers covered every episode.

Royal photographs helped to extend the popular character of the monarchy. The celebrity *carte* provided a strange and new relationship with figures who were nevertheless wholly familiar. Celebrity photographs had a potent imaginative appeal that stemmed from the novelty of the individual and collective experience they generated. They had a notable collective agency because, through their circulation, they went beyond the scope of engraving and lithography. Their ubiquity helped to provide a shared national experience of well-known individuals. Thus, for example, photography was instrumental in creating the familiar and iconic image of Queen Victoria in her widow's weeds. By examining a series of articles that were published in periodicals like *Once a Week*, *All the Year Round*, and the *Art Journal*, we can see how photography accentuated perceptions of the monarchy's media making. For commentators, many of whom were writing from a fine art standpoint, the celebrity *carte* provoked fears of a populist broadening of the public sphere and a more superficial notion of celebrity itself.

Significantly, though, the *carte* was equally notable for the intimate relationship it generated between individual consumers and well-known figures. The widespread dissemination of the *carte* only had a collective impact because of the potency with which they were experienced. Their collection helped to reinforce an individual's sense of themselves as belonging to an imagined national community. Compared to existing graphic media, the lens of the camera offered a more authentic and intimate link with the sitters it depicted. Celebrity *cartes* had an insinuating and sensuous realism. Photographs of Victoria and Albert thus provided a new and more palpable means of participating in the life of the royal family. The extensive dissemination of royal photographs worked to maintain the imaginative prominence of the royal family.

Graham Clarke has argued that a photograph is 'in the end, a sealed world, to which we bring meaning'.[3] As such, this chapter is concerned with the two dominant forces that determined the meanings poured into Victoria's photographs. The first of these is the expansion of the photographic industry in the 1850s and 1860s. The impact of the royal *cartes* is inseparable from the development of photography into a public and a commercial medium. Like the illustrated press and the Books of Beauty, photography reproduced Victoria according to its own technological format and pictorial conventions. It is equally the case, however, that the impact of Victoria's photographs was determined by the ideological and commercial pressures already in place around

---

[3] Graham Clarke, *The Photograph* (Oxford: Oxford University Press, 1997), 24.

the monarchy. The most obvious of these is the desire for a more publicly available and consumable royal family. The uses to which royal photographs were put consequently make them very much part of the broader process of Victoria's media making. The royal photographs are similar to the coverage of the newspaper and periodical press in that they extended the lightness of the monarchy and downplayed its role as a political institution. As David Cannadine has archly noted, 'It is not the British monarchy as *monarchy* that the world is interested in, but the British monarchy as harmless entertainment'.[4] Celebrity *cartes* epitomize this because they were, above all, a form of amusement, gossip, and voyeurism.

The two principal dynamics affecting Victoria's photographs can also be understood through Rosalind Krauss's distinction between photography as an object of discourse and photography as a subject constituting its own critical discourse.[5] The expansion of the photographic industry meant that photography constituted itself as an aesthetic and judicial subject. The advent of specialist photographic journals, supplemented by numerous articles in general periodicals like *All the Year Round* and *Once a Week*, created a body of writing that sought to define the role of photography as a technological and popular media. At the same time, however, the public life of the royal *cartes* turned them into very much an object of commentary. The prominence of Victoria's photographs meant that they necessarily played a part in debates about the overall character of the monarchy. Krauss's differentiation is useful because the full impact of Victoria's photographs has to be understood as the product of the aesthetics of photography interacting with pre-existing discourses concerning the British royal family. It is a process that epitomizes the osmosis between the civic position of the monarchy and its representation in the various print and graphic media.

The first ever photographs of the British monarchy were two daguerreotypes of Prince Albert that were taken by William Constable at Brighton on 7 March 1842. Albert also visited Richard Beard's London daguerreotype studio later the same month. Beard's studio, in Parliament Street, was the first commercial studio to open in the country. These two sittings were the beginning of Victoria and Albert's keen enthusiasm for photography. The couple became patrons of the Photographic Society soon after its inception in 1853. They maintained their personal and artistic interest throughout the 1850s. Prince Albert, for example, contributed £50 in 1855 towards a study by the

---

[4]   David Cannadine, *The Pleasures of the Past* (London: Collins, 1989), 8.

[5]   Rosalind Krauss, 'A Note on Photography and the Simulacral', in Caroline Squiers (ed.), *The Critical Image: Essays on Contemporary Photography* (London: Lawrence and Wishart, 1990), 15–27. Juliet Hacking uses the same distinction in 'Photography Personified: Art and Identity in British Photography 1857–1869', Ph.D diss., University of London, 1998, 15.

Photographic Society into how to prevent the fading of photographs. Through their close links with the Photographic Society, Victoria and Albert employed some of the most prominent photographers of the day. One typical commission was that given to Francis Bedford by Victoria in 1857. Victoria wished him to visit Coburg and take a series of pictures of Albert's homeland as a present for the Prince's birthday. Roger Fenton, better known for his Crimean War pictures, also took several series of royal photographs in the 1850s. These include a well-known set of Victoria's children in *tableaux vivants* in February 1854, of a performance put on by Victoria's children to celebrate their parents' wedding anniversary. Like virtually all royal photographs up to the late 1850s, these were private pictures. They were never intended for publication, and have a very different status from the subsequent celebrity *cartes*.[6]

It was not until the Manchester Art Treasures exhibition, opened by Albert in May 1857, that photographs of the royal family were first put on public display. The exhibition was intended to bring art to a working-class audience and numerous paintings and photographs were lent to the exhibition from the Royal Collection. Photographs of both Albert and the Duke of Cambridge were amongst the exhibits. The portrait of Albert was taken specifically for the exhibition by Lake Price, probably as a sign of his approval and encouragement of the event. It was shown again at the winter exhibition of the London Photographic Society at South Kensington Museum in February 1858, where the *Liverpool and Marchester Photographic Journal* noted that it had been hung in 'the post of honour'.[7] According Albert's picture the principal viewing position reflects the novelty value of so illustrious a sitter exhibiting his picture in public. For the Photographic Society the possession of such a photograph would also allow them to make the most of the royal patronage that the fledgling media enjoyed.

In contrast to the attention attracted by Albert's photograph at South Kensington, the very first public showing of a photograph of Queen Victoria passed by with hardly a notice from the reviewers. More recent critics have consequently missed the existence of its exhibition. The London Photographic Society's fifth annual exhibition, which opened in May 1858, included a group photograph of the royal family at Osborne House (see Fig. 25). Taken by Leonida Caldesi, it depicts Victoria with Beatrice in her lap, Albert standing opposite her, and the rest of their children freely ranged around them. The *Liverpool and Manchester Photographic Journal* described it as being 'well

---

[6] A detailed account of the royal support for photography in its early stages can be found in Frances Dimond and Roger Taylor, *Crown and Camera: The Royal Family and Photography 1842–1910* (London: Viking, 1987).

[7] 'Exhibition of Photographs at the South Kensington Museum', *LMPJ* 1 Mar. 1858, 61.

Fig. 25. Leonida Caldesi, *Royal Family at Osborne House* (1857)

executed and highly interesting, as displaying most vividly the domestic character'.[8] Compared to the posed conventionality of the later studio-bound *cartes*, the picture is genuinely informal in its appearance. Whereas *cartes* were usually single or paired portraits because of the technological constraints upon its format, this group portrait of the royal family appears far less overtly limited. Furthermore, many of the later royal *cartes* must have been shaped by a consciousness that they would be circulated in their hundreds of thousands. In contrast, Caldesi was attending Osborne House as the photographer of Victoria and Albert. The resultant pictures were for their own personal albums. Victoria and Albert were not aware of themselves posing in order to be transformed into a public image. Caldesi's photograph consequently has a much more uninhibited appearance.[9] The difference between the photographs of the 1850s and the published royal *cartes* of the 1860s demonstrates the way that the technological format of photography, in the size and type of picture necessary for it to be available for widespread consumption, influenced the photographic representation of Victoria.[10]

---

[8] 'The London Photographic Society's Fifth Annual Exhibition', *LMPJ* 15 June 1858, 153.

[9] Dominic Colnagni, the well-known printseller, did issue a print of this photograph in June 1859.

[10] Those publications that missed Victoria's picture included *The Times*, *Art Journal*, *JoPS*, the *Saturday Review*, and the *Daily News*. Critics probably did not notice the picture as several of the reviews complain about the overcrowded, poorly lit exhibition rooms, filled with pictures they had already seen at an earlier exhibition. See 'The Photographic Society', *Athenaeum*, 29 May 1858, 692–3.

The first public showing of photographs of Victoria and Albert were undoubtedly watershed moments. The circulation of these pictures was nevertheless negligible. Their audience was limited to those visiting the various exhibitions; the photographs were very firmly neither for sale nor reproduction. The exhibitions at the Photographic Society reflect the limited arena in which photography as a whole operated during the 1840s and 1850s. As Grace Seiberling has meticulously argued, the initial practitioners of photography were predominantly upper-class amateurs, motivated by a mixture of artistic interest and scientific improvement.[11] In its fledgling state, the production of a single photograph was a fraught and finicky process. Photography required time, expensive materials, and a rudimentary knowledge of chemistry. Its pursuit was limited to those with independent financial means and a high level of education. The Photographic Society, and the many other local photographic societies that followed it during the 1850s, were intended to cater for the genteel amateur. Likewise, in the early years of the photographic journals—the *Journal of the Photographic Society* began in 1853 and the *Liverpool Photographic Journal* in 1854—their pages were primarily devoted to discussions of the latest technical advancements. Only as the decade progressed and photography broadened in appeal did aesthetic and commercial questions come to the fore. In 1855, Cuthbert Bede noted that, 'For the present at any rate, Photography has the patronage of aristocratic—may we not add, Royal? amateurs. It has not yet become *too* common; nor, indeed, is it likely to become so.'[12] Victoria and Albert's interest in photography belongs to the tradition of royal patronage. Yet, at the same time, as reputed practitioners, they exemplify the upper-class amateurs to whom photography was an affordable pastime.

It was only in 1851, when Frederick Scott Archer published the details of his collodion process without any patent restraints, that photography began to free itself from the legal and technological shackles that had previously constrained it. During the 1840s commercial photographers were forced to operate under licence. This was because the agents of Daguerre and Henry Fox Talbot rigidly enforced the patent restrictions upon their respective processes. Even after the collodion process was made public, Fox Talbot argued that his existing patent also covered the new method. Archer's method was not freed from its legal restrictions until December 1854, when Fox Talbot lost a legal test case brought against him. The collodion process was a significant advance over previous processes, especially for portrait photography, since the negative plate needed less exposure time than Fox Talbot's

---

[11] Grace Seiberling and Carolyn Bloore, *Amateurs, Photography and the Mid-Victorian Imagination* (Chicago: Chicago University Press and International Museum of Photography, 1986), 1–18.
[12] Cuthbert Bede, *Photographic Pleasures: Popularly Portrayed with Pen and Pencil* (London: Thomas McClean, 1855), 54.

calotypes. It was consequently not until the mid-1850s, by which time the collodion process had been refined and standardized, that photography became viable for use on a widespread basis.

There was a rapid increase in the number of photographic studios during the late 1850s. Evidence abounds of the way that the increasingly commercial character of photography altered perceptions of the medium. In its review of the 1857 exhibition of the Photographic Society, the up-market *Saturday Review* complimented the society for having escaped the 'deluge of portraits of "Ladies and Gentlemen" which might reasonably have been expected from the shoals of professors in this line with which every thoroughfare is now pestered, and whose sole idea of the use of this valuable art seems to be that it is meant to perpetuate imbecile faces by a ghastly and too faithful likeness'.[13] These comments are typical of the distaste towards what was seen as the prostitution of the medium by the burgeoning number of portrait studios. The sardonic reference to Ladies and Gentlemen emphasizes that the accessibility of the new studios was already equated with the loss of photography's artistic distinction. The predominance of professional exhibitors provoked the council of the Photographic Society, in August 1858, to announce its intention to exclude from its annual exhibition any photograph that had previously been seen in public. The ploy was obviously directed against those professional photographers who sold their wares from their studios or from printsellers' windows.[14] Even though the council had later to rescind its decision, there is no doubt that, amongst the well-to-do amateurs who still held sway in the Photographic Society, it was strongly felt that the expansion of photography debased the artistic aspirations they held for the medium.

The commercialization of photography underpinned the publication of Victoria's photographs. Moreover, the perception that photography had either been debased into a vulgar medium or democratized into a universal one had a large influence upon how her published photographs were regarded. It is no coincidence that, at the very moment when photography was moving away from its roots as a leisured occupation, the first attempts to publish series of photographs of famous figures took place. The most long running of these was *Photographic Portraits of Living Celebrities, executed and published by Maull and Polybank.* Forty numbers of this monthly series were published between May 1856 and October 1859. However, with each albumen print measuring 19.5 by 14.5 cm, these large pictures were far removed from the small size and the comparatively low price of the *carte.* The changes of the 1850s are characterized by Seiberling as a movement away from an interest in the medium

---

[13] 'The Photographic Society's Exhibition', *Saturday Review*, 3 (1858), 78.
[14] Dr H. Diamond, Editorial, *JoPS* 21 Aug. 1858, 1.

itself to an emphasis on the particular purposes for which it could be used.[15] A corresponding change can be seen in the relationship between photography and the Crown. Attention shifted from Albert and Victoria's support for photography to the way it could be used by professional photographers to disseminate their likenesses.

A French photographer, André Adolphe Eugéne Disdéri, originally patented the *carte-de-visite* in November 1854. The name derived from the fact that it consisted of a small photograph, around 9 cm by 6 cm, pasted on to a slightly larger piece of card. Its size gave it the appearance of a visiting card, a purpose for which it was rarely used. Instead of one large negative plate being used for a single photograph, the ingenuity of Disdéri's design was that he used a camera with multiple lenses to expose a number of identical portraits on a single negative plate. Disdéri's initial patent specified ten images on one plate. This was subsequently reduced to a standard format of eight images produced using a camera with four lenses and a repeating back mechanism.[16] With single plates containing eight small prints instead of one large picture, individual *cartes* were hence reproduced at a fraction of the cost previously incurred for one full-plate picture. Having eight pictures upon one plate also dramatically increased the potential to reproduce a large number of pictures in a short space of time. As we will see, both of these factors were crucial in being able to create and supply a large market.

The format of the *carte* encouraged distinguished personages to let their photographs enter public circulation. In 1861, the *Saturday Review* claimed that, prior to the *carte*, photography had distorted and exaggerated the prominent features of the face. Celebrities had not been prepared to let themselves be revealed in such unflattering guises.[17] What was different about the *carte* was the type of lens that it used. *Carte* portraits had a long depth of field and a consequent lack of spatial hierarchy. Sitters were characteristically depicted in a full-length format. Their faces were distant enough from the camera to ensure that many signs of age or excess went unnoticed. As an article in the *Quarterly Review* put it in 1864, 'it gives you a kind of panoramic view of your friend, and gives a prominence to his best coat and trousers, which cast his features into the shade'.[18] Disdéri's patent was granted in 1854 but *cartes* did not catch on until late 1858 or 1859, when a veritable explosion of interest in France quickly crossed into Britain. Disdéri's published portraits of Napoleon III, Empress Eugenie, and other dignitaries of the Second Empire

[15] Seiberling and Bloore, *Amateurs, Photography*, 102.
[16] Elizabeth Anne McCauley, *A. A. E. Disdéri and the Carte de Visite Portrait Photograph* (New Haven: Yale University Press, 1985), 32–5.
[17] 'Lord Derby's *carte-de-visite*', *Saturday Review*, 4 May 1861, 446.
[18] Robert Cecil, 'Photography', *Quarterly Review*, 116 (1864), 516.

Fig. 26. John Edwin Mayall, *Queen Victoria and Prince Albert* (1860)

were hugely successful. The role of photography in picturing royalty was a European-wide phenomenon and Disdéri's royal photographs may well have provided a reassuring model for the publication of *cartes* of the British royal family.[19]

With the pleasure of seeing photographs of family, friends, and celebrities for the first time, collecting *cartes* became the latest fashion. They were lovingly fixed in photographic albums and pored over in drawing-rooms (see Fig. 26). Mayall's *Royal Album* was incredibly successful and at the forefront of the rage for celebrity photographs. After only a few days on sale wholesalers had already demanded 60,000 sets.[20] The publication of the *Royal Album* exemplifies the way that the first celebrity *cartes* became part of popular

---

[19] By 1857, Disdéri had begun amassing portraits of the members of the French aristocracy and their entourages. Between 1860 and 1862, he published two 1-franc instalments a week of a *carte* portrait accompanied by a short biographical sketch. See McCauley, *Disdéri*, 44–6.

[20] 'The Royal Album', *The Times*, 16 Aug. 1860, 9.

culture. Initially, *cartes* had a very protean status. Like the copper- and steel-engraved prints of the 1830s, they moved uneasily between being fine art portraits and media images. One photographic retailer, Charles Asprey of 166 Bond Street, advertised the *Royal Album* at £4. 4s. Individual photographs from the album, as well as those of other European monarchs, sold for 1s. 6d. each.[21] At these prices, the complete portfolio was very much a luxury item. Accordingly, the *Royal Album* followed the pattern of expensive steel and mezzotint engravings in its initial mode of publication. A private viewing of the royal photographs took place at Mayall's studio prior to their being put on show as a public exhibition.[22] Paintings were often placed on private view at printsellers before they were engraved and Mayall's exhibition reflects a similar practice. When the *cartes* went on sale they were available in two formats in a manner akin to the distinction between proof copies of engravings and ordinary prints. Despite the fact that there should have been no difference between photographs from the same negative, Mayall's *cartes* were first of all to be available in proof impressions on India paper (emphasizing the quality of the paper was a standard practice for signifying the value of a print). Subsequent impressions were to be available in albums of the kind that would soon become the norm for collecting *cartes*.[23]

Although the *Royal Album* was situated in a fine art milieu, individual *cartes* had a far broader audience and a very different existence. The celebrity *carte* was an industry and subject to the same logistical dictates as any other popular commodity. Celebrity *cartes* had their own London wholesale house, Marion & Co. The firm acted as the central supply point for retailers and as a distribution hub for most of the major photographers. Marion & Co. stocked thousands of celebrity photographs of every kind. In 1862, their manager claimed that 50,000 *cartes* passed through the firm's hands every month.[24] Thus, in many respects, the *Royal Album* was actually out of kilter with the popularity and the nature of individual celebrity *cartes*. Their success stemmed less from their aesthetic qualities and more from the voyeuristic curiosity they aroused over the sitters they depicted. In their initial mode of publication, Mayall's royal photographs suggest that, even at the moment of their release, neither their mass potential nor their appeal was fully perceived.

Demand for Mayall's photographs was so great that it was impossible for him to produce them quickly enough. He was probably able to print only

---

[21] Charles Asprey, *A New and Enlarged Catalogue of Photographic Portraits of the Royal and Imperial Families of Europe, etc.* (London: Charles Asprey, 1861), n.p.
[22] 'Photographs of the Queen and Royal Family', *ILN* 18 Aug. 1860, 118.
[23] 'The Royal Album', 9.
[24] 'Mason v Heath', *PN* 7 Mar. 1862, 116–17.

several hundred pictures from a single negative in a day. Unfortunately, for Mayall at least, photography became commercialized so quickly that it was not yet adequately covered by any copyright law. Forgeries of the royal *cartes* were commonplace and large profits were made out of an immense number of quasi-illegal pictures.[25] The extent of piracy was such that Charles Clifford's well-known photograph of Victoria, taken in November 1861 at the request of Queen Isabella of Spain, had its publication delayed until a copyright act had been passed.[26] One result of the extensive forgery was, of course, to further drive down the price of the royal photographs. The *Photographic News* noted that they had been offered to 'the trade' for as low as three shillings a dozen.[27] At this price, the wholesale value of each *carte* would be approximately 3*d*. Even with taking into account the mark up on the counterfeit pictures, they would have been several times cheaper than the 18*d*. that Asprey's were charging. Counterfeit copies of the royal pictures were instrumental in exploiting the reproductive potential of photography. Mayall's *cartes* were metamorphosed into objects of popular culture through the efforts of the illegal sellers as much as the legal ones. The royal *cartes* would have been impossible without Victoria's sanctioning, but commercial pressures made them into popular artefacts.

The pirated copies of Mayall's photographs motivated him to produce a second series of *cartes*. Owing to the technological constraints that left him unable to match the enormous demand, Mayall visited Buckingham Palace to make a new set of negatives in February 1861.[28] These negatives would obviously allow him to supply the market with far more of his own pictures (see Fig. 27). In publishing a second series, however, Mayall was caught in a self-perpetuating cycle that ensured the market was saturated with royal photographs. The supply of new pictures created further demand for new pictures, an expectation that new pictures would continue to be released, and yet more opportunities for counterfeiters. Interestingly, though, the *Photographic News* commented that for this series Mayall, to whom the piracies constituted a major loss of income, had adopted a plan that would enable him immediately to detect and punish piracy.[29] On each of the *cartes* from this series there is an inscription of 'Mayall. Fecit. March 1st 1861'. The inscription has usually been considered, if at all, as merely an artist's signature or a dating convention, yet it may well have been intended as a specific claim to ownership. With no copyright to cover his photographs, the inscription was

[25] 'Talk in the Studio', *PN* 22 Feb. 1861, 96.
[26] The picture was not released until it was registered for copyright on 9 Feb. 1863, 'Her Majesty the Queen', *PN* 17 Apr. 1863, 183.
[27] 'Talk in the Studio', 96.
[28] See 'Photographs of the Royal Family', *The Times*, 20 Feb. 1861, 12; 'Talk in the Studio', 96.
[29] 'Talk in the Studio', 96.

THE QUEEN & PRINCE CONSORT.

Fig. 27. John Edwin Mayall, *Queen Victoria and Prince Albert* (1861)

Mayall's attempt to trademark his property. Anybody copying his images would have to copy his trademark illegally at the same time.

A letter published by the *Photographic Journal* in May 1862 supports the interpretation of Mayall's inscriptions as trademarks. The letter suggests that, in the case of copyright difficulties, a trademark could be used against those who sold pirated *cartes*. Every photograph could have affixed to it 'an impressed stamp of the initials or monogram of the artist, previously to the photograph being mounted'.[30] The letter appeared twelve months after Mayall's photographs were taken but the suggestion is identical to the practice he adopted. Another significant strand of evidence stems from the fact that many of Mayall's other *cartes* from 1861 are marked in the same way as those of Victoria and Albert. A *carte* of Lord Brougham bears the date of 21 June

---

[30] 'Photographic Copyright', *PN* 1 May 1862, 33.

1861, while another of the Earl of Derby bears the date of 1 February 1861. However, after the introduction of a copyright bill in July 1862, none of Mayall's *cartes* have any kind of inscription. His wedding photographs of the Prince and Princess of Wales from March 1863, for example, carry no mark upon them.

Between the publication of Mayall's first and second series in August 1861, several of the most noted photographers of the day were permitted to follow his example. Other members of the royal family also sat regularly for their photographs, a trend that was to continue for the rest of the century. In the same way as the newspaper and illustrated press often contained accounts of Victoria's tours and visits, the advent of the celebrity *carte* maintained the ubiquity of the monarchy. The overwhelming commercial impetus behind the piracy of Victoria's *cartes* is reflected in the profits that photographers were reputed to be making. In 1869, Andrew Wynter, writing in the *Biritish Journal of Photography*, claimed that Mayall had made £35,000 from Marion & Co. for his royal pictures alone.[31] Between 1860 and 1862, 3 to 4 million copies of Victoria's *cartes* were said to have been sold.[32] In the first week after the death of the Prince Consort, no fewer than 70,000 photographs were ordered from Marion & Co.[33] Photographs of other celebrities might go in and out of fashion, but commentators were unanimous in their conviction that sales of those of the royal family were the most enduring. It should therefore come as no surprise that, in 1885, the eminent photographer William Downey declared that the best-selling photograph so far on record was a picture of the Princess of Wales giving her first son a piggyback. Downey claimed that it had sold at least 300,000 copies.[34]

After numerous protests by the photographic industry, a revised copyright bill finally came into effect on 29 July 1862. To qualify for protection under the new act a photograph had to be registered at Stationer's Hall for a fee of one shilling. Prosecutions took place regularly in the years following the copyright legislation, and testify to a still thriving trade in illegal copies. Reported cases in the early 1860s involved photographs of the Prince of Wales and the Duke of Cambridge, as well as copies of popular paintings such as William Frith's *Railway Station*, Holman Hunt's *The Light of the World*, and Millais's *The First Sermon* and *The Second Sermon*.[35] The paintings by Millais were part of several prosecutions from 1868 that were instigated by the leading printseller Henry Graves, formerly a partner in Hodgson and Graves. He had

[31]   Andrew Wynter, 'Contemporary News. Cartes de Visite', *BJP* 12 Mar. 1869, 126.
[32]   Ibid. 149.
[33]   Ibid. 35. See also 'Talk in the Studio. The late Prince Consort', *PN* 23 Feb. 1862, 106.
[34]   'Notes', *PN* 27 Feb. 1885, 136.
[35]   'Talk in the Studio', *PN* 13 Mar. 1863, 132; 'Photography in Court', *BJP* 11 Nov. 1864, 43; 'Miscellaneous', *PN* 5 June 1863, 275.

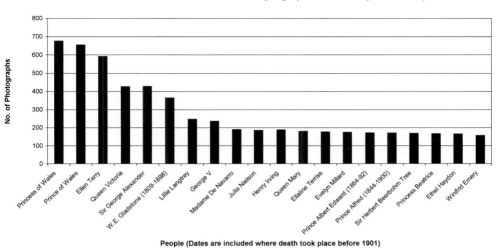

People (Dates are included where death took place before 1901)

Fig. 28. Photographs registered for copyright by sitter, 1862–1901

expended £1,700 upon the copyright of Millais's pictures, and around £25,000 preparing the plate for Frith's *Railway Station*, only to find photographs of both engravings cheaply available.[36]

The Stationer's Hall records are significant because they demonstrate the way photographs helped to forge a national identity around the royal family. The copyright records provide a quantitative index to the commercial photographs in circulation after 1862. They cannot reveal the volumes sold of any one photograph, and there are necessary provisos to interpreting the records (see Fig. 28).[37] They do, however, record the number of portrait photographs registered of any one sitter. Working on the assumption that photographs were registered specifically because they were expected to be commercially successful, the copyright records are a guide to the photographic prominence of distinguished figures. Significantly, though, the photographs registered reveal as much about privileged access to the public sphere as they do about which sitters were necessarily the most popular. A *carte* of a working-class celebrity might sell enormously, even though his or her participation in the media arena was limited to just one photograph. Distinguished personages had significant advantages in that photographic studios often solicited them for a sitting. As well as gaining a lucrative negative, the studio concerned would also share in

---

[36] 'Photographic Piracy', *PN* 15 May 1868, 218–19; 'More Photographic Piracy of Engraving', *PN* 6 Mar. 1868, 116; 'More Piracy', *PN* 13 Mar. 1868, 131.

[37] Russell Harris, *List of Copyright Records in the Public Record Office* (Kew: PRO and Elm Trust, 1996). One qualification to the figures is that an appearance in a group photograph is counted for every individual sitter, thereby double-counting family photographs of the monarchy.

Fig. 29. 'High Jinks', *Punch*, 6 August 1870, 55

the prestige associated with their sitter. The royal family's enthusiasm for photography, for example, gave rise to a large number of photographic studios that were eager to puff their prestige by displaying the royal warrant. Indeed, the misuse of the royal coat of arms was an important factor in the introduction of new regulations over its employment in the 1883 Patents, Designs, and Trademarks Act.

The copyright records reveal that, especially during the 1860s and 1870s, the supply of celebrity *cartes* was saturated by those of royalty, politicians, artists, and the leading clergy. Despite the modernity of the camera, Church and State were highly prominent in the early copyright records. A wonderful *Punch* cartoon from 1870 satirizes the earthly vanity of those preachers achieving public recognition through their *cartes* (see Fig. 29). Only in the 1880s and 1890s did actresses and sportsmen transform a media hegemony that was intimately bound up with the social hierarchy. The first set of photographs ever registered for copyright were two portraits of Alfred Tennyson on 15 August 1862. Four days later came the second ever set of photographs to be registered: a series of seven portraits of the Princesses Helena and Louise. During the first month of the law's operation—when there were eleven sets of photographs registered—six of them involved current members of the British royal family. Out of the first 2,000 photographs registered, up to 11 September 1863, 317 contained one or more members of the British royal family, a proportion of just over 15 per cent. Yet the ubiquity of the royal presence was not only notable in the first month. Figure 28 extrapolates data from a catalogue of the copyright records edited by Russell Harris to provide a sample of the sitters who appear most frequently between 1862 and 1901, while Table 1 provides an additional year-by-year breakdown of the records for five of the most photographed personages of the century, including Queen Victoria, Ellen Terry, and William Gladstone.

Comparing the number of royal photographs registered with those of other prominent politicians, clergymen, and actresses illustrates the extent to which the British royal family was able to dominate the imagined community of the nation. The Prince and Princess of Wales were by far the most photographed personages of the century, with 655 and 676 photographs recorded respectively. Despite the seclusion of Victoria after Albert's death, the only non-royals to surpass or equal her were Ellen Terry (593) and the actor-manager George Alexander (424). The difference in quantity between Victoria and the Prince and Princess of Wales can be partly explained by the high society glamour surrounding Edward and Alexandra. Their affinity for the camera was part of the glamour of their belonging to the fast-living group known as the Marlborough House set. Furthermore, with the Prince and Princess of Wales fulfilling many public duties that the Queen might otherwise have undertaken, and with the interest aroused by the birth of the couple's several children, they provided a more attractive prospect for photographers than the secluded Victoria.

Major royal occasions such as weddings and jubilees provided a tremendous boost to the photographic coverage of the royal family. In 1863, the year of the Prince and Princess of Wales's wedding, there were 75 photographs of Edward and 71 of Alexandra catalogued. This was the highest total for either of them in any one year until Edward's accession in 1901. One factor in the total number of royal photographs registered is the sheer longevity of the Queen and most of her children. Yet even on a year-by-year analysis Victoria exceeds comparable figures such as Gladstone. His life as a public statesman was one of the few to approach Victoria's in length. He even achieved his own iconographic status as the Grand Old Man. Table 1, however, demonstrates that Gladstone was still regularly below the number registered for the Queen and the Prince and Princess of Wales. A similar situation can be seen for Samuel Wilberforce, the well-known Bishop of Oxford, and E. W. Benson,

Table 1. Photographs registered at Stationer's Hall, 1862–1901

Year	Queen Victoria	W. E. Gladstone	Samuel Wilberforce	Ellen Terry	Princess Alexandra	Prince of Wales
1862	5	8	7	0	45	37
1863	44	11	22	0	71	75
1864	9	7	4	5	24	9
1865	9	1	7	0	31	51
1866	2	3	0	0	91	8
1867	14	5	3	0	5	10
1868	2	4	0	0	13	3
1869	0	13	1	0	7	4
1870	0	0	0	0	0	1
1871	3	0	2	0	37	37
1872	6	0	1	0	11	14
1873	0	7	15	0	0	0
1874	0	5	0	0	3	0
1875	1	0	0	0	0	4
1876	6	4	0	0	13	8
1877	7	10	0	0	2	13
1878	0	0	0	0	0	9
1879	4	7	0	6	16	6
1880	0	7	0	8	19	5
1881	7	15	0	0	11	5
1882	27	10	0	0	4	41
1883	0	22	0	38	15	4
1884	0	27	0	44	13	17
1885	0	4	0	14	13	8
1886	26	4	0	57	17	21
1887	40	8	0	11	25	15
1888	13	18	0	13	12	17
1889	18	16	0	101	18	20
1890	2	15	0	35	2	15
1891	2	7	0	43	3	12
1892	4	16	0	33	1	6
1893	13	23	0	44	13	13
1894	4	18	0	0	8	19
1895	0	13	0	34	0	3
1896	14	11	0	25	38	32
1897	47	19	0	37	32	31
1898	30	26	0	20	24	23
1899	37	2	0	13	11	23
1900	26	0	0	2	1	7
1901	6	0	0	10	27	29
Total	428	366	62	593	676	655

Archbishop of Canterbury between 1882 and his death in 1896. When we compare the royal photographs with those of three well-known theatrical figures in Fig. 28, Ellen Terry, Henry Irving, and the precocious Ellaline Terriss, it becomes apparent that most of their pictures were registered late in the century. The photographs of Ellen Terry were registered in a concentrated period between 1883 and 1900, while the first photographs of Henry Irving and Ellaline Terriss were not registered until 1896 and 1893 respectively. The ubiquitous supply of photographs of the British monarchy created an extensive royal media presence that was more the imposition of a collective experience than simply the satisfaction of popular demand.

As Fig. 28 and Table 1 demonstrate, the number of photographs registered is relatively small compared with the proliferation of twentieth-century media photography. Each *carte* therefore possessed a heavy symbolic weight, and the potential commercial value of an individual photograph is exemplified by a legal dispute regarding the ownership of a negative of Prince Albert. The case was heard in the Court of Common Pleas on 28 February 1862. The details revealed by the witnesses provide a unique insight into the way in which relations between photographers and the royal family changed irrevocably with the new commercial status of photography. The case is a perfect example of why we should not take the royal photographs at their face value. The high seriousness of the sitters should not suppress the other factors motivating the existence of the photographs.

The plaintiff in the case was Robert Mason of Paternoster Row, London, a photographic publisher. The defendant was Vernon Heath of Murray and Heath, a well-known firm of photographers.[38] Heath was one of the first photographers to enjoy royal approval, teaching photography to the young Prince Alfred in the early 1850s. The origins of *Mason* v. *Heath* stem from as early as April 1860, when Mason solicited Prince Albert to sit for a photograph to be published in a series entitled the 'British Photographic Gallery'. Albert declined to sit on the grounds that he could not be seen to be promoting the success of any commercial undertaking. Fascinatingly, four months before the publication of Mayall's *Royal Album*, Albert was turning down requests from photographers on the basis that they were instigated for purely commercial ends. As Roger Taylor has argued, before the 1860s royal pictures would probably have been taken by William Bambridge (effectively the photographic factotum of the royal family), or by photographers connected to

---

[38] 'A Dispute about a Negative', *BJP* 15 Mar. 1862, 112; Vernon Heath, 'Mason v Heath. To the Editor', *BJP* 15 Mar. 1862, 112–13; 'A Dispute in Relation to a Negative of the late Prince Consort', *JoPS* 15 Mar. 1862, 17–19; Vernon Heath, *Vernon Heath's Recollections* (London: Cassell & Company, 1892); 'Photography in the Law Courts', *PN* 7 Mar. 1862, 110–11; 'Mason v Heath', *PN* 7 March 1862, 116–17; 'Mason v Heath', *PN* 14 Mar. 1862, 130–1.

Victoria and Albert through their involvement with the Photographic Society.[39] Mayall enjoyed a similarly close association. The decision to sanction the *Royal Album* must have been aided by the fact that, like Heath, he was already well known to Victoria and Albert. Mayall began his career as a daguerreotypist in Philadelphia before moving to London in 1846. He was responsible for taking daguerreotypes of the Great Exhibition and this commission meant the beginning of an acquaintance with Prince Albert that was to continue over the next decade.[40] In contrast, most professional photographers were on a wholly different footing. Their treatment reflects the fact that their photographs were not commissioned as Victoria and Albert's own pictures, which the royal couple might then permit to be made public. They were always already conceived of as public pictures of Victoria and Albert.

Mason's initial failure implies that the publication of the *Royal Album* reversed an existing unwillingness to make Victoria's photographs widely available. Did increasing pressure from photographers cause the change of heart? Mason reapplied upon three or four occasions after his first rebuttal from Albert and it hardly seems likely that he was alone in his attempts. Thus the publication of the *Royal Album* can be seen as a response to external pressures rather than simply a proactive decision on the part of Victoria. Following the *Royal Album*, when Mason renewed his application in June 1861, permission was finally granted. The court case stems from the pictures of the Prince that were subsequently taken. By coincidence, the Prince was about to sit for a photograph by Heath. In order to save Albert time and trouble, Mason was directed to confer with Heath so that only one sitting would be necessary. The arrangement marked the beginning of the dispute. Mason subsequently alleged that Heath had agreed to take two negatives for him at a price of one guinea each. This was the standard rate Mason paid to other prominent photographers such as Kilburn and Mayall. Having two negatives would allow Mason to print twice the number of *cartes* at a time when, as we have seen with Mayall, it was the inability to keep up with demand that was the primary problem for publishers. Mason claimed that he could have sold 40,000 copies of the portrait. His anticipated profit was £1,000, or around 6*d.* upon every picture. Even taking into account any exaggeration of the figures by Mason, his claims provide an indication of the large sums that were at stake for a single photograph.

Needless to say, Heath's version of affairs was very different. According to Heath, Mason told him Albert had made Mason responsible for choosing which photographer would have the privilege of taking the Prince's picture. Heath knew this story to be false. He believed that Mason was trying to

[39] Dimond and Taylor, *Crown and Camera*, 25.
[40] 'Photographs of the Royal Family', *The Times*, 18 May 1860, 9.

defraud him in order to be charged an unduly low price. After four pictures of Albert were taken on 2 July, Victoria had to approve the pictures. Heath was eventually instructed to pass on one negative to Mason, for which he decided to charge the large sum of fifteen guineas. Mason consequently alleged that Heath had broken their agreement to supply him with two negatives. In court, however, the evidence was firmly on the side of Heath as Prince Albert's Private Secretary, Carl Ruland, appeared as a witness to confirm his story. With notable members of the royal household having to appear in court and private correspondence between Ruland and Heath being made publicly available, the royal photographs of Albert are placed within a wholly different frame of reference, that tarnishes the dignified seriousness of their depiction. As a whole, the case sheds light upon the web of protocol that publishers like Mason had to undergo before they could hope to gain a royal photograph. The constraints upon photographers helps to explain why there was such pressure upon those royal photographs that were sanctioned for publication, why there were comparatively few of them, and hence why each individual *carte* had a discursive weight imbued within it.

Why were the royal photographs so successful? What was the nature of their appeal? Reactions to Victoria's *cartes* are made up of a cluster of related concerns, which, in different ways, all emphasize the democratic, intimate, and collective nature of the royal pictures. These responses were the product of a wide-ranging debate over the very nature of photography. A crucial component of this discourse, to which Juliet Hacking has drawn attention, was the employment of an egalitarian rhetoric:

One of the forms through which a number of disparate individuals connected to photography came to recognise and consolidate a mutual interest was the mobilisation of democratic and demotic rhetoric in specialist photographic discourse. All the tropes of Victorian populism are here: photography as universal language, photography as teacher, photography as cheap and efficient means of disseminating a love for the beautiful. The identification of photography as equally subject to aesthetic as well as scientific enquiry enabled specialist photographic discourse to become, simultaneously, explicitly universalising and implicitly political.[41]

Loaded with this democratic semantic, royal photographs altered the character of the monarchy. Victoria's *cartes* were invested with a constitutional agency even though their success owed very little to politics. The realism of photography gave them a demythologizing equality at the same time as they created an intimate familiarity with the royal family. They reinforced the existing ideological demand for a closer relationship between the royal family and it subjects.

[41] Hacking, 'Photography Personified', 26.

The extensive circulation of the royal photographs meant that they were celebrated for the collective experience they provided. In October 1861, the *Art Journal* compared the collection of *cartes* to an ad infinitum multiplication of national portrait galleries. The National Portrait Gallery had first opened its doors in 1858, with the explicit intention of displaying portraits that would embody a grand national history, and the *Art Journal* saw the celebrity *carte* as creating a similar national constituency. In a significant turn of phrase, the *Art Journal* claimed that they reproduced the 'family portrait of the entire community'.[42] *Cartes* constituted and expressed an inclusive communal identity: they integrated public figures into the intimate arena of individual subjectivity. Royal photographs were at the forefront of this shared pattern of experience, and the *Art Journal* was in no doubt of the importance of Victoria's *cartes*:

> The production and the reproduction and the diffusion of the *carte-de-visite* portraits of Her Majesty the Queen, and of the various members of the Royal Family, would furnish materials for no ordinary chapter in the history of popular Art . . . It would be difficult to form an estimation of the extent to which these beautiful little portraits may be reproduced. Without a doubt they will be required in tens of thousands. They will have to find a way into every quarter of our sovereign's wide dominions, and into every city and town, both at home and in the colonies . . . These royal *cartes-de-visite* leave far behind all other agencies for enshrining our Sovereign's person and her family in the homes of her people. They do for everybody, as much as Winterhalter can do for the Prince Consort himself.[43]

Like Hengist-Horne's earlier essay, the *Art Journal* is concerned with conceptualizing the impact of such widespread royal reproduction. The comparison to Franz Xavier Winterhalter is significant because his royal portraits, mostly undertaken during the 1840s and 1850s, were the result of personal commissions from Victoria. By equating Winterhalter's pictures with the possession of a royal *carte*, the *Art Journal* is eulogizing the intimacy of the personal insight that they offered.

The scale of the royal photographs' success meant that the *Art Journal* congratulated the nation 'upon possessing such a means for realising the popular ideal of our sovereign, and of the Prince and Princesses of England'.[44] This statement is crucial for understanding the ideological success of Victoria's photographs. In a fashion akin to Victoria's civic visits, the publicness achieved through Victoria's *cartes* is elevated to the fulfilment of a populist and, by implication, constitutional ideal. The reproductive potential of photography is celebrated for placing the monarch literally inside the homes of her subjects; it ensured a court portrait for every hearth. Such rhetoric exem-

---

[42] 'Cartes-de-visite', *Art Journal*, NS 7 (1861), 306.   [43] Ibid.   [44] Ibid.

plifies the way that the royal photographs were celebrated for extending the intimacy between Victoria and her subjects.

It was not only through the circulation of the *cartes* themselves that photography provided a shared experience of Victoria. The porous interface between photography and other graphic media helped to create a familiar figure of Victoria. Photography did not become a dominant visual media until the 1880s and 1890s, when the development of half-tone engraving allowed periodicals like the *Illustrated London News* and the *Graphic* to reproduce photographs of contemporary news events regularly. However, from the early 1850s the illustrated press regularly used engravings of photographic portraits. As early as May 1856 the *Illustrated London News* printed an engraved portrait of the Princess Royal that had been copied from a photograph by Mayall.[45] The royal image was photographic long before it was disseminated primarily through photographs. Through its insinuating influence over engraving and lithography, photography created an iconic image of the sovereign. When Victoria was thought of, it was likely that she was thought of in photographic terms.

Soon after the introduction of the *carte*, photography was threatening the dominance of printsellers. A review from the *British Journal of Photography* shows photography and engraving striving to capture the same market in the early 1860s:

Those who have been in the habit of inspecting the display of *cartes-de-visite* in the shop windows of the metropolis must have been amused to see the indications of the battle between the engravers and photographers as exhibited therein during the last few weeks. First comes a series of delicately drawn lithographs of celebrities, evidently intended, by the combined force of superior attractiveness and lowness of price, to compete with or take the place of their popular and triumphant rivals, the *carte-de-visite*. Scarcely have these made their appearance before, closely treading on their heels, the same engraving comes out in the form of a very clever and attractive photographic reproduction.[46]

In the free flow of images between the graphic media, photography was increasingly able to outdo engraving and lithography because of its speed, cheapness, and novelty. Prints were driven out of the market by photographic copies. At the same time, engravers were forced to start copying photographs. This was both a way of competing with the camera and a practical means of taking advantage of the new medium. Nevertheless, such copying obviously resulted in engravers being increasingly subservient to photography. Their dependence meant that photography became the dominant media. By the end

---

[45] 'Princess Royal', *ILN* 31 May 1856, 584.
[46] 'Notes of the Month', *BJP* 1 Apr. 1863, 151. See also *Portraits and Memoirs of the Royal Family of England* (London: Ward and Lock, 1862).

of Victoria's reign, the dominance of photography was such that Benjamin Constant's late portrait, exhibited at the Royal Academy in 1901, was the copy of a photograph by the Bassano studio.

After the late 1850s, many engravings and lithographs of the royal family were based on *cartes* or cabinet photographs. Victoria's photographs were also used for her portrayal on a plethora of different objects, ranging from biscuit tins to commemorative pottery. Artefacts were endlessly reproducing Victoria according to the format of photography. This was a condition exacerbated by the fact that the advent of the *carte* coincided with Victoria's widowhood. With Victoria in secluded retirement, engravers had to rely more and more on photographs for up-to-date images. The first time the *Illustrated London News* dedicated its front page to Victoria after her widowhood, when she planted a memorial tree at Windsor on the first anniversary of Albert's death, its engraving derived from a photograph lent to the periodical by William Bambridge. Victoria's refusal to undertake her civic duties after Albert's death placed ever more stress upon the importance of her photographs, heightening the awareness of a media monarchy.

Numerous examples demonstrate the enthusiasm with which the periodical press took advantage of photography. In January 1860, *Cassell's Illustrated Family Paper* announced that it had in preparation a large engraving of the royal family, based on a photograph by Lake Price.[47] Tellingly, like the various reproductions of royal photographs that appeared in the *Illustrated London News*, the engraving predates the *Royal Album* by eight months. Other periodicals followed the example of *Cassell's*. In August 1861, the *Illustrated News of the World* published separate prints of Victoria and Albert. These were based on Mayall's *cartes* and were part of a series entitled the *Drawing Room Gallery of Eminent Personages* (see Fig. 30). Two months later, the first number of *Queen* gave away a small photograph of Victoria. Taken together, the transmission of these different portraits exemplifies the way in which photography created an iconic portrayal of Victoria. Instead of the situation at Victoria's accession described by *Bentley's Miscellany*, where there was an enormous range of different Queens, photography helped to constitute a much more universal and unifying experience of Victoria.

The circulation of the royal photographs certainly helped to further a familiar relationship with the royal family. Equally as important, however, is the intimate way in which the photographs were experienced. The realism of photography was anticipated to make the sitter present in profoundly unmediated way. *Cartes* were expected to be filled with the potent presence of their sitter. Lindsay Smith has recently revisited Benjamin's argument that photography

---

[47] 'Special Notice to the Readers of the Family Paper', *Cassell's Illustrated Family Paper*, 5 (1860), 128.

Fig. 30. Engraving by D. J. Pound after J. E. Mayall, 'Prince Albert', *The Annual Gift-Book: A Drawing Room Gallery of Eminent Personages* (London: London Joint Stock Company, 1859)

and film caused the advent of a revelatory realism that invested new technology with magical properties.[48] The slow-motion film and the microscope were examples of how 'the most precise technology can give its products a magical value such as a painted picture can never again have for us'.[49] The magical character of photographic realism imbued the first *cartes* with the quality of totemic artefacts. In 1861, the *Art Journal* contrasted the photographer with the silhouette artists who travelled around villages and popular fairs. In so doing, it suggested that *cartes* were almost metonymic forms of their sitters: 'These black paper enormities admonish us that but a single step intervened between the first tracing of a much-loved shadow on the wall at Corinth and the almost breathing and sentient portrait of the carte-de-visite.'[50] This

[48] Lindsay Smith, *The Politics of Focus: Women, Children and Nineteenth-Century Photography* (Manchester: Manchester University Press, 1998), 1–11.
[49] Walter Benjamin, 'A Short History of Photography', in *One Way Street and Other Writings*, trans. Richard Jephcott and Kingsley Shorter (London: Verso, 1985), 243.
[50] 'Cartes de Visite', *Art Journal*, 306.

fetishistic realism exacerbated the intrasubjective effect of the royal photographs. Even the preface to *Drawing Room Gallery of Eminent Personages* played upon the transcription of photography. It declared that 'we flatter ourselves that we offer the very best substitute for personal acquaintance in the ensuing series of life-like portaits'.[51]

Stereoscopic photographs took the principle of interactivity even further in that the viewer was literally taken inside the world of the photograph. The term stereoscope derives from two Greek words, στερεο meaning solid and σκοπειν meaning to look at. Seen through specially designed viewers, stereoscopic pictures provided a three-dimensional experience. They were an incredibly popular parlour-room pastime from the mid-1850s. The London Stereoscopic Company was set up in 1854 and by 1858 its trade list included more than 100,000 titles.[52] In 1861, stereoscopes of the interiors of Sandringham, Buckingham Palace, Windsor, Osborne, and Balmoral were published.[53] For the viewer, these cards provided a virtual reality tour of the inside of the royal residences. Later stereoscopic cards included pictures of Victoria's personal cabin on the *Alberta* (see Fig. 31).

The sensuous intimacy of the royal photographs was underpinned by Victoria's desire to release her pictures for general consumption. Victoria and Albert's preparedness to make themselves public was a defining element in the appreciation of their individual *cartes*. George Shadbolt, the editor of the *British Journal of Photography*, found evidence of Mayall's successful efforts in the 'easy and graceful attitudes of his sitters, which add an additional charm to his productions and testify that the sittings have been submitted to *con amore* in every instance'.[54] Other reviews of Victoria's photographs were equally keen to emphasize that they had been personally authorized. *The Times* specifically drew attention to the fact that the *Royal Album* could not have been issued without Victoria's official permission and 'as that is granted, her own approval of Mayall's work is almost officially proclaimed'.[55] *Photographic News* asserted that the publication of the royal photographs was a 'happy thought on the part of her Majesty, and as at once calculated to stimulate and gratify the proverbial loyalty of the people of England'.[56] This frisson of excitement clearly existed because of a distinct uneasiness over the publication of the first royal *cartes*.

The assumption that royal photographs would not be made available was

[51] 'Preface', *The Annual Gift-Book: A Drawing Room Gallery of Eminent Personages* (London: London Joint Stock Newspaper Company, 1859), p. iii.
[52] William C. Darrah, *The World of Stereographs* (Gettysburg, Pa.: W. C. Darrah, 1977), 4.
[53] 'Stereoscopic Views of the Royal Palaces', *Art Journal*, NS 7 (1861), 30.
[54] George Shadbolt, Editorial, *BJP* 17 June 1860, 157.
[55] 'The Royal Album', *The Times*, 16 Aug. 1861, 9.
[56] 'Royal Patronage of Photography', *PN* 23 Aug. 1861, 375.

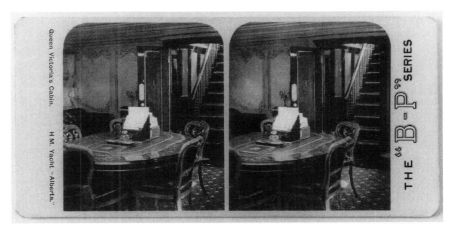

Fig. 31. 'Queen Victoria's Cabin, H. M.'s yacht *Alberta*', *B-P Stereoscope Views of Portsmouth and Portchester* (Birmingham: W. Tylar, *c.*1880)

very much part of the amateur milieu in which photography still, to some degree, operated. In August 1860, John Watkins was requested by Victoria to take photographs of the Prince of Wales and his entourage just prior to his visit to Canada. The *Art Journal* subsequently noted that 'The portraits though, of course, not intended for circulation, may be seen at the rooms of the photographist'.[57] In the same month as the publication of the *Royal Album*, the *Art Journal* was automatically presuming that such family photographs would not be published. Connoisseurs could, however, visit Watkins's studio to appreciate them. Photography remained a medium that the royal family used extensively for their own private benefit. The degree of revelation attached to the publication of their photographs was in inverse proportion to the extent to which they were simply celebrity *cartes*, displaying a public persona rather than offering a private insight. Once Victoria's photographs were habitually made available, their essential complexion was irredeemably altered. In the early 1860s the royal photographs were not simply *cartes* of Victoria and Albert; they were Victoria and Albert's own *cartes*, their own personal family records.

Reviews constantly drew attention to Victoria's personal approval of the publication of her photographs. In so doing, they emphasize the relationship between photography and her earlier media making. Newspapers and prints were often characterized by an idealized and fabricated Victoria. In contrast, the necessary link between sitter and photograph required Victoria's personal involvement. The corresponding control that could be exercised over the

[57] 'Minor Topics of the Month', *Art Journal*, NS 6 (1860), 253.

publication of her *cartes* gave them an aura of authenticity. Yet, despite the revelatory realism of the royal photographs, their novelty exists on a continuum with the coverage of the newspaper and periodical press. What made photography an important part of the narrative of royal populism was the agency it gave to Victoria as the catalyst of the monarchy's own progressive reinvention. The personal credit given to her is similar to the praise heaped upon her willingness to undertake tours and visits. There was no need to unravel the aristocratic mystique around the monarchy because Victoria was willing to demythologize herself before the camera. In 1868, the *British Journal of Photography* made one of many comparisons between Elizabeth and Victoria's attitudes to their images. It declared that, while Victoria had not been much flattered by photography, 'we may feel thankful that we do not live in the days of "good Queen Bess" whose personal vanity was such that she caused a proclamation to be issued preventing any artist or engraver taking liberties with her famous face'.[58] Victoria's enthusiasm for photography was a key factor in their symbolizing the shift to a more inclusive style of monarchy.

What is initially striking about Mayall's pictures is their sobriety. The plainness of the background and the relative lack of any accessories give the *cartes* a bare minimalism. The meaning of the pictures has to be found almost entirely within Victoria and Albert themselves: there are none of the external signs of sovereignty reminiscent of state portraiture. Significantly, articles on photography in *All the Year Round* and *Once a Week* recommended that if an individual truly wished to know themselves they should forgo any props or painted backgrounds and should let themselves be posed in their everyday dress.[59] Such advice was value laden in that it slid together social and aesthetic authenticity. Understood through this rubric, the 'ordinariness' of Victoria and Albert's *cartes* is a sign of their willingness to put their true selves on display before the camera. Simultaneously, though, the realism of the camera reveals their true selves to be ordinary. The photographic portraits of the couple certainly project an air of formal respectability rather than of regal status. Royal display—in all its forms—was a potent symbol both of aristocratic mummery and of the monarchy's fabrication. The pared-down realism of the *cartes* consequently gave them an added charge in that they were ostensibly a counterpoint to the panoply of fictional narratives around Victoria.

The 'ordinary' royal family portrayed by Mayall's *cartes* was something the initial reviews were keen to celebrate. *The Times* noted that 'The illustrious personages are shown without those stately appurtenances which are usually

[58] 'Personal Vanity of a Queen', *BJP* 5 June 1858, 273.

[59] 'The Philosophy of Yourself', *All the Year Round*, 9 (1863), 393; Andrew Wynter, 'Photographic Portraiture', *Once a Week*, 6 (1862), 148.

copied in portraits, and are represented as members of a private circle, engaged in domestic pursuits alone'.[60] The *Athenaeum* similarly praised their intimacy, effusively claiming that each study reproduced 'with a homely truth, far more precious to the historian than any effort of a flattering court painting, the lineaments of the royal race'.[61] The *carte* appeared to offer an authentic disclosure of what *The Times* called the inner life of royalty.[62] The truth of self-hood was invariably located in the private sphere and Victoria's photographs were more real because they seemed to permit a view behind the walls of Windsor. The intimate glimpse of the monarchy offered by photography there-fore accentuated the bond between the royal family and its subjects.

The bourgeois royal family expressed by the camera was only one strand in the dense cluster of meanings that fed off the realism of the royal *cartes*. Pho-tography did more than reveal; it provided an unflattering and potentially dan-gerous exposure. Numerous reviews refer delicately to photography's lack of success in picturing Victoria. *Once a Week* was typical in its response. In 1863, Andrew Wynter confessed to its readers that the royal family had fallen into very bad hands through their photographers for their pictures were all slanders upon them.[63] Wynter was one of the most notable writers upon pho-tography during this period; his essays in *Once a Week* and *Good Words* were reprinted in the major photographic journals. Wynter declared that one pho-tograph of Victoria and Albert showed them looking at each other like two wooden dolls; hardly a confirmation of their domestic intimacy. His review is an indication that their pictures could appear formal and posed to contempo-rary commentators. In the *British Journal of Photography* another critic noted that, 'my loyalty, I hope, will not be questioned when I say that photography has not hitherto flattered the appearance of the Royal Lady'.[64] Similar deroga-tory comments continued to appear until the very end of Victoria's reign. In 1897, for example, *Photographic News* meanly commented that the Queen preferred being taken in profile because 'when you are the possessor of more than one chin, profile *is*, perhaps the best'.[65] Nevertheless, it is precisely because of the camera's uncompromising portrayal that Victoria's *cartes* were so potent. The unflattering nature of Victoria's pictures is an extension of the logic that lauded her ordinariness. Both responses are part of the demytholo-gizing and egalitarian character of the celebrity *carte*. The realism of photog-raphy, for example, was perceived to have an equalizing impact because the camera lens recognized no social distinction among those who sat before it. Only by tracing the egalitarian nature of the celebrity *carte* is it possible to

---

[60] 'The Royal Album', 9.   [61] 'Our Weekly Gossip', *Athenaeum*, 18 Aug. 1860, 230.
[62] 'The Royal Album', 9.   [63] Wynter, 'Photographic Portraiture', 149.
[64] 'The Lounger', *BJP* 12 May 1865, 250. See also 'Our Editorial Table', *BJP* 11 Aug. 1865, 419.
[65] 'Chit chat', *PN* 15 June 1897, 43.

demonstrate the role of photography in shifting the political character of the monarchy.

In the ongoing dispute over the status of photography as an art during the 1850s and 1860s, Juliet Hacking has argued that critiques of the *carte* oscillated between 'what were figured as antithetical regimes of likeness: truth to the nature of material appearance and truth to the sitter's nature'.[66] On one side of this equation is the aesthetic distinction that notable photographers invested in the production of their pictures. In their attempt to raise both their own status and that of photography itself, the portrait studios for high society sitters saturated themselves in the discourses of fine art. One of the primary ways in which they did so was by taking up the notion of the ideal. Photographic discourse assimilated the aesthetic hierarchy that had been codified in the eighteenth century through Joshua Reynolds's influential *Discourses of Painting*.[67] Writing in the *Photographic News* of 1863, Disdéri himself published a series on the aesthetics of portraiture. His instructions underline the pictorial effect that he felt photographers should aim at:

The first step that the photographer should take to obtain a good likeness is to penetrate the numberless aspects under which he sees his model, and to ascertain the real type and character of the individual. It is thus alone that he is enabled to commence an appropriate representation and to chose the particular attributes and expression, as well as the distance, light, and accessories of the picture.[68]

As Disdéri makes clear, the photographer's role was to capture the inner and ideal self of the sitter, to go beyond the mere mechanical reproduction of surface appearance. The pose of the sitter and the background accessories were all intended to be significant in manifesting his or her expression of selfhood. Thus, a photograph of Prince Albert by Camille Silvey surrounds him with a statuette, globe, and open book, symbols of his commitment to learning, industrial progress, and the fine arts.

The traditional pretensions of the ideal required the painter to express the sum of their sitter's character. In practice, however, this often meant flattering their well-heeled sitter or aristocratic patron. Despite photographers' attempts to mimic fine art conventions, the ideal was undermined by the unadorned realism of photography. The camera was lauded for truthfully seeing alike all who sat before it. The aristocratic connotations of the ideal meant that photographic realism had both a demythologizing and equalizing agency. In *Once a Week*, Wynter declared that: 'Tompkins or Hopkins may submit to go down to posterity as livid, corpse-like personages; but the Lady

---

[66] Hacking, 'Photography Personified', 33.
[67] See Audrey Linkman, *The Victorians: Photographic Portraits* (London: Tauris Parke, 1993), 34.
[68] A Disdéri, 'The Aesthetics of Portraiture', *PN* 10 July 1863, 330.

Blanche or the fair Geraldine forbid it, Oh heavens!'[69] The photographer could not sustain the flattery of the court painter: the advent of photography literally and figuratively transformed the public face of the monarchy.

The democratic eye of the camera existed alongside the uniformity of the *carte* as an object. The mania for *cartes* owed much to their nature as artefacts. Their size and format conditioned their use and, consequently, the way in which they offered an intimate relationship with the royal family. *Cartes* had an equalizing agency because they created an experience of photography as something both familiar and everyday. In 1863, the *Athenaeum* condescendingly declared that photography could never be an art, precisely because of the type of pleasure given by the medium: 'As pleasant memoranda of things seen and enjoyed, as suggestions of the unseen substantialities of art (for we doubt one feels awed by a photograph of the pyramids), *photographs are handy*.'[70] 'Handy' is here being used to describe a lack of sublimity, a predisposition towards the ordinary. Small, ephemeral commodities which were widely available, easy to hold, easy to pass around, easy to look over by the dozen within a drawing-room, *cartes* possessed little distinction in themselves. As the *Reader* put it, 'the poorest carries his three inches of cardboard; and the richest can claim no more'.[71] *Cartes* were literally touchy-feely artefacts—not to be looked at with deferential awe or revered from a distance but catalogued and collected, gossiped and commented upon. By the very literal handyness of their use, *cartes* imbued their subjects with the quotidian qualities of their material format.

Closely connected to the equalizing nature of the *carte* as an object was its status as a freely circulating artefact. In *Once a Week*, Wynter compared the National Portrait Gallery, with its reclusive opening hours of only three days a week, to the accessibility of the street-portrait galleries of the many photographic establishments. Wynter claimed that scarcely a dozen people made their way to see the portraits at Great George Street, Westminster, where the National Portrait Gallery was then located. He had often been alone in the rooms for several hours at a stretch:

Certainly our street portrait galleries are a great success: no solemn flight of stairs tends to pompous rooms in which pompous attendants preside with a severe air over pompous portraits; no committee of selection decide on the propriety of hanging certain portraits. Here, on the contrary, social equality is carried to its utmost limit, and Tom Sayers is to be found cheek-by-jowl with Lord Derby, or Mrs Fry is hung as a pendant to Agnes Willoughby. The only principle governing the selection of the

---

[69] Wynter, 'Photographic Portraiture', 148.
[70] 'Talk in the Studio', *PN* 24 July 1863, 359. Sections of the article from the *Athenaeum* were reprinted in the *PN*.
[71] 'Photography', *Reader*, 9 Aug. 1862, 118.

carte-de-visite portraits is their commercial value, and that depends upon the notability of the person represented.[72]

For reviewers, many of whom were writing from a predominantly fine art standpoint, the democracy of the *carte* was constituted by the space of their circulation and exhibition. At the National Portrait Gallery, all portraits had to be of historical figures. The only living figure whose portrait was permitted was that of the sovereign. Despite attempts to make the gallery appeal to a broad public, sitters from a historical national élite dominated the portraits on show.

In contrast to the National Portrait Gallery, the *carte* was both contemporary and egalitarian. Several other articles drew attention to the uncanny equality achieved through the display of disparate personages together.[73] As the *Art Journal* put it: 'the most curious contrasts may be drawn and the most startling combinations affected . . . when even the most hurried of passing glances reveals to us the fac-simile of Lord Shaftesbury and Cardinal Wiseman, and of the French Emperor and Sims Reeves side-by-side.'[74] Celebrity *cartes* were caught up in a simultaneity that brought an unlikely diversity of sitters together through their photographs. This simultaneity eroded class difference and created an accentuated expression of collectivity. Each studio window was a bricolage of images that provided a novel embodiment of the nation as an imagined community; one that was remarkable because of its contrast with the official polity imposed by bodies like the National Portrait Gallery.

The democracy of the celebrity *carte* thus stems from the power they gave to individual consumers. It was through their choices that celebrities were formed, and this is one of the reasons why photography accentuated the populist character of the monarchy. The celebrity *carte* created a new order of cultural visibility, one less connected to traditional notions of status and wealth. This was a phenomenon to which the *Reader* specifically drew attention in 1864:

Photography is levelling and undiscriminating. Brown or Jones makes as good or better photographs than men of the stamp of Newton or Napoleon. We do not recognise men by the light of their photographs, though we usually recognise photographs when we have become familiar with the countenances they represent . . . On canvas or in marble let us preserve the resemblance of our great men for the benefit of our children, and take little heed about the permanence of photography.[75]

[72] Andrew Wynter, 'Cartes de Visite', *Once a Week*, 6 (1862), 135.
[73] See 'Photography', *Reader*, 9 Aug. 1862, 118.
[74] 'Cartes de Visites', *Art Journal*, 307.
[75] 'Photographic Improvements', *Reader*, 8 Oct. 1864, 457.

The *Reader* wonderfully captures the way that the extensiveness of the *carte* produced a recognition value that was independent of the social status of the sitter. The broad appeal of photography meant that there was increasing cause to latch on to popular figures such as sportsmen or actresses. Hence, it is significant that the earlier quotation from *Once a Week* singled out Tom Sayers as an example of the disturbing equality of the *carte*. Sayers, a well-known boxer, is one of the earliest examples of a working-class figure being turned into a celebrity through the aid of his photographs. In April 1860, Sayers fought the American champion, John Heenan, in what was effectively a fight for the undisputed championship of the world. The bout attracted widespread attention, including a mock epic poem by Thackeray in *Punch*. Sayers was also beset with photographers claiming the honour of paying for his sitting. His reported answer was 'It's no good, gentlemen, I've been and sold my mug to Mr Newbold'.[76] Newbold was a publisher of one of the sporting papers, and 50,000 *cartes* of Sayers were reportedly sold around the time of his fight.[77] Newbold's treatment of Sayers is akin to Mayall's attempt to copyright his royal photographs. Both are examples of photography beginning to be used in the aggressive creation and exploitation of celebrities.

The equalizing propensity of the *cartes* was underpinned by their status as commodities. For *Once a Week* and the *Art Journal*, all of the sitters are equal because all commodities are equal. Marx famously claimed that exchange-value creates only equivalences. It was the equivalence embodied in the simultaneity of the photographic displays—where *cartes* of disparate personages were placed together—that made them so disconcerting. Entrance into the public gallery of *cartes* was no longer dependent on status but on market value. Public notability was increasingly less commensurate with social nobility. Thus, while the *cartes* may have removed one type of artistic distinction, in their own way they were equally able to fetishize their subjects. The recognition value of celebrity *cartes* soon meant that they were increasingly able to manufacture their own kind of aura around a sitter.

Royal photographs, because of the station of the sitter, were particularly subject to this equalizing impulse. Numerous articles in the periodical press took a gleeful delight in examining what celebrity *cartes* revealed about the sovereigns of Britain and Europe. There was a desire for well-known figures to justify the imaginative investment in them and a satisfying pleasure when they were demythologized by the camera. In a typical article, *All the Year Round* amused its readers by wondering whether Elizabeth I's *carte* might show her to be a 'coarse ill-favoured old hag' or whether George IV's would show him to be all padding and crinoline.[78] Contemporary European

---

[76] Wynter, 'Cartes de Visites', 135.   [77] Ibid.
[78] 'The Philosophy of Yourself', *All the Year Round*, 9 (1863), 392.

monarchs fared little better in their treatment from *All the Year Round*. The periodical went so far as to hail the various royal *cartes* as revolutionary artefacts:

It has done much—a thousand times more than democrat or demagogue could ever do—to demolish the Right Divine to govern wrong. From the *carte-de-visite*, we learn the astounding fact that kings and queens are in dress and features exactly like other people. Marvellous, preternatural, as this may seem, it is true. Wings do not grow upon the shoulders of monarchs. They are compelled to tread like common mortals; and many of them look like very coarse and vulgar mortals too . . . this destructive *carte-de-visite* mania has made short work of the fictions of etiquette. The ex-Queen of Naples appears in knickerbockers. The ex-king stands sulkily with his hands in his pockets of a pair of very ill-made peg-tops. The Emperor of Austria, in his scanty white tunic, looks very much like a journeyman baker listening to the second report of Mr Trewenhere; the bluff King of Holland has a strong family likeness to Washington Irving's Peter Stuyvesant; the King of Italy is like Tony Lumpkin with a pair of enormous moustaches . . . As for the incomparable *carte-de-visite* of the Emperor Napoleon the Third, in a plain frock and shining hat, with his pretty, graceful wife on his arm, his moustaches carefully twisted, and a waggish smile on his face— what does he look like? The dark and inscrutable politician? The arch plotter? The gloomy man of December? Not a bit of it. He looks like a confident gentleman who knows a thing or two, who is going down into the City to do a little stroke of business and who will afterwards buy his wife a new bonnet on Ludgate Hill, or a new dress in St. Paul's churchyard.[79]

There is a voyeuristic *schadenfreude* at being able to see the authentic coun-tenances of kings and queens for the first time. It is nevertheless crucial to realize that this was revolution not to be feared but revelled in. *Cartes* did not bring down Napoleon III or Queen Victoria: they remade them as respectable citizens. *All the Year Round* might trumpet loudly over the republicanism of the *carte*—a *lèse-majesté* available to all—but they did not drive their pur-chasers to the barricades. They encouraged them to the printsellers for more photographs to pore over.

The irreverent attention bestowed on the royal photographs is another version of the familiarity and ordinariness celebrated by many other reviews. Yet, before we dismiss the sedition of the royal photographs entirely, there is one notable absentee from the exhaustive catalogue of foreign monarchs dwelt upon by *All the Year Round*. Victoria's *cartes* were not so devoid of import that the same relentless scrutiny could be applied to her. The royal photographs derived their *schadenfreude* only in relation to an underlying deference towards the monarchy. The *lèse-majesté* of *All the Year Round* and *Once a Week*

---

[79] 'The Philosophy of Yourself', 393.

was bourgeois radicalism of the kind that could still savour its proclaimed superiority over a moribund aristocracy. Yet, at the same time as the royal photographs threatened to remove all monarchical mystique, the same process reduced Victoria to an ordinariness that is implicitly valorized. The photographic revealing of an 'ordinary' Victoria was merely the latest narrative perpetuated in the populist reinvention of the monarchy.

The familiarity created through celebrity photographs was far from being a wholly benevolent affair. The camera was already disreputably associated with a more intrusive form of celebrity. Photography helped to make the monarchy available for public consumption, but it encouraged expectations that could not be controlled or contained. The irreverent comments upon the royal *cartes* suggest how easily the intimacy of photography could spill over into a more undesirable form of attention. A series of engagement *cartes* of the Prince of Wales and Princess Alexandra, taken by the Belgian photographers royal, Ghémar Frères, and registered at Stationer's Hall on 21 October 1862, exemplify the tension aroused by the camera's intrusive potential. Ghémar's engagement *cartes* depict the affections of the affianced couple. Several of the photographs show Edward or Alexandra standing with their arms resting lovingly on the shoulders of the other (see Fig. 32). These displays of intimacy were far removed from the formality of a state portrait and typify the appropriation of photography for family occasions. The romance they conveyed made these *cartes* highly successful. In 1866 the *British Quarterly Review* reported that the sale of Ghémar's portraits of Victoria, and the Prince and Princess of Wales, had exceeded 2 million copies.[80] The photographs were nevertheless found to be distasteful by some commentators. Edward and Alexandra were felt to be indiscriminately making available their most private feelings. In particular, there was a prurient reaction against the excessively overt female sexuality that was perceived to be on display.

Three articles, two from the *London Review* and one from *Once a Week*, heavily criticized the publication of Ghémar's royal *cartes*. *Once a Week* was one of the most highly regarded journals of the 1860s; its contributors included Millais, Mrs Henry Wood, and George Henry Lewes. It was more successful and had a far higher circulation than the *London Review*, which ran for only nine years between 1860 and 1869. Both of these periodicals were nevertheless located towards the upper end of the publishing market. The *London Review* condemned the *cartes* of Edward and Alexandra as fabrications. It refused to believe that they could ever have consented to release such intimacy for wholesale consumption:

---

[80] 'Photographic Portraiture', *PN* 9 Nov. 1866, 534. The article from the *British Quarterly Review* was reprinted in the *PN*.

Fig. 32. Ghémar Frères, *Edward and Alexandra* (October 1862)

a vast number of these supposed portraits from the life are 'cooked up' by foreign artists, whose main object is to make everything look pretty and sentimental. The result is often miserably false and bad. Here, for instance, we have before us a card which contains portraits of the Prince of Wales and Princess Alexandra, issued several weeks before there were married. His Royal Highness sits in a chair, while the Princess stands over the back of the chair, with her two hands resting on his shoulders. Pretty, is it not?—Sentimental, sweet, and lover-like? Very—only not quite probable or in the best taste. That a young lady may have stood, in that attitude of tender watching at the chair of her future husband, is likely enough,—but she would never think of being photographed at so confiding a moment. The 'lover' would certainly object to the artist 'posing' his intended in such a way, and the lady herself would object to it with still greater vehemence. Can Paterfamilias possibly believe that the Prince and Princess allowed themselves to be shown after this fashion to the general gaze?[81]

[81] 'Photography and Bad Taste', *PN* 10 Apr. 1863, 174. The article was reprinted from the *London Review*.

The impropriety of the picture does not stem from the scene having taken place. It derives from it having deliberately been photographed, and, even worse, of it being made publicly available.

In *Once a Week*, Andrew Wynter echoed the criticisms of the *London Review*. For Wynter, like the *London Review*, the principal culprit of the *cartes* was Ghémar Frères. The studio had taken advantage of the natural frankness and amiability of Edward and Alexandra 'to pose them in a manner which, to say the least of it, jars on the good taste of the fastidious beholder'.[82] Wynter attacked the impropriety of the photographer, thereby carefully avoiding any criticism of Edward or Alexandra. The *London Review* went further in that it disputed the very realism of the photographs. Its scepticism reveals that the celebrity *carte* spawned its own critique at the moment of its coming to prominence. Ghémar's portraits were condemned not simply for their intimacy but for their pandering to the sentimental and sensational taste of the public. For the *London Review*, the *cartes* were not truly private moments revealed. They were spectacles of privacy manufactured in the knowledge of their appeal. The censure of the *London Review* is premissed on its belief that the intrusiveness of the camera is undermining the separation between public and private. Much of the impact of the photographs stemmed from the supposed distinction between the two separate spheres.

The *London Review* article went even further in censuring what it regarded as the contrived nature of the latest *cartes* of Victoria. The photographs in question are those released after the death of Albert, where Victoria is in full mourning, often gazing melancholically at a bust or photograph of the Prince (see Fig. 33). Although these photographs are well known and have been reproduced in many biographies, their position in the genealogy of the celebrity *carte* has been downplayed. Despite Victoria's complete retirement after the death of Albert, several series of these mourning *cartes* were released. The *cartes* were public demonstrations of the depth of Victoria's grief, which, paradoxically, justified her inability to contemplate performing any state engagements. Notwithstanding the custom for a decorous period of retirement, the first mourning photographs were being advertised as early as March 1862.[83] Further series of *cartes* were registered at Stationer's Hall on 17 October 1862 and 16 January 1863, by William Bambridge and Ghémar Frères respectively. These photographs, and others like them, dominated Victoria's representation in the first years after Albert's death.

With Victoria's total retirement and with the depth of grief displayed in the *cartes*, the viewer became a voyeur of the Queen's suffering. The mourning *cartes* provided an unprecedentedly charged insight into the life of such a

---

[82] Wynter, 'Photographic Portraiture', 149.
[83] 'Ashford Brothers & Company', *Stationer*, 4 (1862), 66.

Fig. 33. William Bambridge, *Mourning the Prince Consort* (1862)

well-known figure. As such, they produce the same contradiction embedded in the engagement photographs of Edward and Alexandra. At the same time as the *London Review* found the mourning photographs to be profoundly uncomfortable because of their intimacy, it found them distastefully theatrical because of their perceived fabrication. The critic from the *London Review* was convinced that photographs depicting the innermost feelings of Victoria could not have been published. They were roundly denounced as forgeries: 'It is quite lamentable that any one should believe these fancy pictures to be photographs from life, or real scenes: yet we doubt not that they are generally so accepted.'[84] The *London Review* critic was coruscating upon those who were ignorant enough to suppose that Victoria, 'who has withdrawn herself from public life ever since her great affliction, would have permitted a photograph for his trading purposes, thus to invade the privacy of her grief'.[85] The incredulity of the article, along with its mistaken interpretation of the photographs, captures the extent to which celebrity *cartes* could undermine a belief in the realism of the medium.

---

[84] 'Photography and Bad Taste', 175.   [85] Ibid.

When the article from the *London Review* was reprinted in *Photographic News*, an editorial aside noted how woefully misinformed the commentator was.[86] Importantly, though, it agreed that there was ground for the charges of bad taste, and that, as a whole, the article was worthy of serious consideration. The belief in the impropriety of these two sets of royal photographs was certainly not shared by all. Yet the adverse reviews show the inherent risks of the celebrity *carte*. Its familiarity could easily tip over into discomfort at having the life of the monarchy played out to such an extent through the camera. These concerns dogged the first royal photographs, with the *London Review* publishing another article attacking the over-familiarity between photographers and the royal family. As it declared, 'whether it be joy or grief affecting the royal family, in some way the lens of the camera appears to spy into it in the most offensive manner . . . sacred feelings are turned to commercial account'.[87] The *London Review* and *Once a Week* emphasize that the shared experience provided by the celebrity *carte* was not just a matter of making the monarchy available; it meant the sharing of love and grief between the royal family and a wider public. The potency of this interaction is evident in the fact that it was so overcharged with both affect and discomfiture. It is, of course, a situation that continues to this day.

For consumers, poring over photographs was one of the principal pleasures. Nevertheless, because of this constant attention photography soon lost much of its novelty. The articles in *London Review* and *Once a Week* illustrate the development of a sceptical attitude towards the uses to which photography was being put. There was a widespread recognition that the realism of the *carte* was a metamorphosis as well as a mimesis. Victoria's photographs were invested with a heavy ideological mixture of ordinariness and intimacy. Yet the values overloaded on to them have to be set against a sophisticated engagement with the nature of photography as a mass media. The bourgeois identities revealed by the *carte* are far more equivocal than has been realized. The commentaries upon Victoria's photographs should not disguise the fact that they were a performance of ordinariness, a display of uniformity. Various articles suggest that the royal pictures would have been comprehended as such by many of those who viewed them. The critiques of the celebrity *carte* in the periodical press are similar to the crop of responses to Victoria's media making in *Punch*, *Reynolds's Newspaper*, and the *Penny Satirist*.

Cartes of the early 1860s have a conventionality that is immediately apparent when they are viewed together in large numbers. In addition to the standard full-length format, the prevalence of the same props and poses gave the celebrity *carte* a marked uniformity of representation. Poses such as the sitter

---

[86] Ibid.   [87] 'The Medley of Portrait Cards', *London Review*, 20 June 1863, 658.

reading or standing by a draped column were repeated endlessly. Royal photographs were no exception to this homogeneity. When the photographs of Mayall, Ghémar, and Heath are examined as a body of work, we can see just how similar many of the photographs are. The composition of the pictures of Victoria and Albert are indeed notable for their uniformity, while photographs of their children, as well as those of other distinguished figures, repeat the same conventions. The portrayal of Victoria and Albert owes much more to the conventions imposed by the photographic studio than to any inherent bourgeois identity the couple possessed. Or rather, it is inconsequential as to whether or not Victoria and Albert were portraying a genuine identity. This is because the way in which they were represented was so copied that their photographs came to seem as stereotyped as any other of the plethora of *cartes* in circulation (see Fig. 34).

The conformity between the different photographs does not answer the question as to why the different *carte* portraits should look so alike. An examination of just one of the most evident similarities between the sitters, that of the seemingly dark and sombre nature of their dress, reveals that it too was one of the conventions of the *carte*. The clothing commonly worn for the *carte* in the early 1860s stems from the fact that the silver nitrates used in the wet collodion process did not have an equal sensitivity to the different colours of the spectrum. Light colours were extremely difficult to photograph with the correct definition. White dresses risked making you appear ghost-like whilst yellow or mauve dresses were immediately transformed into jet-black garments. To counter the potential for failure, it was common practice for photographers to issue instructions on the appropriate dress that sitters should wear when having their *carte* taken. In 1855, Cuthbert Bede noted that Mayall's instructions to his sitters were as follows:

LADIES are informed that dark silks and satins are best for dresses; shot silk, checked, striped, or figured materials are good, provided they not be too light. The colours to be avoided are white, light blue, and pink. The only dark material unsuited is black velvet.
For GENTLEMEN, black, figured, check, plaid, or other fancy vests and neckerchiefs are preferred to white.
For CHILDREN, plaid striped, red, or figured dresses.[88]

As Bede noted, 'Thus does King Camera prescribe his court costume'.[89] Sitters were literally forced to wear similar costumes and it is hardly surprising that many of them looked alike. The more that the *carte* became popular, particularly amongst those who were able to ape the dress of those thought of

---

[88] Bede, *Photographic Pleasures* 41.   [89] Ibid.

Fig. 34. Montage of *Cartes-de-Visite*, *c*.1860–1865

as their social betters, the more its costume was translated into an equalizing uniformity.

The homogeneity between the various *cartes* was also caused by the way photographic studios sought to enhance their aesthetic status. Many studios copied the backgrounds, props, and poses used by eighteenth-century portrait painters like Reynolds and Gainsborough. The conventions used for picturing Victoria, Albert, Gladstone, Disraeli, and Derby were imitated endlessly. West End studios serving high society sitters, like that of Camille Silvey's, were sumptuously decorated, using genuine objets d'art for their props. Alongside such ornateness, however, a whole sub-industry grew up to provide the majority of photographic studios with cheap wooden balustrades and papier-mâché adornments. The uniformity of the *carte* was further ensured by the photographic journals themselves. They were full of detailed articles on how to pose and light a sitter and what sort of background it would be appropriate to use. Numerous inexpensive manuals on photography were also produced, such as Jabez Hughes's *The Principles and Practice of Photography Familiarly Explained* (1861). The widespread dissemination of the same props and formal conventions caused the aesthetic practices employed by studios such as Silvey's to be repeated in a perfunctory fashion.

The cheaper photographic studios did not only copy visual conventions. All of the associated connotations of aesthetic and social prestige were easily and deliberately mimicked. Accusations of bad taste against the cheaper photographic studios and their working-class sitters were rife, particularly by well-to-do periodicals like *Chamber's Journal*, *Once a Week*, and the *Reader*.[90] These critiques reveal that the portrait studio was as much a space for fantasy as it was for stern and unadorned revelation. *Cartes* were a pleasurable opportunity for theatricality and pretence. A satirical treatment of the social performance characteristic of *carte* portraits was thus central to the musings on the mediating effects of photography. *Once a Week* drew attention to the typical disjunction between the status of those sitting for their *carte* and the fine art conventions that were being used to represent them. The most notorious of these was the stereotyped false background:

There is Mrs Jones, for instance, who does the honours of her little semi-detached villa so well: how does she come to stand in that park-like pleasure-ground, when we know that her belongings and surroundings don't warrant more than a little back-garden big enough to grow a few crocuses? Or Miss Brown again, why should she shiver in a ball dress on a veranda, and why should we be called upon—instead of looking at her good honest face—to have our attention called away to the lake-like prospect at her back? Then there's Mr Robinson, standing in a library with a heap of books put within reach of his hand. Now, all Mr Robinson's little world know that he never looked at any book but a ledger in his life. It will be observed that it is the photographic artist who courts the lower-station of the middle-classes, who most delight in these scenic arrangements, and no doubt know what they are about.[91]

Similar comments can be found in many articles on photography from the early 1860s. There was an acute awareness of the *carte's* appeal to class-based aspirations. It perpetuated an ideal of refined gentility. All signs of labour were discarded in favour of the kind of refined poses adopted by Victoria and Albert.

[90] 'Modern Priests and the Temple of the Sun', *Chamber's Journal*, 17 Jan. 1863, 33–6; 'Photography and Bad Taste', 174–5.
[91] Wynter, 'Photographic Portraiture', 149.

What was at stake in the various attacks upon the bad taste of the *carte* was not simply the social identity it could no longer confidently claim to declare. The use of lavishly painted backgrounds and contrived props called into question the authoritative mimesis of photography itself. As Sarah Kember has recently argued with respect to computer-enhanced digital photographs, 'the panic over the loss of the real is actually a displacement or projection of a panic over the potential loss of our dominant and as yet unsuccessfully challenged *investments* in the photographic real'.[92] In a comparable fashion, the attacks on the cheap photographic studios reveal the bourgeois investment in photographic realism. For many of the working-class sitters that were condescendingly attacked, the pleasure of the *carte* was not in its realism but in its ability to enact a magic grotto-like transformation. Posing and the pleasure of performance were integral to the experience of visiting a studio. It was consequently not simply the social performance of the *cartes* of working-class sitters that made them distasteful. The threat they posed was in their implicit suggestion that all such class identities were performative. They undermined the transparent and authentic selfhood of photographic portraits by suggesting just how they could be fashioned. There is an elegant irony to the *carte* portrait. While many studios used backgrounds and props to elevate their sitters' class status, the photographs of Victoria, Albert, Napoleon, and Eugénie, were notable for the way they elided their aristocratic status. They were lauded for their ordinariness at the same time as the *cartes* of the working class were derided because the sitters refused to accept their own ordinariness.

The awareness of the distorting potential of the *carte* was widespread. There was a broad sensibility that was both sceptical and knowing towards photography. As early as August 1863 the *Stationer* carried an advertisement for a large series of 'Rock's Comic *Carte-de-visite*'. Many of the pictures were proclaimed to be especially adapted for the seaside.[93] Each of the 150 or so advertised pictures was accompanied with a caption such as 'A monkey like you with C-de-V', 'And £5000 a Year', 'One of the Upper 10,000', and 'The Juvenile Stuck-Ups'. Some of the *cartes* portrayed drawings of elaborately dressed cats and monkeys, twirling their whiskers and proudly holding their top hats. Each of the comic photographs plays knowingly upon the social performance of the *carte*. Rock's comic *cartes* have a relationship towards the authenticity of photography that is wholly contrary to the complaints against the cheap studios. Their very appeal lies in their performativity and their knowingness towards the contrivances of the *carte*. They express a sophisticated comprehension of the 'realistic' conventions of photography.

[92] Sarah Kember, *Virtual Anxiety: Photography, New Technology and the Body* (Manchester: Manchester University Press, 1999), 18.

[93] 'Rock's Comic Carte-de-visite', *Stationer*, 10 Aug. 1863, 245.

Victoria's photographs were given a demotic agency because they appeared to eschew mediation. Yet the mythology around Victoria's pictures has to be set against the widespread scepticism towards the contrivances of the *carte*. Royal pictures were by no means excluded from the accusation that *cartes* were overstylized. In *Once a Week*, Victoria and the Prince and Princess of Wales were criticized for letting themselves be subject to the photographer's whims. There was a picture of Victoria 'so posed that a tuft of verdure in the background appears to form a headresss such as Red Indians wear—the ludicrous effect of which must be imagined'.[94] The critiques of Ghémar Frères illustrate that the *cartes* of the royal family could be seen as just as much a performance as those that were criticized for their class pretensions. In Victoria's case, however, it was precisely their lack of social display that made them such a potent fabrication. A revealing testimony to Victoria's use of photography for a performance of ordinariness can be seen in a photograph from 1863 of her sitting at a spinning wheel in the guise of a poor, homely weaver (see Fig. 35). The picture was published by Elliott and Fry and the *cartes* from the *Royal Album* should be seen as on a par with this photograph. The equality and performativity of the *carte*, and consequently of Victoria's photographs, were two sides of the same equation. Furthermore, it was a uniformity that was wholly beyond the sitter's control. Victoria's photographs do emphasize her role as wife, mother, and, later, mourning widow. They do downplay her position as monarch. Yet they do so through a conventionality that, as the scepticism of the comic *cartes* and the various articles on photography testify, would have been immediately apparent to many of those viewing her pictures.

The performative character of the royal photographs is also evident in responses to a hitherto unrealized practice: the habitual and extensive retouching of Victoria's pictures. Blemishes and wrinkles were removed in the same way as the knife of the plastic surgeon now operates on ageing celebrities and Hollywood stars. The initial unadorned realism of the royal photographs—so potent in furthering the impression of a popular intimacy with the monarchy—was replaced by accusations of their excessive fabrication. These critiques extend the scepticism expressed towards the elemental realism of the camera, and responses to the retouching of Victoria's pictures are another example of the way photographic practices intervened in preexisting debates about the authenticity of Victoria's figure. There is nothing remarkable about the manipulation of royal photographs per se since it was a common process. Yet retouching was an issue because it inevitably challenged the candid realism associated with Victoria's photographs. In the same way as newspapers were accused of mystifying the monarchy through

[94] Wynter, 'Photographic Portraiture', 109.

Fig. 35.　J. E. Mayall, *Queen Victoria at a Spinning Wheel* (1863)

deferential journalism, the retouched royal pictures meant that photography became part of the distrust felt towards the media making of Victoria's figure.

Why were the photographs of Victoria retouched? The answer to this question is twofold because there are two different phases when retouching had a significant impact upon Victoria's photographs. The first is from the mid-1850s to the early 1860s; the second is from the 1870s onwards to the end of her reign. Separating the two phases are significant differences in the practical process of retouching, and its broader impact upon perceptions of the royal image. The colouring and retouching of photographs were prominent concerns as early as the 1857 Art Treasures exhibition in Manchester. Of the 240 portraits exhibited, a large number had been reworked. A review in the *Liverpool and Manchester Photographic Journal* drew attention to both the number of touched photographs and the extent of their alteration. It noted that, in some cases, 'no trace of the original picture is visible, its only use apparently being to secure identity and truth, the visible picture being laid over the other in oil and water-colour'.[95] At this stage, any manipulation would usually have been carried out on the albumen print rather than on the glass-plate negative.

Coloured photographs were intended to alleviate the unflattering and mechanical harshness of the monochrome picture. The practice made the resultant pictures more akin in appearance and status to miniature portraits. As such, colouring is another example of photography's initial subservience to fine art aesthetics. The *London Review* claimed that coloured photographs approached more closely to oil paintings because they were the result of study and generalization, which were qualities lacking in an ordinary photograph.[96] On a more pragmatic level, miniature painters put out of business by photography soon found themselves employed by photographic studios. In 1857, Elizabeth Eastlake claimed that there was no photographic establishment that did not employ artists for finishing pictures, at salaries of up to £1 a day.

In order to counter the hybridity of coloured pictures, there were numerous claims that the realism of photography was its unique element. Manipulation of photographs was felt to undermine the most valuable quality of the medium. Efforts were consequently made by the London Photographic Society to prevent any retouched photographs being shown at their annual exhibition. The rules of entrance for the 1857 exhibition at South Kensington, for example, included precise instructions regarding retouched photographs. They would be admitted only if accompanied by untouched copies of the same picture. Positive pictures from touched or painted negatives also had to be described accordingly. These instructions continued to be repeated but judging by the complaints of some reviewers they were far from being universally followed. In 1864, the London Photographic Society barred from their annual exhibition any coloured or touched pictures. Although the exhibition was much reduced, the rules did enforce a pure photographic aesthetic where there was a clear demarcation between authentic and fabricated pictures.

The first exhibited royal photographs were by no means excluded from the complaints against any form of alteration. In its review of Prince Albert's portrait at the South Kensington exhibition, the *Liverpool and Manchester Photographic Journal* noted that its estimation of the picture had been lowered because there was 'a stopping out of the background by artificial means'.[97] It did, however, state its belief that the figure itself had not been altered and that,

[95] 'Exhibition of Art Treasures at Manchester', 126.
[96] 'The New Picture Galleries', *Photographic Journal*, 15 Feb. 1862, 380. The article was reprinted from the *London Review*.
[97] 'Exhibition of Photographs at South Kensington Museum', 61.

given the present preponderance of retouching, the interference was 'perhaps as little as could be done where any at all had been resorted to'.[98] Similarly, in its review of the picture of the royal family that was exhibited by Caldesi in 1858, the *Liverpool and Manchester Photographic Journal* also noted that there was some evidence of it having been touched.[99] Thus, the very first publicly exhibited photographs of Victoria and Albert were subject to a degree of manipulation. There never was any utopian kernel of royal realism that was rendered up for mass consumption.

When *cartes* became the latest fashion in the early 1860s, photographs of Victoria and Albert were routinely available in coloured versions. Unlike in subsequent decades, though, there seem to have been no complaints that the royal photographs were perceived to be in any sense artificial. The full-length format usually adopted by the *carte* meant that sitters were distant enough from the camera not to require any flattering manipulation. The only example of reworking that is documented is when Mayall's pictures of the Prince of Wales's wedding were published as engravings. In April 1863, *The Times* noted that royal hands had been at work on the pictures. The Princess Royal and Princess Alice had retouched Mayall's photographs, 'lightening the local colour, and taking off that affect of age which the deepened-tones of the sun-picture, in hair and complexion, give to the likeness of both Prince and Princess'.[100] The Princesses' attention provides a rare and intriguing glimpse of the royal family's personal involvement in their published appearance.

During the 1870s and 1880s, retouching significantly increased in prevalence. This second phase of retouching differed from the early years of photography in that the dominant means of manipulation was through working upon the negative rather than painting upon the positive print. Photographic manipulation became particularly common after the introduction of the dry-plate negative in the early 1870s. This is because these were easier to rework than the existing wet-plate negatives. Another factor is that the introduction of a larger format of cabinet photograph presented a greater threat to a sitter's vanity. The cabinet portrait was introduced partly as an attempt to overcome the technical limitations of the smaller *carte* format. It had a greater depth of field than the *carte* and any blemishes or wrinkles were more likely to be evident. The value of producing flattering pictures certainly encouraged the widespread use of retouching. As one article in *Photographic News* noted, photographers knew that 'those portraitists who retouch most effectively secure the largest share of public patronage'.[101] Another equally important reason for the practice was the removal of technical imperfections and the

---

[98] Ibid.   [99] 'The London Photographic Society's Fifth Annual Exhibition', 152.
[100] 'Portraits of the Prince and Princess of Wales', *The Times*, 9 Apr. 1863, 7.
[101] 'Retouching and Photographic Truth', *PN* 16 (19 Jan. 1872), 25.

desire for greater realism. The amount of light used by photographic studios, for example, considerably deepened any wrinkles and accentuated the signs of age. Retouching was actually argued to be a means of making a photograph into a better likeness and a more realistic image.

How was retouching carried out? The specialist photographic journals often contained advice on how to manipulate negatives, and there were numerous instruction manuals published. These suggest that, at its best, retouching was a complex practice that required a high degree of artistic skill and an intimate knowledge of facial physiognomy. All too easily, however, zealous manipulation gave sitters' faces a wax doll or billiard ball appearance. Many articles were not against the practise *per se*. Yet they were concerned that too much unskilled work would destroy popular faith in photographic realism. As one manual put it, 'The clever pupil of the celebrated Professor Scratchpaw took in other pupils until the scratchpaw aborigines flooded the market with *re* or *misre*-presentations of somebody or other.'[102]

Retouching was carried out using a variety of soft lead pencils upon a glass negative coated with a solution that allowed the pencil to bite. Elaborate professional equipment, including desks with inbuilt lights and reflectors, aided the task. Figure 36, an Ensign Retouching Desk, is typical in that it has a mount for holding the negative and a mirrored bottom that would aid the sight of the retoucher. Most manuals recommended the use of lines to accomplish any desired alterations, much in the way a steel or wood engraver would work. Work varied from the carefully precise to the brutally extensive. As *The Art of Retouching* noted:

Do not on any account forget to touch ladies' waists in a specially hearty matter, if you want to keep on good terms with them. You are always safe in cutting off an inch on each side, and in some cases, where corpulence is rather conspicuous, two or more inches will never be missed. Creases or folds in the wrong place in ladies' dresses must never be allowed to remain, or else the portrait will surely fail to give entire satisfaction.[103]

Instruction manuals nevertheless contained far more information than simply the removal of waistlines and double chins. They included details of how to soften the lines around the temples; how to remodel the furrows around and under the eyes where the studio light would cause dark shadows; and how to thicken and darken hair through careful manipulation. Necks, cheeks, jowls, all were subject to the retoucher's pencil. Carried out with skill and subtlety, retouching could add *gravitas* as well as beauty to a sitter's appearance.

Complaints against the manipulation of Victoria's photographs can be

---

[102] J. Hubert, *The Art of Retouching* (London: Hazell, Watson and Viney, 1891), 7–8.
[103] Ibid. 49.

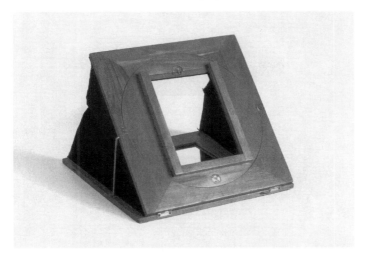

Fig. 36. Ensign Retouching Desk, *c.*1890

found intermittently in the 1880s and 1890s. As well as the increasing prevalence of retouching, Victoria's advancing years probably quickened the impulse to rework her pictures. The Crown might never die but Victoria's photographs were concerned with showing a monarch whom age did not touch. It was not simply that Victoria seemed an unchanging figure in a disorientating world: judging by her photographs she *was* unchanging. In May 1887, a theatrical periodical, the *Bat*, complained that the public 'who have to depend on the pictures in the *Illustrated News* and the *Graphic*, or the unnatural productions of the photographer, are justified in asking what the Queen is really like'.[104] Likewise, in August 1887, *Photographic News* noted that a new set of pictures by Hughes and Mullins conformed to the accustomed fabrication of Victoria's photographs: 'Like all published photographs of the Queen, these are ungenuine in the sense that they have been manipulated by a retoucher; indeed, it is hard that the public cannot purchase a real photograph of the Queen; but they have to be content with unreal mixtures of photography and monochrome intricacy.'[105] These comments betray a complete lack of surprise at the retouching. They presume that, because the photographs had been made public, they had necessarily been retouched. *Photographic News* even complimented Hughes and Mullins because, in contrast to other photographers, they had not attempted to exaggerate Victoria's height by duplicitous means. Responses to the royal retouching were invariably critical. In its next issue, *Photographic News* criticized a picture of Victoria in her jubilee dress

---

[104] 'Nothing in the Papers', *Bat*, 17 May 1887, 419.   [105] 'Notes', *PN* 12 Aug. 1887, 504.

Fig. 37. Alexander Bassano, *Queen Victoria* (1882)

for being reworked to such an extent that 'it makes it appear as if the Queen was suffering from a peculiar and hitherto undescribed form of oedamatous disease'.[106] Oedamatous was a condition caused by the excessive build up of fluid in body tissue and *Photographic News* is attempting to describe the wax-like skin texture caused by excessive retouching.

A set of original negatives from the Bassano studio demonstrates the extent to which Victoria's pictures, and those of other members of the royal family, were retouched. The Bassano studio took numerous series of royal photographs. Alexander Bassano initially trained in the studio of painter Augustus Egg and made his reputation in the 1870s. During the 1880s and 1890s, the Bassano studio was one of the foremost photographic studios for

[106] 'Notes', *PN* 9 Sept. 1887, 569.

Fig. 38. Alexander Bassano, *Queen Victoria* (1882)

high society sitters. Lord and Ladies, Generals and Princesses, and even the Zulu King Cetewayo; they all flocked to Bassano's exclusive Old Bond Street studio. Each sitting cost two guineas. For this sum, the sitter not only received the personal attention of Bassano. They also benefited from the three full-time retouchers that the studio employed to finish the photographs.

Two photographs taken by the Bassano studio in 1882 (see Figs. 37 and 38), are part of a large series of twenty-seven cabinet portraits registered at Stationer's Hall on 16, 17, and 18 May, and exemplify the extent to which Victoria's photographs were retouched. Unfortunately, there is no way of providing before and after versions of the retouched pictures, one needs to depend on the marks of the retoucher's pencil that are evident on the negative.

The most obvious manipulation of Fig. 37 is that Victoria's waistline has been slimmed down by several inches where the sash meets her right arm. Curves have been created where none previously existed. Under Victoria's chin, the heavy marks of the retoucher's pencil are also conspicuous. Not only has her double chin been erased, the retoucher has altered the line where Victoria's chin meets her neck. He thus gives her more of a statuesque appearance. A moderate proportion of Victoria's face has disappeared under the gentle touch of the retoucher's pencil. Her forehead and an area of cheek have been thoroughly smoothed. The rest of her cheek also has a suspiciously stippled effect that suggests some delicate and skilful work. The effect is to remove any wrinkles, as none are evident in the final photograph. Another way in which years have been removed from Victoria's appearance is by a heavy retouching of her hair. A series of lines on the negative darken and thicken her hair at the temples. The final picture shows a Queen who looks more youthful than her sixty-two years.

The alteration of Victoria's picture is typical of the work carried out by the Bassano studio. In those photographs where Victoria is posed with one of her daughters, the faces of both figures have been retouched. More work though is usually evident on the Queen's features and figure. Figure 38, a portrait of Victoria standing by a chair, shows that similar areas of the face and neck have been reworked. The thinning of her chin can even be seen on the final photograph. Figure 38 is also notable for the way that the edges around her figure have been softened. This is exemplified by the long vertical burr around the edge of the white bottom half of her dress. Victoria's height has also been exaggerated; she can be seen standing on a raised platform that is substantially hidden by the swathes of her dress. Other royal photographs use similar devices to create a more imposing and reassuring figure. Victoria's official Diamond Jubilee portrait, for example, positions her on a step above the line of the camera. The viewer is made to look up towards the Great White Empress.

It is hard to gauge the depth of scepticism towards Victoria's later photographs; complaints are only occasional and limited to the specialist photographic journals. None the less, they are an index to the continued ideological stress laid upon the authenticity of Victoria's figure. It is also typical that the labour invested in Victoria's photographs stemmed from the photographic studios rather than from the royal family. The retouched pictures are not evidence of orchestrated manipulation. Rather, the practice exemplifies the way technical developments in individual media impacted upon public perceptions of the monarchy.

After the initial mania for *cartes* had subsided, many new royal photographs continued to be released. Victoria, along with the Prince and Princess of

Wales in particular, continued to be photographed by many of the most notable photographers of the day. What is significant about Victoria's later pictures is that, from the 1870s onwards, they reflect the establishment of photography as the dominant visual media. Compared to the *carte*, which was often defined against the formality of portraiture, Victoria's later photographs absorbed some of the traditional functions of court portraiture. Portraying her as part regal and imperious, part devoted grandmother and mourning widow, Victoria's late photographs seem increasingly like official portraits. At the same time, they continue to capture her domestic role. In keeping with this continuity, it is notable that photographers were granted official warrants in the same way that Wilkie, Lane, Collen, and Hayter all held various court appointments. To take just two examples of the several firms that held official titles, W. & D. Downey were appointed Photographers in Ordinary to Her Majesty in March 1879, and Alexander Bassano was appointed Photographer to Her Majesty in June 1890.[107]

The two pictures taken by Bassano in 1882 are typical of how Victoria's photographs came to depict her more in her role as Queen and Empress. Befitting her imperial reinvention as the Great White Empress, Victoria dominates the pictures with an all-encompassing regal hauteur. Pictures such as Fig. 39, taken by Chancellor of Dublin in 1899, also illustrate the hybridity of Victoria's later photographs. The picture combines the intimacy of family photography with the iconography of state portraiture. Depicting Victoria with the Prince of Wales, the Duke of York (later George V), and the young Prince Edward of York (later Edward VIII), the picture is an expression of domestic affection. Equally, though, the photograph stresses primogeniture and the continuity of the royal lineage; it promotes the monarchy as a source of stability amidst the disorientation of modernity.

If the royal photographs did not quite provide the Patron Portrait that *Bentley's Miscellany* had called for many years earlier, they at least helped to provide Victoria with a stable and immutable public presence. Her photographs retained a high degree of homogeneity. They picture her endlessly with her sons and daughters, and with a succession of grandchildren and great-grandchildren. With Victoria's seclusion, photography substituted for much of the cultural work previously carried out by her public appearances. In 1880, the *Photographic News* noted that the photographic profession continued to owe much to Victoria:

Indeed, while Her Majesty continues to lend her countenance to the camera, it does not matter very much whether she appears in public or not. Any loyal subject can gaze

---

[107] *Crown and Camera* provides a list of these appointments. Dimond and Taylor, *Crown and Camera*, 213.

Fig. 39. Chancellor, *Four Generations* (1899)

upon the counterfeit presentment of the highest lady in the land for the small sum of one shilling; whereas for half-a-guinea, on one of the rare occasions on which she assists at public proceedings, he may only be gratified by the sight of her back hair.[108]

By the time of the Diamond Jubilee, the central role of photography in the making of a media monarchy was officially recognized. An official photographic portrait was sanctioned for the first time (see Fig. 40).[109] Tellingly, its issue was in response to a large number of requests from printsellers for an authorized image.[110] Its release was therefore part of the continual pressure on the royal family to make themselves available for media consumption. Conversely, the official blessing given to Downey's picture actually sets it apart from other portrayals of Victoria then in circulation. It recreated a frisson similar to that which met the personal authorization of the very first royal

---

[108] 'Photography and Royalty', *PN* 19 Mar. 1880, 133.
[109] The photograph was taken by W. & D. Downey in 1893 at the wedding of the Duke of York.
[110] 'Trade Topics', *Printer's Register*, 8 May 1897, 2.

Fig. 40. W. & D. Downey, *Official Diamond Jubilee Photograph* (1893)

photographs. Photography had long lost the aura of novelty. Yet it had become ever more able to create a degree of public charisma around an individual. The official sanctioning of the Diamond Jubilee photograph helped to imbue it with an aura that the medium itself could no longer provide.

The second important aspect of the Diamond Jubilee photograph is that it was deliberately not registered for copyright, a decision that allowed it to be reproduced at will.[111] Wholly protean, the image appeared on biscuit tins, commemorative plates, and souvenir artefacts of every description. It was engraved for most of the illustrated periodicals and exported throughout the British Empire. The Diamond Jubilee photograph is thus one small culmination of a media monarchy. Much of the populist discourse around Victoria's photographs stemmed from the reproductive ability of the camera to make the monarchy accessible. The decision not to control this official photograph through the law of copyright is thus part of a genealogy that includes the

[111] 'From the Editor's Chair', *PN* 14 May 1897, 307.

pirated royal photographs of the early 1860s and the tension raised by the uncontrolled plethora of prints in the late 1830s. In the Diamond Jubilee photograph an excess of reproduction was officially sanctioned. The overarching figure of Victoria was constituted by the very lack of control over the photograph. There was little reason to pay to reproduce an alternative picture when an official portrait could be published without charge. For the first time the means of mass reproduction were harnessed to ensure one authoritative and iconic picture of Victoria. In a defining moment, the court portrait and the media image had become one.

Victoria was the first British sovereign to be subject to the lens of the camera. Its presence indubitably shaped the style of monarchy she embodied. Victoria's enthusiasm for photography created precedents that subsequently allowed the camera to continue its work in making the monarchy available. Other members of the royal family, notably the Prince and Princess of Wales, followed the lead set by Victoria and Albert. When Edward visited the Near East in 1862, Francis Bedford accompanied the royal party as the resident photographer. Princess Alexandra was also a keen photographer and took lessons at the London Stereoscopic School of Photography. In the autumn of 1897, she participated in an exhibition organized by the Eastman Company at the New Gallery in Regent Street. A selection of Alexandra's photographs appeared in the *Graphic* in August 1905. They were subsequently published in 1908 as *Queen Alexandra's Christmas Book*, with all of the proceeds going to charity. The album consisted of over 120 photographs. Many of them were Kodak pictures individually pasted into the pages. They portrayed family scenes from Balmoral, Sandringham, and from cruises abroad the *Victoria and Albert*. Like the first royal *cartes*, the size and intimacy of the pictures emphasized that these were Alexandra's own personal photographs.

The equalizing aspect of Victoria's photographs is another important strand in the political rhetoric applied to her media making. The same critical and celebratory paradigms expressed in relation to prints, newspapers, and illustrated periodicals also governed the responses to the royal *cartes*. Concerns over unravelling the mystique of monarchy continued to be expressed alongside the promotion of a homely royal family. Similarly, the modernity of the camera, like that of 'news', was claimed to reform the nature of the monarchy. Victoria was explicitly dissociated from her predecessors through her tours and her promotion as a moral exemplar. Her *cartes* were likewise promoted as the agents of a similarly progressive and popular reinvention. The relationship between Crown and camera was assimilated into an ongoing narrative— ultimately ideological in its concerns—which emphasized Victoria's break from an autocratic past.

5

REPORTING ROYALTY

Dinner, tea, lunch, supper! Royal weddings forbid the fourth estate from
ever dreaming of such luxuries. They have to live on telegraphic mes-
sages. They may eat their notebooks and drink ink if they like, but they
must not hope for most substantial nourishment.

(George Augustus Sala, *Illustrated London News*, 14 March 1863)[1]

The expanding scale of the newspaper and periodical press inevitably
brought to the fore the relationship between journalists and the royal family.
As the epigraph from George Augustus Sala suggests, royal occasions were
notorious for the labour reporters had to expend. Upon Victoria's first highland tour in 1842, the *Illustrated London News* puffed itself for sending two
artists to shadow the royal party.[2] Such limpet-like attention was highly novel
in the 1840s. The development of new and existing media meant that it was,
however, commonplace by the end of Victoria's reign. At the Diamond Jubilee
procession through London, numerous cinematic cameras vied with scores of
professional photographers.[3] The Lord Chamberlain likewise received applications for press passes from newspapers as diverse as the *Ceylon Times* and
the Australian *Coolgardie Pioneer*. The gathering and distribution of royal
news often resulted in trenchant encounters between reporters and the royal
household. The practices of royal reportage reveal the monarchy's increasingly formal relationship with the different media.

The growth of professional journalism went hand in hand with the evolution
of a double-edged dynamic between the monarchy and the press. There was a
reciprocal yet unequal dependency between these two institutions. Reporters
and the royal family were locked within a pattern of mutual benefit and
antagonism. This double-edged relationship is evident both in the public

---

[1] George Augustus Sala, 'Echoes of the Week', *ILN* 14 Mar. 1863, 270.
[2] 'September 10, 1842', *ILN* 10 Sept. 1842, 278.
[3] See John Barnes, *The Beginnings of the Cinema in England* (London: Bishopgate Press, 1983), ii.
170–99. PRO LC 2/140 2–55 contains all the applications for Diamond Jubilee press passes.

perception of royal reportage and in the interaction between newspapers and court functionaries. On the one hand, a mutually beneficial relationship grew up between the monarchy and the press. As the daily and weekly newspaper became a habitual source of information and pleasure, the combined forces of supply and demand meant that there was an increasing desire for royal news stories. Readers of metropolitan and provincial newspapers would obviously expect an account of major events such as a royal wedding or Victoria and Albert's opening of the Great Exhibition. The pressures of reader demand were none the less more than compensated for by the commercial benefits that the press derived from its royal reportage. Royal events, and sometimes scandals, were important means of selling newspapers. At the wedding of the Prince of Wales, for example, *The Times* sold 108,000 copies compared to an average circulation of between 60,000 and 65,000 copies. Newspapers had an incentive to supply a fulsome coverage of Victoria's activities. In so doing, they simultaneously helped to promote a philanthropic and industrious royal family.

Unsurprisingly, despite the benefits that the British royal family derived from its press coverage, the consequent interaction with journalists was a source of personal tension. The newspaper and periodical press's desire for royal news meant that they placed an increasing amount of pressure on the royal family. Numerous fractious encounters took place between journalists and court functionaries. At the same time as the monarchy and the media fed off the other, there was an inbuilt strife within their relationship. Yet the mutual gains of the royal family and the press cannot be separated from their conflicts. The contrary nature of the dynamic was inescapable. Even the monarchy was forced to acknowledge that, whether it desired it or not, the press played a necessary role in maintaining its public position. Such awareness underpinned notable changes in the treatment of reporters. The growing respectability of journalism is particularly evident in the actions of the Lord Chamberlain, the court functionary who dealt with the press. From the 1840s, the Lord Chamberlain instigated formal procedures for managing the requests of reporters. Newspapers received more official access at the same time as the advent of a cheap telegraph system improved the whole national structure of news distribution. With the slow coming into being of journalism as a profession, the years between Victoria's coronation and the marriage of the Prince of Wales saw the development of a series of institutional processes intended to incorporate journalists into royal occasions.

Newspapers' attempts to gain journalistic access were not just confined to negotiation behind the scenes, however. In the same way as Victoria's authorization of her photographs gave their realism an added charge, any official access given to journalists was loudly trumpeted and used to vouchsafe the

GROSS OUTRAGE;

OR, PAUL PRY IN THE HIGHLANDS, MAKING A SKETCH OF THE ROYAL CHEST OF
DRAWERS THROUGH THE KEYHOLE.

Fig. 41. 'Gross Outrage', *Punch*, 15 (1848), 131

realism of their sketches or reports. The promotion of an intimate news
realism nevertheless has to be set against the offensive practices commonly
associated with royal reporting. Numerous satires, published by *Punch*,
Figaro in London, and *Penny Satirist*, derided its intrusiveness as much as
its bathetic language. These critiques make up part of the double-edged
dynamic between the monarchy and the press in that they derive from two
contrary standpoints. On the one hand there was a general repulsion towards the irreverent and zealous intrusions of reporters. Public distaste was
a product both of the increasing demand for royal news and the sanctity
attached to Victoria's domestic life. Nowhere is this attitude more succinctly
conveyed than in a full-page cartoon from *Punch*. Set amidst one of Victoria's
regular highland retreats from the formality of Windsor, the engraving shows
a Paul Pry peeping through Victoria's bedroom keyhole in order to sketch the
royal chest of drawers (see Fig. 41). The opprobrium heaped upon the special
artist sums up the stigma of much royal reportage.

The outraged articles on journalistic intrusion nevertheless exist alongside a contradictory series of critiques. For radical newspapers, reporters were distasteful because of their excessive deference rather than their lack of it. Press intrusion was motivated by a desire to fetishize the monarchy rather than to expose it. Reporters were therefore an obvious target for anti-monarchist writing. The satires on Jenkins that were discussed in Chapter 2 obviously belong in this category. Closely connected to these critiques was a series of attacks on the provision of news by the royal household, especially upon the court newsman himself. The post of the court newsman was the most notable response by the royal household to the pressure exerted by the press, and his work suggests the volume of royal news was more than simply a product of the demands of readers or the loyalism of newspapers. *Punch's* satires upon the court newsman do not just mock the bombastic language of the *Court Circular*. They are attacks upon the news values engendered through the flow of information that he provided. The contrary attacks upon royal reporting express both the commercial pressures at work and their perceived political impact. Journalists were attacked for both their professional disrespect and their political deference.

When Victoria came to the throne, 'the Press' was often conceived of as a fourth estate, a principal means of spreading knowledge, progress, and reform. Such heavy symbolism was disproportionate to its size. Most newspapers had very limited resources. It is only in the light of this situation that we can fully understand the novelty of the subsequent attention Victoria received. Limited printing and communications technology; a widespread lack of leisure time; the 'taxes on knowledge' levied on each newspaper; these were all heavy burdens that kept expenses high and held back circulation. Even after the reduction in Stamp Duty in 1836, *The Times* still sold for 6*d*. and individual copies of the paper passed through many different hands. The high circulation of unstamped newspapers during the early 1830s, often sold for a penny, testifies to the potential reading audience that would soon be supplied by cheap journals and fiction. In 1829, there were thirteen daily stamped newspapers in London, seven published in the morning and six in the evening. The *Westminster Review* estimated that the total circulation of daily newspapers was 28,000 in the morning and 11,000 in the evening. Of these, *The Times* had by far the largest circulation at 10,000, with its nearest rival, the *Morning Herald*, having a circulation of around 8,000.[4] Of the six evening newspapers, which often simply regurgitated information from the morning editions, their collective circulation was claimed not to exceed much more than the circulation of *The Times*. Outside London, provincial newspa-

---

[4] Gibbons Merle, 'Newspaper Press', *Westminster Review*, 10 (1829), 217.

pers were growing in number as towns increased in size. None the less, they remained relatively small concerns. Larger provincial newspapers like the *Manchester Guardian* and the *Leeds Mercury* were only published twice a week. Most of their political news was taken from the London press. Some of the smaller provincial publications remained no more than news-sheets made up by the local printer or bookseller.

There were only a small number of full-time opportunities for reporters because of the scale of the newspaper press. Morning newspapers consisted of an editor, a sub-editor, and between ten and fourteen reporters. Evening newspapers like the *Standard* employed between three and four reporters in the 1830s. Many of those employed were using their newspaper work simply as a stop-gap activity on the way to more permanent careers. Law students attempting to qualify for the Bar were particularly well known in this respect. Prior to his famous reporting of the Crimean war, William Howard Russell was one correspondent who was initially called to the Bar in 1850. Reporting was hardly a profession in its own right and newspaper work was consequently held in very low regard. As a neologism for newspaper reporting, 'journalism' was itself only coined in the early 1830s. In comparison with the distinguished gentleman of letters, the association of journalism with paid labour also gave the work a distinctly unsavoury taint. The stereotypical image of those struggling in the lower reaches of periodical and newspaper production was of a debt-ridden hack bowed down by dissipated pursuits. Debtors' prison was more of an occupational expectation than a hazard. In the *London Review* of 1835, Henry Brougham and John Roebuck claimed that the men of the press were far from fit to be seen in respectable society:

the Newspaper Press is thus degraded from rank of a liberal profession: the employment of the class engaged in it sink: and the conduct of our journals falls too much into the hands of men of obscure birth, imperfect education, blunt feelings and coarse manners, who are accustomed to a low position in society, and are content to be excluded from a circle in which they have never been used to move.[5]

Journalism was certainly anything but a homogeneous occupation and there were acute distinctions between leader writers, parliamentary reporters, and those connected with the radical press. Similarly, most provincial correspondents operated in an entirely different milieu from their metropolitan counterparts. Yet even the small and influential group of privileged reporters who worked for the London press was very much looked down upon by those who worked for the quarterly reviews and the monthly magazines. In terms of

[5] Quoted in Alan Lee, *The Origins of the Popular Press in England 1855–1914* (London: Croom Helm, 1976), 105.

newsgathering, neither print nor graphic reportage was fit to be seen in good company, especially regal company.

During the first years of Victoria's reign, royal reporting was frequently disparaged. It was seen as the occupation of the penny-a-liner, unashamed inhabitants of Grub Street who possessed little social status and even less literary merit. Notorious as the principal suppliers of domestic news in the 1830s and 1840s, penny-a-liners were column-fillers who provided newspapers with their accounts of fires, street accidents, police cases, and royal visits. They hung around coroner's courts and police stations, hoping to pick up snippets of news that they could sell at the standard rate of three half pence per line. Owing to the incentive to make their accounts as lengthy as possible, their sobriquet became synonymous with mawkish triviality and needless circumlocution. Their working practices were also heavily frowned upon. Privacy and propriety were claimed to be scruples unknown to the penny-a-liner. Driven by the need to sell their copy, sensationalized and fabricated stories were commonplace. In 1845, *Chamber's Edinburgh Journal* estimated that there were around sixty penny-a-liners working in London, with a corresponding number adopting their guise in order to sell fabricated stories to editors.[6] Each of the London daily newspapers was said to pay £1,000 p.a. for their reports. When the smaller sums paid by the evening and Sunday journals were also taken into account, *Chamber's Edinburgh Journal* estimated that around £7,000 p.a. was shared by the metropolitan penny-a-liners.[7] Such expenditure adds up to 1,120,000 lines a year. Despite the derision they aroused, penny-a-liners played a very necessary role in the news provision of the period.

The marketability of royal news was an important element in determining the copy that penny-a-liners sold for their living. At the same time as penny-a-liners were responsible for a large amount of royal news, however, the stigma of their role exemplifies the low status of reporters. Writing in the *Westminster Review* in 1833, Gibbons Merle derided them as 'persons who have not had the education of decent butlers'.[8] Their royal reportage in particular was regarded as distasteful for its intrusions and excesses. *Punch*, *Figaro in London*, and the *Spectator* were among the journals that consistently equated the fawning attention that the metropolitan press gave to Victoria with its undue reliance upon penny-a-liners.

Chamber's singled out one genus of the penny-a-liner because of its recent expansion. This was the type devoted to following Victoria and Albert. On their progresses across Scotland, in addition to the few reporters specifically

---

[6] 'Penny-A-Liners', *Chamber's Edinburgh Journal*, NS 3 (1 Feb. 1845), 65.
[7] Ibid. 68.   [8] Gibbons Merle, 'Journalism', *Westminster Review*, 18 (1833), 199.

accredited to the various newspapers, the couple had to endure the incessant attention of the penny-a-liners following in their wake:

they described with painful minuteness every inch of her journey, giving facts, however small, wherever they could get them, and substituting surmises when facts were not to be obtained. No respect had they for royal privacy; and the colour of the royal gown or bonnet, or of the royal spouse's hat and hat-band, and shooting-jacket, were carefully noted from day to day—always with a view to the three half-pences that were thus to be acquired. Every place that her majesty passed, or obtained even a glimpse of in passing, became of consequence immediately in their eyes.[9]

Thanks to the efforts of the penny-a-liners, there was an excess of easily attainable royal news flowing towards the editor's office. Such zealous attentiveness explains why they were associated with the worst excesses of royal reporting, and, in so doing, why they also helped to create the ubiquitous presence of Victoria.

Chamber's Edinburgh Journal's attack on the penny-a-liners' intrusiveness testifies to the journalistic deference that was expected. The penny-a-liners were reviled for simply recording the colour of Victoria's dress. Prior to this, caricaturists like Gillray had often focused on the most personal activities of members of the British royal family, particularly when it came to exposing their sexual affairs and extravagant habits. Yet the actual physical proximity of the penny-a-liners created a different order of intimacy. Their close attention caused an uncomfortable sense of scrutiny and surveillance. Moreover, it is important to emphasize that the type of personal attention that Victoria received was a significant departure from the standard style of dryly factual news description. The popular and illustrated press's royal reporting, with its prevalence of human-interest details, prefigures the New Journalism of the 1870s and 1880s. In a famous article from 1887, T. P. O'Connor compared the old and New Journalism. O'Connor declared: 'There was a day when any allusion to the personal appearance, the habits, the clothes, or the home and social life of any person, would have been resented as an impertinence and almost an indecency.'[10] Such strictures never really applied to Victoria and Albert. The type of close attention they received was always more redolent of the New Journalism. Such royal coverage has to be seen as significant as the quantity of column inches in creating a popular intimacy with the reading public.

The nature of graphic reportage at the beginning of Victoria's reign replicates the uncertain status and the inventions of the penny-a-liners. As previously mentioned, the *Observer* and *Bell's Life in London* were the most prominent of the few newspapers who provided occasional news illustrations

---

[9] 'Penny-A-Liners', 66.   [10] T. P. O'Connor, 'The New Journalism', *New Review*, 1 (1887), 424.

during the 1820s and 1830s. The engraver responsible for the illustrations of Victoria's coronation printed in the *Observer's* and *Bell's Life in London* was the 18-year-old wood-engraver Henry Vizetelly (1820–94). In a career spanning the next fifty years, Vizetelly would later become a well-known special correspondent and the editor of several periodicals, including the *Pictorial Times* and the *Illustrated Times*. His memoirs provide an invaluable guide to the changing treatment of reporters because his attendance at royal occasions began with Victoria's coronation and lasted until 1865, when he moved to Paris as the continental representative for the *Illustrated London News*.[11] Vizetelly's career started in 1835 when, after attending the occasional Royal Academy lecture on drawing, he chose to become an engraver. He was subsequently apprenticed to G. W. Bonner, a friend of the family and one of the few engravers then operating in London. Upon Bonner's early death in 1836, Vizetelly became a pupil of Orrin Smith at Judd Street, near Russell Square. At Smith's establishment, he mingled freely with a range of artists, engravers, and writers, including John Leech, Kenny Meadows, Douglas Jerrold, and Laman Blanchard.

Despite the effort that went into the *Observer's* coronation edition, its illustrations demonstrate the extent to which the lowly status of engravers, coupled with the technological constraints, limited the scope of graphic reportage. The *Observer's* coronation engravings stemmed from a number of sketches that Vizetelly made prior to the event. Such pre-preparation was absolutely necessary. It was technically impossible for Vizetelly to have commenced his engravings after the ceremony, which took place on a Thursday, and have them ready for publication in the weekend editions of the *Observer* and *Bell's Life in London*. Vizetelly's engravings are typical of both the illustrations published in the press and those sold individually by printsellers on the day of the coronation. The extensive discrepancies between the various prints in their supposed portrayal of the same scene inside Westminster Abbey reveal their pre-preparation. Illustrations of Victoria's coronation did not rely on the unimpeachable fidelity of their graphic reportage. Rather, their appeal stemmed from the novelty of their communicative or commemorative acts. In the 1830s, the employment of wood-engraving still owed much to the non-naturalistic tradition of the popular print: realism and graphic news were neither synonymous nor predominant.

An older apprentice, who graduated from Bonner's workshop the year before Vizetelly entered it, was W. J. Linton. Linton is better known as a radical poet and a notable British republican but he was also a renowned

---

[11] Henry Vizetelly, *Glances Back Through Seventy Years*, 2 vols. (London: Keegan Paul, Treck & Co., 1893).

wood-engraver.[12] In the autumn of 1842 Linton went into partnership with Orrin Smith. One year later, their workshop became the principal engravers for the *Illustrated London News*.[13] Like Vizetelly, Linton was also heavily involved in numerous journalistic activities. For example, he took over the editorship of Douglas Jerrold's ailing *Illuminated Magazine* in 1844. Linton and Vizetelly are significant because of the different ways that their lives are caught up in the commercial development of the newspaper and periodical press. They started their careers at the beginning of the rapid development of graphic reportage. At the same time, though, they still belonged to a sphere of highly skilled artisans. Linton's republicanism is the prime example of their formative political influences, but Vizetelly's memoirs also describe the most democratic opinions being expressed in Bonner's workroom. The apprentices eagerly read radical thinkers outside their working hours. Paine's *Rights of Man* and Shelley's *Queen Mab* were amongst their favoured literary fare.[14] There is consequently a marked contrast between the personal politics of those individuals involved in the burgeoning production of illustrated news and the various periodicals' wholly supportive approach towards Victoria. The forces at work upon the careers of Linton and Vizetelly embody wider ideological tensions that can also be found in the royal reportage of *Reynolds's Newspaper*.

The woodcuts accompanying Catnach's cheap ballads are similar to the coronation illustrations provided by a variety of more reputable newspapers and printsellers. The resemblance emphasizes why the use of engraving for graphic reportage was accorded a low aesthetic status. The fabrication of the numerous coronation engravings aligns them with the more dubious practices of the penny-a-liners and the sensational claims of the street-patterers. Moreover, the formal affinity between the various individual prints, panoramas, and news illustrations stems from the reliance of newspapers and publishers on a small number of London artists and engravers, and the range of work they thereby undertook. Kenny Meadows, when in financial straits, did work ranging from fine steel-engravings of 'Byron's Beauties' to sensational woodcuts for cheap fiction.[15] In 1837, he was producing one of the many flattering portraits of Victoria. This contrasts with his work for *Punch* in the early 1840s, which included engravings satirizing the attention given to the monarchy. The variety of work done by engravers and journalists means that

---

[12] See F. B. Smith, *Radical Artisan: William James Linton 1812–97* (Manchester: Manchester University Press, 1972); Anne Janowitz, *Lyric and Labour in the Romantic Tradition* (Cambridge: Cambridge University Press, 1998), 195–216.
[13] Smith died in late 1843, leaving Linton as sole proprietor.
[14] Vizetelly, *Glances Back*, i. 121.
[15] Ibid. 152.

Victoria's figure was not simply contested by publications with opposing standpoints. Contrary portrayals of Victoria were produced according to particular publishing dictates. They were equally capable of deriving from the same individual.

Vizetelly's own work at the coronation had a typically broad artistic and geographical range. With the sketches that he had left over from his work for the *Observer*, he produced a panorama around 12 ft in length, for which the publisher, Robert Tyas, paid him at a rate per foot.[16] Vizetelly's commissions also stretched as far as south-west England, well beyond his work for Tyas and the *Observer*. Before the coronation, the *Western Times* announced that it had engaged one of the finest London engraving firms, Messrs Vizetelly & Co. of Fleet Street, to supply the engravings for its illustrated coronation edition.[17] The scope of Vizetelly's work reveals the proliferation of a popular visual reportage. Paradoxically, though, it also illustrates its reliance on a relatively small number of London artists, publishers, and engravers.

The second principal factor causing Vizetelly to produce his engravings before the coronation was that, as a young wood-engraver, he possessed neither the professional status nor the social connections necessary to procure a ticket for Westminster Abbey. A typical lack of official regard underpins the coronation engravings of Vizetelly and his fellow illustrators. Vizetelly gained authorization to sketch inside Westminster Abbey and at the royal stables before the coronation. However, his position obviously precluded him from having the personal sittings with the Queen that Royal Academy artists would regard as customary. The *Observer* wrote to the Duke of Wellington requesting permission for Vizetelly to use the roof of Apsley House. Wellington's reply was typically acerbic: 'The Duke has no knowledge of the writer, neither is he interested in any way in the *Observer* newspaper. Apsley House is not a public building but the Duke private's residence.'[18] In contrast to Wellington's brusqueness, Leslie and Hayter were granted access to Westminster Abbey for the purposes of painting the coronation ceremony. Leslie was sent one ticket for the Earl Marshall's box through the patronage of Lady Holland, and a second by virtue of being a Royal Academician.[19] In the early years of the *Illustrated London News* and *Pictorial Times*, attempts to cover major public events were subject to many difficulties. Artists from the periodicals went to the relevant locations in order to prepare their sketches, but, according to Vizetelly, official permission was rarely given. This was because the illustrated newspaper, 'not then the social power it has since become—met with but scant favour in official quarters'.[20]

[16]   Vizetelly, *Glances Back*, 157.   [17]   'Her Majesty's Coronation', *Western Times*, 23 June 1838, 3.
[18]   Vizetelly, *Glances Back*, i. 156.
[19]   C. R. Leslie, *Autobiographical Reflections*, ed. Tom Taylor (London: John Murray, 1860), ii. 165.
[20]   Vizetelly, *Glances Back*, i. 237.

The advent of the illustrated press in the 1840s nevertheless caused a distinctive shift in the role of the special artist. There was a link between its promotion of a realist aesthetic and the coming to prominence of the issue of journalistic access. In spite of the professional and technical factors that continued to constrain engravers, the initial prospectus of the *Illustrated London News* claimed that if ever the pen was led into fallacious argument 'the pencil must be oracular with the truth'.[21] Brian Maidment has argued that the endorsement of a realist aesthetic was an important means by which the illustrated press was able to emphasize its superiority over the ideographic tradition of the popular woodcut.[22] Maidment is correct; however, his argument needs to be extended to take into account the way in which such claims were predicated upon the increased scale of resources that could now be profitably devoted to graphic reportage. The privileged epistemological weight the *Illustrated London News* attached to engravings went hand in hand with the ability to have its special artists present at major public occasions. In terms of the extensive coverage of Victoria's tours and visits this meant that there was an important circularity between the desire to gain access to a royal event in order to provide an authentic narrative, and the use of journalistic access to substantiate the realism of royal reportage.

The *Observer's* illustrations of the Queen's marriage in February 1840 demonstrate the way in which their attempts to achieve a graphic news realism meant that press representatives increasingly came into contact with the royal household. The paper was at pains to solicit its readers' understanding towards any poetic licence that might have been employed: 'Our readers will no doubt make due allowance for any imperfections which may be discovered, when they reflect that the whole of the labour of the artists and engravers has been accomplished in less than a week, and this under circumstances of difficulty, in obtaining admission to scenes to be sketched, almost insurmountable.'[23] The acknowledgement of the less than faithful nature of the illustrations is explicitly linked to the problem of journalistic access and the demands of quick publication. Conversely, despite this admission, the *Observer* was keen to proclaim that its pictures were taken upon the spot and not the fanciful creations of speculative artists.[24] Its five engravings purported to show the most intimate scenes of the ceremony, including the exchanging of the rings and the signing of the marriage register. The kudos of having gained any kind of access was used to invest the intimacy of its illustrations with a documentary news value.

[21] 'Our Address', *ILN* 14 May 1842, 1.
[22] Brian Maidment, *Reading Popular Prints 1770–1870* (Manchester: Manchester University Press, 1996), 145–6.
[23] Quoted in Mason Jackson, *The Pictorial Press: Its Origins and Progress* (London: Hurst & Blackett, 1885), 263.
[24] 'Celebration of Her Majesty Queen Victoria', *Observer*, 16 Feb. 1840, 5.

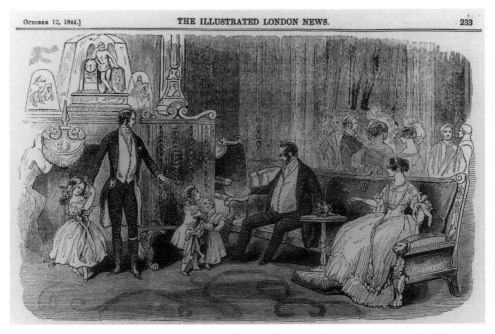

Fig. 42. 'The Crimson Drawing Room', *Illustrated London News*, 12 October 1844, 232

In the subsequent decade, the *Illustrated London News* repeatedly stressed that the value of its engravings derived from the authentic historical record that they constituted. The preface to its first volume proudly proclaimed that the year two thousand would be ten times more assured of the splendid realities of Victoria's highland visit than those who enshrined in fiction the glories of Queen Bess.[25] The *Illustrated London News* consistently equated its ability to have its artists following the royal party with what it called a 'Daguerrotypic fidelity'.[26] A sketch of the visit of Louis-Philippe reveals how its artists frequently assumed a confidential standpoint towards the royal scene they were depicting (see Fig. 42). The periodical invariably went out of its way to thank any royal official who was condescending enough to grant its artists any access.[27] When Ebenezer Landells was in the process of covering the Queen's second highland tour in September 1844, he was invited to submit some of his engravings to Victoria for her approval. The *Illustrated London News* milked

[25] 'Preface', *ILN* 6 Jan. 1843, p. iv.
[26] 'Her Majesty's Belgian Excursion', *ILN* 30 Sept. 1843, 212.
[27] For examples see *ILN* 26 Sept. 1846, 261; *ILN* 8 July 1848, 8; *ILN* 6 May 1843, 297.

the occasion for all it was worth.[28] Royal recognition was the highest possible acknowledgement for the new illustrated press. It promoted the artist's privileged position close to the royal entourage, whereby Victoria herself was the validator of the sketches' authority and realism. Such episodes should not, however, disguise the fact that it was standard practice for the *Illustrated London News* to base many of its engravings on reports that had already appeared in the London press. Similarly, in the transition from artist's sketch to published engraving, many details would probably have been changed to ensure maximum visual impact.

The efforts of the *Observer* and, later, of the *Illustrated London News* document the pressure exerted upon the royal household because of their demands for press recognition. Journalistic access was never a question of the court simply opening itself up to an already existing barbarian horde of reporters. It was a product of the slow and uneven development of journalism, and of the consequent negotiations and stand-offs that took place between newspapers and the royal household. Vizetelly did accomplish one major achievement at the coronation. He was provided with a pass from the Chief Commissioner of Police that authorized him to move through the streets that had been closed off by Westminster Abbey. The police constables on duty, however, merely laughed disbelievingly at his pass. Their reaction reveals the unprecedented nature of Vizetelly's achievement. A correspondent working for the *Standard* had a similar experience at the Queen's wedding. When the reporter presented his pass to the police he was told 'We are not to be deceived by such things as them'.[29] The Metropolitan Police Act was only passed in 1829 and the awarding of police passes therefore must have been a relatively recent invention. In his *Masters of English Journalism*, Thomas Escott claimed that, at Victoria's coronation, Vizetelly was the first ever reporter to obtain a press pass from the police for a public ceremony—a watershed moment if ever there was one.[30] The difficulties recounted by reporters suggest that royal occasions were at the forefront of their efforts to have their role authorized by various governmental bodies.

Numerous incidents from the 1840s suggest that a frosty relationship between correspondents and the royal household was a habitual part of royal reportage. Newspapers could cause offence for a variety of reasons. At Victoria's wedding, the *Morning Post* found itself without an admission pass, even though eight or nine tickets had been sent to other London newspapers. The *Morning Post* had been at the forefront of attacks upon Victoria's Whiggish sympathies, and believed that the court was taking its revenge. It

[28] 'Diet et mon Droit', *ILN* 28 Sept. 1844, 198.
[29] 'The Royal Nuptials', *Standard*, 10 Feb. 1840, 3.
[30] Thomas Escott, *Masters of English Journalism* (London: Fisher Unwin, 1911), 224.

launched a scathing attack on the Lord Chamberlain for having the power 'to prostitute his office to the gratification of a mean and indignant party spirit'.[31] Lack of professional and social status was also an ongoing problem. In 1843, when Victoria and Albert stayed with Louis-Philippe at the Chateau D'Eu, the Lord Chamberlain struck out the name of every special artist from the list of proposed invitations. According to Vizetelly, who was by now the editor of the *Pictorial Times*, the reason was that 'birth and rank, as well as mere talent, were necessary qualifications to render them a fit subject for representation to the British Queen'.[32] Vizetelly's allegation emphasizes the extent to which the royal household, initially at least, was not proactive in the attention given to Victoria's tours and visits.

Given the difficulties encountered by newspapers and periodicals, they seem to have relied heavily on personal connections to gain them access to royal occasions that they would not otherwise have received. Even here, however, there is no simple dependency upon traditional models of patronage. Rather, an embryonic professionalism sought to exploit whatever patronage was available. In 1845, Andrew Spottiswoode, the owner of the *Pictorial Times* and also the Queen's printer, used his influence to get John Gilbert into one of Victoria's official drawing-rooms. This allowed Gilbert an unrivalled opportunity to sketch the event. Such connections could nevertheless cut both ways. In early 1844 the *Pictorial Times* printed some irreverent French caricatures of Victoria and Albert's visit to Eu by the French caricaturist, Cham. They were reproduced as part of a review of the *Comic Album*, the periodical in which the satires had originally been published. They aroused considerable royal indignation and Spottiswoode reputedly found himself in serious trouble.[33]

The wariness of the royal household towards the press was far from being unjustified. Reporters' desire for an exclusive insight into Victoria's domestic life caused behaviour that did little to improve their reputation. A particularly fractious encounter took place in 1844 between Prince Albert and the ubiquitous Rumsey Forster, aka 'Jenkins' of the *Morning Post*.[34] In the process of purchasing Osborne House, Albert had to travel to the Isle of Wight. The private nature of his visit meant that only the immediate members of his household accompanied him. Forster, however, had been following the Prince's party. On his return journey across the Solent in the *Victoria and Albert*, he surreptitiously managed to join the ship's small crew. Albert noticed Forster when he was standing only a few feet away from him on deck. After being sternly lectured on the liberty he had taken in conspiring to get on

[31] 'The Dignitaries of Her Majesty's Household', *Morning Post*, 12 Feb. 1840, 5.
[32] Vizetelly, *Glances Back*, i. 261.   [33] Ibid. 257.
[34] The details of this incident are based on Vizetelly, *Glances Back*, i. 327.

board Forster was roughly banished to a small boat being towed astern. He quickly found himself completely drenched. As soon as the royal yacht reached low water on its approach to Portsmouth, two sailors were ordered to take the boat and put Forster off close to the shore. A wade of half a mile through soft mud was the reward for his labour. He was also honoured in a long satirical jibe by the periodical *Pasquin*:

> So here, the caitiff stealthily had fled,
> (Liners rush in, where Premiers fear to tread!)
> As cobwebs clustering in some favourite room,
> Fly at the touch of the active housemaid's broom,
> As weeds are rooted out from each fair spot,
> And left on dung hills lingeringly to rot;
> Just so, the wretch was hurled into the flood
> And left to wallow in congenial mud,
> Smeared o'er with filth, he struggled to the shore,
> And gained his safe obscurity once more.
> Such the adventure whence he drew his fame,
> And gained a ducking, and a mudlark's name.[35]

Mudlark was the name given to those who scavenged in the banks of the Thames for items to sell: Jenkins is thereby tarred with an occupation carried out only by the desperate and destitute. His exploits also underline a paradox in the imaginative appeal of Victoria and Albert's private lives. Much of Victoria's public persona depended upon the idealization of her domestic activities. The ideological investment in Victoria's family life nevertheless only fuelled the desire for more intimate insights into what was taking place behind the curtains of Buckingham Palace and Windsor Castle. The attention of the newspaper and periodical press compromised the boundary between public and private space, while at the same time attempting to uphold it.

Numerous articles in *Punch* attacked the intrusions of journalists during the 1840s and 1850s.[36] As a cumulative bloc, they embody the prominence of royal reportage in popular culture. Typical of *Punch's* satires is a parody upon the exertions of the journalists sent by the morning dailies to Scotland. The article describes the correspondent from *The Times* leaving his bed at 5 a.m. in order to have the first peek through the park railings at the Queen's morning promenade; the *Morning Post's* commentator sitting in a bed of stinging nettles for hours in the expectation that Victoria would come his way; the

---

[35] 'Horae Satyricae', *Pasquin*, 1 (1847), 60–1. 'The Reporter and the Prince', *Punch*, 6 (1844), 156, imagines a similar event taking place to *Punch's* own royal penny-a-liner. *Punch's* article is a clear satire at Forster's expense.

[36] 'Prince Albert's Tour', *Punch*, 6 (1844), 156; 'The Queen's Visit', *Punch*, 7 (1844), 133.

correspondent of the *Morning Herald* being 'honoured with an exclusive squint through a fissure in the panelling of the room where Her Majesty was tasting some brose', the details of which were immediately rushed off to London.[37] Another article feigned to sympathize with the difficulties of reaching the Queen's retreat at Balmoral for those who were employed to eavesdrop under the windows of royalty.[38] *Punch* suggested that Balmoral had been chosen for its very seclusion in the hope of baffling those who would otherwise 'waylay them in their walks and dodge their movements, in order to contribute a column or two of trash to "our own reporter's" department of the newspapers'.[39] The extent of the attention that journalists gave to the monarchy encouraged a set of royalist news values. The necessary intrusion demanded by that attention nevertheless resulted in journalistic behaviour that was far from deferential.

There is a second episode which underlines the efforts of journalists to exploit the appeal of royal domesticity. It was the theft of a number of etchings that had been produced by Victoria and Albert. The etchings, many showing Victoria's children and close friends, were privately printed at Windsor. Mindful of their significance, precautions were taken at the printers. The amount of paper distributed in the workshop was only enough to print the required number of copies. The plates themselves were also kept under lock and key. A journeyman printer nevertheless managed to take copies of the etchings. Shortly afterwards, these copies found their way into the hands of a Windsor journalist, Jasper Judge. In August 1848, Judge approached a publisher, William Strange of 21 Paternoster Row, to plan a London exhibition. Strange was one of the publishers who occupied premises in and around the notorious Hollywell Street. Strange had previously been the publisher of *Figaro in London* and *Carpenter's Political Magazine*. In 1857, he would be prosecuted with William Dugdale for selling *Paul Pry* and *Women of London*, a legal case that led to the passing of the Obscene Publications Act in the same year.

Around fifty copies of a catalogue, the *Royal Victoria and Albert Gallery of Etchings*, were printed in readiness for the exhibition. The catalogue comprised sixty-three etchings, some of them sketches by Victoria of the royal nursery, which had then been etched by Albert. Upon hearing of the proposed exhibition, an injunction was sought by the Prince in order to prevent the etchings being displayed. The Solicitor-General, Sergeant Talfourd, appeared in court on their behalf. Affidavits from Albert and his secretary, George Anson, also had to be presented. The injunction had to be renewed several

[37] 'The Reporters at Blair Atholl', *Punch*, 7 (1844), 158.
[38] 'Penny-a-liner under Difficulties', *Punch*, 19 (1850), 140.
[39] Ibid.

times and the case regularly went through the courts between November 1848 and January 1849.[40]

Events in court focused on both the demarcation and definition of royal privacy. The prosecution successfully argued that the etchings were the product of the artistic labour of Victoria and Albert. It was therefore their legal right to publish them when they chose. Privacy and the rights of private property were mutually supportable. Talfourd argued that the publication of the catalogue was an infringement of Victoria and Albert's property, and by implication their privacy, because it wholly changed the status of the etchings. The judge agreed, declaring that the case showed a sordid spying into the privacy of domestic life, 'into the home—a word hitherto sacred amongst us—into the home of a family, a family whose private life forms not their only unquestionable title to the most marked respect'.[41] The case further solidified the barriers around the royal private sphere and, in so doing, helped to maintain its fetishized appeal.

Prince Albert v Strange is an example of commercial opportunism at its exploitative worst. The responses to the case are none the less highly revealing. Newspapers and periodicals condemned the actions of Judge and Strange. Yet their attitudes to the etchings themselves, once the catalogue had been made public, were far more ambivalent. *Punch*, for one, was guilty of taking a contradictory if not hypocritical approach to the issue of royal privacy. It thought that the theft might actually have done Victoria a service. *Punch* claimed that if the engravings had been placed upon show they would have greatly delighted her subjects:

The people at large, who have a notion that kings and queens wear diadems instead of hats . . . had doubtless been much astonished to find that HER EXCELLENT MAJESTY can let her Imperial notions subside into the homeliness of common life; and forgetful for awhile of the jangling of Cabinet councils, can busy her thoughts with the 'Head of an Arab Gypsy and Child, and Head of an Old Woman' (No. 60). The Windsor rogues have, all unwittingly, 'drawn the curtain and shown the picture' of HER MAJESTY's retirement in its pleasant aspect; and very pretty, very charming, we must confess the exhibition to be. We do not believe that LOUIS-PHILIPPE left any such etchings at the Tuileries as 'The Apotheosis of MIGNON'; neither, so far as yet known of the matter, did the EMPEROR OF AUSTRIA, on his late drive from the capital, leave such memorandum as 'Pigeons at the Royal Aviary', in charge of his beloved Viennese.[42]

---

[40] 'Prince Albert v Strange', *The Times*. 7 Nov. 1848, 6; 11 Dec. 1848, 7; 14 Dec. 1848, 6; 15 Dec. 1848, 6; 17 Jan. 1849, 6; 21 Jan. 1849, 6; 27 Jan. 1849, 6; 29 Jan. 1849, 6; 30 Jan. 1849, 7; 23 May 1849, 7; 2 June 1849, 7; 4 June 1849, 7.

[41] 'Prince Albert v Strange', *The Times*, 17 Jan. 1849, 6.

[42] 'The Royal Etchings', *Punch*, 15 (1848), 212. See also 'Jasper Judge Right Royally Judged', *Punch*, 16 (1849), 116.

Not only did the etchings confirm the feminine recreations of Victoria because they had been taken unawares: *Punch* ascribes to them an important political agency. Previously any prying had been heavily censured; now that monarchies across Europe were tumbling, the revelation of a virtuous private life was seized on as the crucial feature which distinguished the British monarchy from its continental counterparts. The Chartist threat against the Crown had been defeated, not on the fields of Kennington Common, but in the drawing-room of Windsor Castle. Royal respectability triumphed over Chartist revolution. Palace propriety quelled the proletariat. Such was the rhetoric propounded over the etchings, with journals like the *Spectator* echoing *Punch*'s sentiments. Although full of trouble for the parties themselves, the *Spectator* was glad of the legal proceedings which 'legitimately supply the insight commonly withheld . . . and cannot be altogether unwelcome to the public'.[43] *Punch* and the *Spectator* are caught within an ideological contradiction. Despite and because of the idealization of the royal hearth, they are unable to condemn the voyeuristic pleasure of the etchings.

The tension between journalists and the royal household meant that reporters were slowly and grudgingly accommodated at royal events. The emergence of journalism as a profession resulted in the introduction of a series of precedents for dealing with reporters. In July 1845, the *Spectator* claimed that, with Victoria's own permission, reporters from the leading London newspapers were to be allowed to attend a state ball that was shortly to take place inside Buckingham Palace.[44] Instead of relying on the embellished accounts of penny-a-liners, henceforth, each of the leading newspapers was to have their own court representative, who would be able to attend court functions. As the *Spectator* put it; 'In the army of "Our Own" a brigade is to be enrolled as "the Queen's own". The uniform may be black and white— "foolscap turned up with ink", and a goose-quill embroidered on the collar.'[45] The formalization of relations between the press and the royal household is a defining index to the establishment of a media monarchy.

The weddings of the Princess Royal and the Prince of Wales demonstrate the improved treatment of reporters. Compared with Victoria's coronation, an important shift had taken place for a few privileged newspapers. By focusing on the Princess Royal's wedding it can be seen how just one event throws into relief the interlocking nature of improvements in journalistic access, news distribution, and the rising status of reporters.

[43] 'Art in the Palace', *Spectator*, 11 Nov. 1848, 1090.
[44] Significantly, the invitation did not reach the reporters in enough time to allow them to acquire the appropriate dress. They were consequently not allowed into the ball proper and had to be content with a post in the ante-chamber.
[45] 'Our Own', *Spectator*, 12 July 1845, 663.

At the time of the wedding of the Princess Royal, the press's confidence in its social role was buoyed up by a growth in publications and circulation after the repeal of the Stamp Duty in 1855. The *Manchester Guardian*, for example, consequently became a daily publication. It was also able to reduce its price from 5*d.* to 2*d.*, and reduced it again to 1*d.* in 1857. By the late 1850s a few reporters also enjoyed an exceptional amount of distinction, particularly the type of special correspondent epitomized by William Howard Russell. Special correspondents came into their own after their reporting of the series of revolution across Europe in 1848 and, of course, their subsequent despatches from the Crimean War and Indian Mutiny. Although special correspondents were part of a distinguished coterie, since the 1840s there had been intermittent attempts to improve, or, rather, to invent the general professional status of reporters. In 1846, *Fraser's Magazine* made the oft-repeated argument that the significance of the press was no longer commensurate with the low status of those it employed. Journalism had been raised to the rank of a profession yet reporters still held a position that was 'deemed equivocal by the arbiters of social etiquette, and viewed with jealousy, mixed with a stimulated contempt, by the leaders of the political factions'.[46] Nevertheless, many journalists were still gentleman amateurs. It was not until the 1870s, when the increasing number of newspapers meant a rise in the number of university men entering journalism, that the profession acquired a stable respectability.

The state of graphic reportage, and the status of the special artist, followed a similar pattern to that of the special correspondent. One telling sign that the special artist was metamorphosing into a respectable figure is the number of commissions given to them by various members of the royal family. As early as September 1844, when Victoria was on her second highland tour, she had requested two sketches of the Falls of Braar from Ebenzer Landells. Special artists, like photographers, could serve a popular market at the same time as they were fulfilling commissions from Victoria or the Prince of Wales. In 1860, the Prince of Wales brought a series of illustrations from his tour of the USA and Canada from George Henry Andrew, the artist covering the tour for the *Illustrated London News*.[47] In subsequent decades, the royal family regularly purchased drawings and watercolours from artists employed by the *Illustrated London News* and the *Graphic*, especially from Richard Leitch, John Gilbert, William Simpson, and Sydney Prior Hall.

The autobiography of William Simpson, a special artist for the *Illustrated London News*, recounts how his long-standing coverage of royal events led to

[46] 'English Journalism', *Fraser's Magazine*, 34 (1846), 633.
[47] Oliver Millar (ed.), *The Victorian Pictures in the Collection of Her Majesty the Queen* (Cambridge: Cambridge University Press, 1992), i. 68.

friendship with the Prince of Wales. Simpson first met Victoria in 1854 while working for a lithographic firm, when he was invited to show her his sketches from the Crimea. His first royal commission soon followed and, through numerous other sketches, he became well known to the young Prince of Wales and the Princess Royal. He later attended the wedding of the Czarevitch in Moscow in 1866, travelling with the Prince of Wales in his special train. He also followed Edward through India in 1875 and, on assignments at Sandringham and Balmoral, was treated very much as a personal guest.[48] Simpson carried out his work for the *Illustrated London News* while continuing to receive numerous commissions from Victoria for watercolours of various minor royal family occasions. The commissions given to the special artists thus mark an emblematic reversal in the power relations between traditional court painters and popular graphic media. Royal Academy painters had traditionally had their official court portraits reproduced as prints for a wider audience. In contrast, artists employed by the illustrated press now found themselves receiving royal commissions precisely because of their news reportage for a large audience. On occasion, this meant that the royal family was actually buying back its own publicity.

The wedding of the Princess Royal marks a further progression in the establishment of a formal relationship between the royal household and the press. Vizetelly's memoirs claim that, even at this stage, newspaper representatives were often refused access to court ceremonies. On occasions of more than ordinary interest, editors still had to depend on the *Court Circular* for their scant information.[49] These were highly circumscribed working conditions. Vizetelly, who was by now the editor of the *Illustrated Times*, consequently wrote in protest to the Lord Chamberlain, the Marquis of Breadalbane. The Lord Chamberlain's archives provide a fascinating record of all the various newspapers that applied for permission to report the wedding ceremony in the Chapel Royal. His records catch *in situ* the double dynamic that governed the treatment of reporters at royal occasions. They explicitly show the still questionable importance of journalists, but they also reveal that the organization of royal events was now including the press as a matter of course.

Most of the applications from the various newspapers were received from the end of December onwards. Significantly, though, royal functionaries had already arranged the number of reporters and their seating positions. On 21 December 1857, Spencer Ponsonby, the assistant to the Lord Chamberlain,

---

[48] One example of Simpson's good royal relationships is that, at the coronation of the Czar in 1886, the Duke of Edinburgh arranged a good position near Moscow Cathedral for George Augustus Sala and Simpson. William Simpson, *The Autobiography of William Simpson* (London: T. Fisher Unwin, 1905), 299.

[49] Vizetelly, *Glances Back*, ii. 5.

wrote a memorandum to Thomas Biddulph, Master of the Queen's Household. Ponsonby proposed that admission be restricted to six journalists and two artists because there was no space for any more. The reporters were to be seated high up on the left-hand side of the Chapel Royal. The location was deliberately given to them because 'it would be more out of the way than any other place in the Chapel, for I suppose we could not call upon the reporters to wear full dress'.[50] The position of the journalists therefore embodies a continuing official ambivalence towards their presence. Reporters could not be excluded; nevertheless, they were literally to be placed at the edge of proceedings. Ponsonby's comments combine a jibe about their low social status with a realization that they could not be forced into court regalia.[51] Royal officials compensated for the lack of court dress by having a red silk curtain screen the members of the press. The presence of journalists was to be ignored or conveniently overlooked by the aristocratic congregation. As the *Illustrated London News* tellingly puts it, the press were the 'representatives of an estate which, always felt, is supposed by the fiction of court and parliament to be always absent, and consequently invisible'.[52] Reporters could no longer be dismissed as penny-a-liners and justifiably debarred. Yet the literal refusal to see them epitomizes an unwillingness to acknowledge their communicative role.

Only the crème de la crème of the London press were granted admission to the wedding ceremony. All requests for admission from provincial, weekly, and foreign newspapers were turned down on the grounds of lack of space. Notable publications like the *Saturday Review* and the *News of the World* had their applications turned down. Most privileged of all was *The Times*. John Delane, its famous editor, received two guest tickets to attend the ceremony in his own right.[53] Delane enjoyed close relations with the royal household and, especially after 1860, received frequent letters from Lord Torrington containing the latest court gossip. Torrington often referred to himself as Delane's own 'Windsor Special'. When Delane was on a trip to Scotland in 1866, he found himself unintentionally staying at Guisachen with the Prince of Wales and his entourage. Ironically, Delane's biggest fear was that his attendance would be printed in rival newspapers. He wrote to the *Scotsman*, *Inverness Courier*, and the *Morning Post* begging for his name to be excluded from the list of

---

[50] PRO LC 2/79 158.

[51] The *Court Journal* similarly noted it was decided that the reporters would not have to submit to court dress in case they feared that their pens were being put into royal harnesses. 'The Royal Wedding', *Lloyd's Weekly Newspaper*, 17 Jan. 1858, 5.

[52] 'The Chapel Royal and the Marriage Ceremony', *ILN* 30 Jan. 1858, 97. The *Illustrated Times* also noted that, 'According to a popular court fiction, however, no reporters were supposed to be present'. 'The Marriage of the Princess Royal', *Illustrated Times*, 30 Jan. 1858, 99.

[53] PRO LC 2/79 9.

attendees. He told George Dasent, his assistant editor, 'I need not ask you to strike it out if it is sent up to you'.[54] As famed editor of *The Times*, Delane enjoyed high connections, but it seems that the independent reputation of the paper had to be protected at all costs.

The newspapers given access to the Chapel Royal for the Princess Royal's wedding were *The Times*, *Morning Post*, *Morning Chronicle*, *Daily News*, *Morning Advertiser*, *Daily Telegraph*, *Star*, *Sun*, and the *Globe*, while the *Standard* and the *Morning Chronicle* shared a ticket. The illustrated periodicals granted access to sketch the event were the *Illustrated London News*, the *Illustrated Times*, and the *Illustrated News of the World*.[55] Vizetelly thus got the access he desired. However, while his memoirs present his protest to the Lord Chamberlain as very much a liberal championing of press freedom, his still extant letter is somewhat more prosaic. Vizetelly's letter draws attention to the fact that that the daily newspapers were being allowed to attend the ceremony and demands the same treatment for the illustrated press: 'Their circulation far exceeds that of every other newspaper . . . [and it is] only by their medium that the great mass of the people can obtain anything approaching an idea of the splendour and interest of the ceremony itself.'[56] Promoting the circulation and loyalty of your newspaper was a common ploy when pleading for press passes.[57] Loyalty, however, was also encouraged by commercial interests. Vizetelly, for example, made the appropriately royal sum of £1,200 from the wedding. His arguments exemplify the way in which newspapers' pursuance of their own commercial interests aided the creation of royal events as both populist and national.

The Princess Royal's wedding seems to have established a protocol of journalistic invisibility. It marked a semi-official understanding between reporters and royal functionaries, if not quite an *entente cordiale*. It was certainly an organizational principle that was in place at least until the 1870s. In 1873, the *Printer's Register* published two accounts of the tribulations faced by reporters at Balmoral. Even though there was a carriage of journalists ever ready and eager to follow Victoria, they were expected to stay out of sight and preserve their supposed non-existence. Unsurprisingly, it was an etiquette littered with problems. One incident occurred on a royal excursion from Inverlochy Castle to the pass of Glencoe. A correspondent for *The Times* who,

[54] Arthur Dasent, *John Thadeus Delane, Editor of 'The Times'* (London: John Murray, 1908), ii. 176.
[55] PRO LC 2/79 157.
[56] Ibid. 142.
[57] See PRO LC 2 71. On the Queen's first highland tour in 1842, the *Scotch Reformer's Gazette* wrote to the *London Gazette* office desiring a list of the people who were to be presented to Her Majesty. The letter emphasizes that the paper had been 'most conspicuous for its *Loyalty* and *Devotion* to *the Queen*. It is at the top of the newspaper Press in Scotland for extensive circulation—and is bringing out a supplement with a medallion representation.'

interestingly, was also engaged in sketching views for an illustrated paper, inadvertently came within sight of the Queen's party. Despite the fact that he was 200–300 yards away John Brown, having seen the offender, confronted the luckless reporter. Violence was only prevented through the intervention of a peacemaker.[58] On another occasion, a carriage of reporters was following Victoria on a drive through E— W—   nly to be caught unawares when the
ed around. The reporters' carriage
Victoria pass. She reportedly had
Printer's Register noted that other
hilar difficulties because of the dis-
Ponsonby had apparently made it
aving her footsteps dogged as if by
order to frustrate the reporters at
out her excursions until the last
defeating. The journalists conse-
t their posts in case she suddenly

t occasions so important is that it
e of news distribution. There was
he small number of journalists
ber of newspapers that desired to
n which news distribution func-
tors, most notably the provincial
f any national communications
cial newspapers, there was little
s to cover royal occasions taking
to the hallowed precincts of the
Herald only had an editor, two
l of the Stamp Duty in 1855 was
ess, but most provincial papers
his forced them to cut and paste
ropolitan daily press. Given the
news from beyond their own locality, this dependency was both endemic and a pragmatic necessity. Even those provincial newspapers that published a letter from their own 'London correspondent'—a hack figure who would probably write several such columns—would borrow substantially from the metropolitan press. Significantly, the limited reach of the London newspapers into rural areas, along with their slow

[58] 'Facts and Scraps', *Printer's Register*, 6 Oct. 1873, 183.
[59] 'Facts and Scraps', *Printer's Register*, 6 Nov. 1873, 216.   [60] Ibid.
[61] Lucy Brown, *Victorian News and Newspapers* (Oxford: Clarendon Press, 1985), 83.

distribution around the community, meant that this borrowing of copy was far from a repetition of already established news.

At Victoria's coronation, the reportage of the *Manchester Guardian*, the *Leeds Mercury*, and the *Newcastle Courant*—to take just three examples— were all amalgams of copy that had already appeared in the London press. Of these, the *Leeds Mercury* was the only one to claim to have its own correspondent in attendance. However, his brief report, two-thirds of a column, has to be set against the three and a half columns that were taken from the metropolitan press.[62] There was very much a centrifugal diffusion of news, a slow filtering out from the metropolitan daily press. Such practices were still prevalent in 1858 at the marriage of the Princess Royal. In the same way that the royal image was photographic well before it was disseminated through photographs, the dynamics of royal news distribution meant that there was a national royal news narrative well before there was a national press. A comparison of the accounts of the Princess Royal's wedding printed by a variety of provincial newspapers reveals that many of them have identical paragraphs repeated from original sources that have been cut down to fit the available column space. The coverage of the *Liverpool Mercury* acknowledged that its wedding columns were culled from various London newspapers.[63] Yet its account is almost identical to that published by the *Sheffield Telegraph*, the *Birmingham Daily Post*, and the *Norwich Mercury*.[64] The principal source for many provincial newspapers was invariably *The Times*. Five provincial newspapers of different sizes and serving different geographic regions, the *Manchester Guardian*, the *Leeds Mercury*, the *Scotsman*, the *Western Times*, and the *Hampshire Independent*, all relied heavily on copy that they had taken from *The Times*.[65] Even the *Illustrated London News* supplemented the work of its artists by borrowing substantially from it.[66] The circulation of such reports points to a cascading of news with *The Times* as the central hub.

The structure of news distribution did not simply create a shared national narrative, however. It had a political impact because popular radical newspapers relied on the same cut and paste techniques. *Reynolds's Newspaper* and the *Northern Star* were not immune from the need to provide their readers with coverage of the latest royal tour or visit. They were also well aware of the implications of such borrowing. At Victoria's wedding, the *Northern Star*

---

[62] 'The Royal Coronation of Her Gracious Majesty Queen Victoria, in the Abbey church of Westminster, on Thursday last', *Leeds Mercury*, 30 June 1838, 4.

[63] 'Marriage of the Princess Royal with Prince Frederick William of Prussia', *Liverpool Mercury*, 26 Jan. 1858, 5.

[64] *Liverpool Mercury*, 26 Jan. 1858, 5; *Norwich Mercury*, 27 Jan. 1858, 2; *Sheffield Telegraph*, 26 Jan. 1858, 3; *Birmingham Daily Post*, 26 Jan. 1858, 1.

[65] *The Times*, 26 Jan. 1858, 7; *Manchester Guardian*, 27 Jan. 1858, 2; *Leeds Mercury*, 28 Jan. 1858, 3; *Hampshire Independent*, 30 Jan. 1858, 2–3; *Western Times*, 30 Jan. 1858, 1–2.

[66] See 'The Colonnade', *ILN* 30 Jan. 1858, 118.

noted that it had deliberately taken its account from the *Sun* because it was 'the least fulsome of the ministerial papers on the occasion, and yet sufficiently so as to be positively sickening to any well regulated Christian mind'.[67] When it came to the wedding of the Princess Royal, *Reynolds's Newspaper* and *Lloyd's Newspaper* took their reportage directly from *The Times*. For both newspapers, this practice was repeated at the funeral of Prince Albert and the wedding of the Prince of Wales. Such borrowing obviously worked against any extensive criticism of the monarchy. Before the wedding of the Prince of Wales, *Lloyd's Weekly Newspaper* had attacked the expense of catering for a Germanic and aristocratic court.[68] Similarly, *Reynolds's Newspaper* had printed yet another scathing attack on the Jenkins-like sycophancy of the press.[69] Although it is difficult to know precisely how many newspapers throughout this period relied on the metropolitan press because so many sources are unacknowledged, there was a clear hierarchy in terms of the access to royal news, which helped to ensure that the news values of the press embodied a predominantly deferential standpoint towards the monarchy. This reliance was probably at its height in the 1850s and 1860s. The formation of the Press Association in 1868 subsequently provided a readily available source of official news for the provincial press.

The tension embodied in *Reynolds's Newspaper*'s coverage of royal events—the contradiction between its editorials and news reportage—epitomizes the problems facing a broad-based anti-monarchism. Similar conflicting forces were at work upon the life and career of W. J. Linton. As previously mentioned, in 1843 the firm of Linton and Smith became the principal engravers for the *Illustrated London News*. Thus, at the same time as Linton was becoming increasingly involved in radical politics—he befriended Mazzini and the veteran radical publishers Henry Hetherington and James Watson in the early 1840s—his workshop was busy churning out the populist engravings of Victoria's civic visits. The contradiction between Linton's personal politics and the professional demands of the engraving profession existed before his work for the *Illustrated London News*. Upon the christening of the Prince of Wales in July 1842, the *Observer* and *Bell's Life in London* published a large celebratory engraving that was signed by Linton and Smith.[70] In the same period, though, Linton was publishing anti-royal odes in the *Odd Fellow*, including one poem decrying 'On the Birth of another Guelph'.[71]

[67] 'The Royal Exhibition', *Northern Star*, 15 Feb. 1840, 4.
[68] 'The Royal German Legion', *Lloyd's Weekly Newspaper*, 24 Jan. 1858, 6.
[69] 'The Marriage of the Princess Royal', *Reynolds's Newspaper*, 31 Jan. 1858, 10–11.
[70] Orrin Smith and William Linton, 'Christening of the Prince of Wales', *Observer*, 30 Jan. 1842, 2. See also Victoria's visits to the midlands in Dec. 1843, especially an elaborate heraldic frontispiece engraved by Linton in the *ILN* 2 Dec. 1843, 361. Signed engravings also appear on pp. 369, 372, 373, 374, and 375.
[71] William Linton, *Prose and Verse* (London: n.p, 1895), vi. 46. See also 'The Royal Bounty', ibid. v. 11.

In the mid-1840s, Linton's name is appended to various engravings of royal tours and visits in the *Illustrated London News*. The most telling example of this is when Victoria and Albert visited Coburg in 1845. Prince Albert lent the *Illustrated London News* a set of topographical engravings of his homeland; a prestigious coup for the periodical. The sketches were engraved by Linton and published with his initials.[72] While he was working on these engravings—a fact remarkable enough in itself—in the *Illuminated Magazine*, now edited by Linton, he was publishing a poem castigating the royal party's attendance at a *battue* in Coburg.[73] Linton's firm ceased engraving for the *Illustrated London News* in 1847 and his name subsequently disappears from its pages for several years. As late as 1855, however, he was still doing occasional work for the paper in connection with a royal visit. Upon Victoria's visit to Napoleon III, he engraved two topographical prints of the Palace of St Cloud, the residence where the British Queen would be staying.[74] In 1848, Linton travelled with Mazzini to Paris as a delegate of the People's International League to welcome in the new revolutionary order. Seven years and one *coup d'état* later, he was helping to produce a narrative, albeit only in a small way, that celebrated the reign of Napoleon III and Queen Victoria. That two of the more prominent republicans of the mid-nineteenth century, Linton and Reynolds, were so involved with royal events is fascinating. However, I believe it would be wrong to interpret Linton's activities as either a simple matter of political contradiction or as a sign of the monolithic dominance of a royal culture industry. In the same way as Reynolds was subject to the demands of a successful newspaper, Linton was one of the most renowned wood-engravers of his day. As such, he could hardly avoid carrying out a wide range of work for the periodical press.

The structure of royal news dissemination is also apparent in the activities of a shadowy figure who has so far received no critical attention: the court newsman. The changing role of the court newsman is the most evident response by the royal household to the pressure exerted by the press. He first came into existence in the reign of George III. The King, annoyed at the inaccuracies of the press, instigated the post in order to supply the London morning newspapers with a daily bulletin of his activities.[75] The court information printed by *The Times* in the 1790s and early 1800s consists merely of short unsigned paragraphs. Nevertheless, the court newsman slowly began to supply more information. His role consequently acquired an official status. In

---

[72] 'Queen's Visit to Germany', *ILN* 16 Aug. 1845, 104. Linton's signed engravings are on pp. 104, 105, 137, 140, 153, 164, 165.
[73] Linton, *Prose and Verse*, vi. 105.
[74] 'Palace of St Cloud', *ILN* 18 Aug. 1855, 208. See also 209.
[75] 'The Court Newsman', *The Times*, 15 Jan. 1864, 9.

the 1820s, the *Court Circular* achieved its own titular masthead in *The Times*. Twenty years later, the implications of this development were remarked upon by the *Birmingham Journal*:

The title did more, it exhibited this mistily grand affair, the court; instead of being waited upon and wooed by the magnates of the fourth estate, each striving who should first be permitted to chronicle its excellent things, as being itself no better than an humble candidate for that publicity which the press could alone bestow; instead of being attended by 'gentlemen of the gallery', as compelled to compass a notice by entertaining, on its establishment, a special penny-a-liner for the purpose. This was, however, scarcely a correct view of the matter. The court, in respect to its *Circular*, was patient rather than active—it permitted the publication, rather than authorised it.[76]

For the *Birmingham Journal*, the advent of the *Court Circular* could be understood as the royal household's recognition of the power of the press. The court newsman was the monarchy's own penny-a-liner; an institutional attempt to exploit the benefits of publicity. The article suggests, however, that the *Court Circular* was actually more accepted than authorized, more endured than encouraged. The ambiguities of the court newsman's position stem from the fact that he seems to have been funded by the press as well as the court. Details are scant, but when George Budgman, a former court newsman, died in August 1832, he was receiving a pension from the Treasury and from several London newspapers.[77] Similarly, in 1916, the court newsman was given only a retainer from the Lord Chamberlain. The majority of his income derived from supplying newspapers and the Press Association with the *Court Circular* (he was paid a guinea a week by each newspaper for his reports in 1916).[78] The court newsman evolved within two contrary schema, whereby the royal household veered between being passive and proactive towards the press. In Victoria's reign, his changing role plays out in miniature the development of a professional relationship between the press and the royal household. He metamorphosed from a semi-official hanger-on—a recorder to the *haut ton*—into an established royal functionary. He was, perhaps, the first Public Relations professional in the nineteenth century.

Much of the information on the court newsman is both fragmentary and politically charged. *Punch*'s treatment of him, for example, is very similar to its attacks upon Jenkins. It first mentioned the court newsman in 1845 as part of a mock literary appreciation of the *Court Circular*. Thereafter, *Punch* intermittently satirized his output.[79] *Punch*'s critiques of the court newsman qua

[76] 'Saturday, September 2', *Birmingham Journal*, 2 Sept. 1843, 3.
[77] 'The Court Newsman', *The Times*, 28 Aug. 1832, 2.
[78] PRO HO 139/15.
[79] 'A Hint for the Court Newsman', *Punch*, 14 (1848), 55; 'Singular Force of Habit', *Punch*, 19 (1850), 187; 'The Court Newsman Converted', *Punch*, 21 (1851), 145.

reportage are indicative of his increasing provision of official news. At the coronation, most metropolitan newspapers only relied on the *Court Circular* for the order of service. However, by the late 1850s the role of the court newsman had grown beyond merely preparing a daily report that blandly detailed the Queen's activities. Upon occasions such as balls and court levees, he guaranteed that the metropolitan press received an account of the event.[80] Whereas the penny-a-liners ensured a constant flow of news of the smallest incidents connected with Victoria's tours, the court newsman was relied upon for an account of the more exclusive palace occasions. Unsurprisingly, then, the court newsman came to symbolize not only the communicative excess surrounding the monarchy. He was explicitly aligned with the servility of the court and the official perpetuation of an aura around the sovereign.

The prominence of the court newsman increased to the extent that he was assimilated into radical attacks upon the monarchy. *Sketches of Her Majesty's Household*, published in 1848 by William Strange, is one example of how he was regarded. *Sketches*, which follows the format of John Wade's famous *The Black Book* (1819), is further evidence of the contrary nature of popular publishing. Strange published a book attacking court corruption in the same year that he attempted to organize the exhibition of Victoria's etchings. He capitalized on the revolutionary fervour of 1848 while simultaneously seeking to exploit public fascination with Victoria. In *Sketches*, Strange catalogues, in precise detail, the incomes of the various offices of Victoria's court. The book sought to expose the sinecures that provided a lucrative living for their noble holders. Listed along with such grossly arcane offices as the Gentlemen of the Wine and Beer Cellar (£500 p.a.) and the Gentleman Ushers of the Privy Chamber (£200 p.a.) was the role of the court reporter.[81] *Sketches of Her Majesty's Household* positions him within the framework of Old Corruption, part of the expensive paraphernalia of the court. The current court reporter was said to have inherited the post from his father. When the incumbent, Joseph Doane, retired in 1864, *The Times* noted that his grandfather had been the first to hold the post under George III. Prospective applicants, it seems, need not apply.

Sketches put the court newsman on a par with the other anachronistic court posts. In tracing his historical evolution, however, the book describes an increasingly professional role that reflects the changing nature of journalism as a whole. Not only did the duties of the post expand; the function of the court

[80] On 2 Mar. 1863, for example, the *Standard* printed three columns from the court newsman that gave an account of a royal drawing-room. 'The Drawing Room', *Standard*, 2 Mar. 1863, 6.
[81] *Sketches of Her Majesty's Household* (London: William Strange, 1848), 130–6.

newsman changed specifically in response to the increasing presence of the newspaper press. Thus, after June 1844, the remit of the court newsman was extended beyond London.[82] Previously, when Victoria was at Brighton or Windsor, local correspondents had been responsible for sending court news to the London press. One of the reasons for the change was that at this time, and for a long time beforehand, three reporters engaged by the London press resided at Windsor. Every evening they received the court news of the day from the Secretary to the Master of the Household. However, following numerous incidents when the Windsor correspondents discovered sensitive information, *Sketches* claims that they were banned from the Castle. Henceforth, when the court was at Windsor, the official bulletin was sent directly to the court reporter in London. He would then distribute it to the morning papers. In Strange's account, the court newsman had become the interface—even the screen—between the monarchy and the press.

Sketches of Her Majesty's Household went far further than the mockery of *Punch* in that it tried to expose the repressive treatment of journalists by the court. The book alleged that one of the Windsor journalists, who had discovered some embarrassing gossip, found himself subject to constant persecution. The journalist was in debt to one of the local Windsor tradesmen who also supplied Windsor Castle. A high-ranking court official allegedly attempted to buy the bills of debt from the tradesman so that he could bankrupt the reporter. *Sketches* claims that the Lord Chamberlain subsequently offered £100 to the penny-a-liner in exchange for his silence and a promise to leave town. He also found his engagements to supply royal news to various newspapers superseded by promises from the court newsman to provide the requisite information. There is clearly no easy way of proving the veracity of these allegations. More important than their truthfulness, though, is their testimony to perceptions of the nefarious influence of the royal household. While the court newsman did not become as much of a totemic figure as Jenkins, *Sketches* expresses his inclusion in anti-monarchist critiques.

The growing demands upon the court newsman are most evident upon the retirement of Joseph Doane on 2 January 1864.[83] His replacement was Thomas Beard, not a member of the court but an experienced journalist and long-time friend of Charles Dickens. Beard had gained Dickens his first position as a parliamentary reporter upon the *Morning Chronicle* in 1834. He was also the best man at Dickens's wedding. It is through a letter to Wilkie Collins celebrating Beard's appointment that Dickens provides details of his new

---

[82] This is partially verified by looking at *The Times*'s coverage of Victoria's first tour. Although the *Court Circular* continued to be published, it contained no details of her engagements.

[83] Doane's resignation letter is in PRO LC 1/129 164.

salary, £400 p.a.[84] Editors of the London morning papers were then receiving between £600 and £1,000, with their reporters being paid around £200 a year.[85] Beard's income was well above that of most reporters and sub-editors of the leading London papers. His salary is testimony to the prominent nature of his new role. The replacement of a court sinecure with a respected journalist is a significant shift. It is a concession to professionalism and a corresponding recognition of the new media environment in which the monarchy existed. Beard would serve as court newsman for nearly twenty-three years, finally leaving his post in December 1886.[86]

How can we trace the working of the court newsman? Details of his work are sketchy but the impact of his role is most in evidence at large royal occasions run by the Lord Chamberlain. At the wedding of the Princess Royal the court newsman supplied extensive press releases that were directly reproduced by all strata of the newspaper press. Five leading newspapers, *Lloyd's Weekly Newspaper*, the *Daily Telegraph*, the *Standard*, the *Morning Chronicle*, and the *Daily News*, all drew heavily on the column inches he provided. The *Daily Telegraph*'s use of the court newsman underlines the extent of his influence. It was the most successful of the newspapers to emerge after the reduction in Stamp Duty in 1855 and, by 1858, its large circulation was outstripping *The Times*. The *Daily Telegraph*'s coverage of the wedding began in earnest on 23 January, two days before the wedding, when it published half a column directly from the court newsman on the preparations in the Chapel Royal.[87] Its wedding reportage consisted of two and two-thirds columns from its own reporter and three columns taken directly from the court newsman.[88] The wedding editions of the *Standard*, the *Morning Chronicle*, and the *Daily News* were similar. The *Standard* printed three and a half columns from the court newsman alongside seven columns from its own reporters.[89] Even the *Illustrated London News* and *Queen* utilized the information that he provided. The *Illustrated London News* published three-quarters of a column from the court newsman describing the bridal dress and the various official uniforms on show.[90]

The post of the court newsman survived until 1918, when his role was taken over by the Press Association.[91] During the nineteenth century, the court

[84] Charles Dickens, *The Letters of Charles Dickens 1862–1865*, vol. x, ed. Graham Storey *et al.* (Oxford: Clarendon Press, 1998), 346.
[85] Lee, *Origins of the Popular Press*, 108.
[86] 'Monarchy', *News of the World*, 11 Dec. 1886, 2.
[87] 'St George's Chapel', *Daily Telegraph*, 23 Jan. 1858, 1.
[88] See the reports of *Daily Telegraph* 26 Jan. 1858, 2–3.
[89] 'The Royal Marriage', *Standard*, 26 Jan. 1858, 4–6; 'From the Court Newsman', *Daily News*, 26 Jan. 1858, 5–6; 'From the Court Newsman', *Morning Chronicle*, 26 Jan. 1858, 5–6.
[90] 'The Costumes', *ILN* 30 Jan. 1858, 123.
[91] PRO HO 139/15.

newsman was a crucial interface between the royal household and the press. He was an official source providing much needed, if rather bland, information. The degree to which his output aided the metropolitan press's desire for information demonstrates the extent to which the royal household helped to disseminate the public presence of Victoria. Significantly, though, the court newsman remained caught between conflicting forces. He was derided for his official oversupply of news, while simultaneously cast as a court flunkey designed to mitigate press intrusion. Unable to satisfy the demand for information, yet attacked for supplying too much, the court newsman constitutes part of the double-edged dynamic between the monarchy and the press.

The wedding of the Prince of Wales in March 1863 provides the clearest indication as to how much the role of journalists had changed since the late 1830s. The consideration now shown to members of the press has to be seen in relation to the accretion of different media around royal events. Photography was a significant part of the royal news dynamic for the first time. The commentaries upon the Prince of Wales's wedding also emphasize the ongoing derision associated with the kow-towing nature of royal reportage. Except, on this occasion, one of the reporters present actually responded to the by now familiar jibes. George Augustus Sala used the wedding reportage as an argument for elevating the overall professional status of reporters.

Sala is a significant forerunner to the New Journalism and a key figure in the development of the popular press. He wrote for a number of publications during the 1850s, including *Household Words* and the *Illustrated Times*, but achieved his notoriety as a leader writer for the newly established *Daily Telegraph*. Famed for his bohemianism as much as for his engaging editorials, Sala's human-interest style was heavily identified with the constitution of a penny daily press. By 1863, he was conducting his own journal, *Temple Bar*, and writing a weekly column for the *Illustrated London News*.[92] Sala's commentary on the Prince of Wales's wedding consequently exemplifies larger shifts in the newspaper industry. He justified the royal reporters' work through their labour in making the event available to the nation. Sala's populist claims mark a change in the perception of their role. Instead of being particularly abused for their royal reportage, Sala lauded the worth of journalists precisely because of their efforts at royal occasions. Journalists were promoting themselves as the link between the royal family and the mass reading public. Professional self-worth was now competing with anti-monarchist critiques of their role.

At the wedding ceremony in St George's Chapel, Windsor, the journalists

---

[92] On the details of Sala's career, see Paul Edwards, *Dickens's Young Men: George Augustus Sala, Edmund Yates and the World of Victorian Journalism* (Aldershot: Ashgate, 1998).

were stationed in the organ loft, a position they would occupy at future royal events at least up until Victoria's funeral. In addition to Vizetelly, who was representing the *Illustrated Times*, there were between twelve and fifteen special correspondents in attendance.[93] Again, it was the case that all applications from provincial papers were turned down on the grounds of lack of space.[94] The reporters present included such luminaries as Sala for the *Daily Telegraph*, Nicholas Woods for the *Times*, James Grant, the editor of the *Morning Advertiser*, and the Revd J. C. M. Bellew, who was reporting for the *Morning Post*. William Howard Russell was also present, but the nature of his attendance deserves special attention. The presence of such recognzable names as Sala and Russell reveals how seriously the newspapers treated the event. It captures the emergence of the news journalist as a professional, even prominent, figure.

While the reporters might have been positioned conveniently out of sight in the organ loft, William Powell Frith, commissioned by Victoria to produce a painting of the marriage, was given a prime position from which to observe the ceremony. Frith was stationed in one of the seats in the right-hand side of the chancel. Only a row of royal personages was seated between him and the wedding group around the altar. Vizetelly's memoirs jealously describe Frith, wearing his own court dress, sketching 'in the midst of a little crowd of ladies, all desperately coquetting to ensure their portraits figuring in his picture'.[95] The only journalist who attended the ceremony in his own right was William Howard Russell. According to Sala, Russell was not in the organ loft but was by Frith, seated near the altar wearing court dress.[96] If Sala's account is correct, Russell was at the ceremony both as a special correspondent and as a personage who was famous for being a special correspondent. This was a situation that could not have been possible thirty years previously.

Nowhere is the effort to confirm the rising status of the reporter more strenuously expressed than in several articles Sala published immediately after the wedding. In its edition immediately following the marriage, the *Spectator* attacked the sycophancy and hysteria of the royal press coverage.[97] A highfalutin account from the *Daily Telegraph*, probably from Sala's pen, was singled out for particular derision. Clearly piqued by the criticism, Sala responded to the *Spectator* through his regular articles in *Temple Bar* and the *Illustrated London News*. The spat reveals Sala's perception of his own professional position and, fascinatingly, the timetable of reporters on the day of a major royal

---

[93] 'Metropolitan On Dits', *Court Journal*, 28 Feb. 1863, 206.

[94] Ibid.

[95] Vizetelly, *Glances Back*, ii. 77.

[96] George Augustus Sala, *The Life and Adventures of George Augustus Sala* (London: Cassell & Co., 1895), ii. 26.

[97] 'Hysteria of the Press', *Spectator*, 14 Mar. 1863, 1750.

event. Like many journalists, the self-made Sala was acutely aware of his less than genteel status. It was not until 1858 that he began to work in earnest for the *Daily Telegraph* as a leader writer. Prior to this, he had had several novels serialized, all of which met with only a limited success. Sala's riposte is insepable from his aversion to being cast as no more than a penny-a-liner; the attack upon his language cut to the heart of his literary pretensions.

In Sala's regular 'Echoes of the Week' column in the *Illustrated London News*, he linked the sensationalism of royal reporting to the conditions under which the reporters were forced to write. Sala contrasted the pressure upon the professional journalists working frantically at the royal wedding to the gentlemen-writers working for the weekly published *Spectator*, who had four or five days to compose a single article. For Sala, the *Spectator's* criticisms merely reveal that it had no understanding of the restrictions under which the journalists of the *Daily Telegraph* had to write. Proclaiming that they were not the type of men who lounged around in embroidered dressing-gowns, writing with gold pens upon mauve paper with scented ink, Sala cast the reporters in the role of upstanding and hard-working bourgeois citizens.[98] Instead of being gentleman amateurs or bohemians, they were 'plain middle-aged men who had been fagging all the previous week—and many previous weeks—in heated editorial sanctums, or in the reporters gallery of the House of Commons'.[99] Sala appropriates the facets of journalism that were used to denigrate the profession—the writing to deadlines and the association with paid labour—and redeploys them in an attempt to demonstrate the worth of reporters. Nevertheless, the deliberately staid self-image that Sala is promoting is still in marked contrast to the impecuniousness associated with the lives of many journalists. In December 1858, Sala himself, with his bohemian lifestyle, had been temporarily committed to the Queen's Bench prison in Whitecross Street for debt.[100]

Sala's articles attempt to improve the respect accorded to journalists by cataloguing their honest toil. In so doing, he provides an unparalleled glimpse of the special correspondent's activities at a major royal event. Before the wedding itself on 10 March, Sala had also reported on Edward and Alexandra's procession through London on 7 March. The Corporation of London had permitted the representatives of the press to travel behind the civic procession in two open carriages that would convey them as far as Temple Bar. Thus, in a telling shift, reporters were no longer attempting simply to gain access to the occasion: they had themselves become part of the spectacle. To attend the wedding ceremony itself, the journalists then had to

---

[98] George Augustus Sala, 'Echoes of the Week', *ILN* 21 Mar. 1863, 279.
[99] Ibid.   [100] Edwards, *Dickens's Young Men*, 53–4.

travel down to Windsor on the Monday evening by the midnight train. That had only been the start of their work. Many had a staff of outdoor reporters to whom they had to give instructions, a task that is itself indicative of expanding resources of the press. Most of them did not get to sleep before 2 a.m. By 9 a.m., they had to be at the south door of St George's Chapel. Between 10 a.m. and 10.30 a.m. they were in the gallery rushing backwards and forwards noting down all of the preliminaries. At 1.30 p.m., after the ceremony had been completed, the journalists made their way to the railway station as quickly as possible. According to Sala, they had to fight their way through an aristocratic throng, hotly pursued by policemen who perhaps imagined them to be pickpockets. Officials of the South-Western Railway had provided a special train for them in order to hasten their journey back to London. By 3 p.m., the special correspondents were at their desks. They then wrote without cease until midnight. With the correction of the proofs, they did not finish their final accounts until around 1 a.m. All this so that, as Sala proudly boasts, on the following day the British public 'were enabled to read an account, ranging from five to six columns of close type written by a single hand, in each morning newspaper'.[101] Sala's dramatization is clearly aimed at impressing the reader with the labour of the reporters. His journalistic timetable none the less emphasizes the organizational effort required for royal occasions.

The accounts in the *Illustrated London News* and *Temple Bar* exemplify the official facilities that the members of the press were now receiving from a variety of diverse sources. Concern for their needs illustrates a steadily growing acceptance of their presence. The facilities provided by the City of London authorities, South-Western trains, and the royal household, albeit for a few privileged reporters only, signify a marked shift in the treatment of the press. When the official resources are taken together with the extensive efforts made by the various newspapers and the individual artists, journalists, and photographers, we have a moving testimony to the labour that went into broadcasting the royal family. It was the cumulative endeavour around the wedding—the institutional, professional, and personal investment in the British monarchy—which was responsible for the production of its ubiquitous presence. The reporters and officials sustained and reinvented the role of the monarchy at the same time. The wedding of the Prince of Wales was not simply an occasion covered by the media: it was a media event.

In the edition of *Temple Bar* following the wedding, Sala also ruminated upon his experiences as a special correspondent. He played upon the importance of the wedding as a way of demonstrating the social worth of journalism. For Sala, the wedding needed the presence of the press. It was the press's role

---

[101] Sala, 'Echoes of the Week', 21 Mar. 1863, 299.

to communicate the occasion, to make the wedding into a national event. Yet, notwithstanding the fact that his work for the *Daily Telegraph* was one of the principal sources of his income, Sala describes his own journalism as if it was a task to which he had condescended, a *littérateur* slumming it for a day. Sala's piece is worth quoting at length because it dramatizes his own uneasy relationship to his journalism, the stereotypes of reporters in circulation, and the arguments used to elevate their status:

Yielding to the representations of some very good friends of mine—who conduct a newspaper, I consented for some twenty-four hours to abdicate the honourable position of a rent-and-tax paying English gentlemen, and to become a penny-a-liner. Now there is nothing intrinsically despicable in the status of the meritorious and useful individuals whose more courteous designation is that of 'occasional reporter', and who furnish graphic, and in the main, truthful narratives of fires, murders, accidents, and Lord Mayor's shows, for a certain sum in copper per line, for publication in the columns of the metropolitan press. These chroniclers, whether they be paid at the rate of a penny, or three-halfpence, or two-pence halfpenny a line, form an exceedingly industrious, inoffensive, and intelligent class, and are often much better worth their salt than more pretentious scribblers—I name no names—who are remunerated for their lucubrations at the rate of five guineas a page. But the gluttonous, bibulous, inconstant, ungrateful British public have taken it into their concerted heads that an occasional reporter is necessarily a ragged creature, with a soiled note-book, a battered hat, and a bulging umbrella; a kind of cross between Paul Pry, a detective policemen, and a man in possession; that he is poor and miserable, as well as humble and obscure; and that it is therefore expedient to laugh at and to despise him. Only the other day, travelling by the South-Western Railway, I overheard a gross, muddle-headed, city kind of man, swelling with an overweening sense of his own importance, criticising the account of the marriage of the Prince of Wales that had appeared that morning in the *Times* newspaper. 'What stuff these penny-a-liners do write, to be sure!' quoth my gross *vis-à-vis* to his neighbour. It would have been as much probably as either of them could in the literary line to have written 'cash, Dr.; contra, cr.' at the head of a ledger having reference to transactions in cheese or black-lead. The 'penny-a-liner' whose stuff excited their ineffable spleen happened to have been, on the one part, a gentlemen who was 'the Pen of the War' throughout the Crimean campaign, during the Indian Mutiny, and in the earliest and most momentous episodes of the American struggle. On the banner of William Howard Russell (who was in the nave of St George's Chapel at the Prince's Marriage) are emblazoned the words 'Sebastopol', 'Cawnpore', and 'Potomac' . . . These men have gone through all that the most approved warriors go through . . . and their sole reward—beyond the applause of a select few who know their worth—is to be called 'penny-a-liners' by a fat, ignorant cheesemonger; ay, and the taunt can be glibly and imprudently and mendaciously repeated by thousands who are neither fat, nor ignorant, nor cheesemongers.[102]

---

[102] George Augustus Sala, 'Breakfast in Bed', *Temple Bar*, 8 (1863), 74–5.

Sala captures wonderfully his own ambivalence towards the status of being a reporter. He regards his own reporting as a downward move from the editorship of *Temple Bar*, but is equally at pains to stress the worth of the special correspondent.

Sala bases his argument around the emergence of the special correspondent, arguing that the courageous exploits of Russell had made the penny-a-liner tag unsustainable. Russell's individual achievements are used to cast a chivalric and heroic glow over the whole profession. Yet the access to royal events demonstrates that Russell and Sala were exceptional. They were part of a very small coterie of eminent reporters. Writing for the press was merely one part of the diverse bricolage of literary, editorial, and journalistic activity that they engaged in. For example, at a comparable event, the maiden voyage of the *Great Eastern* in 1859, the privileged reporters in attendance included all of the usual suspects: Sala from the *Daily Telegraph*; Vizetelly for *Illustrated Times*; Murphy for the *Daily News*; Nicholas Woods for *The Times*, and John Hollingshead for *All the Year Round*.[103] When it came to the Prince of Wales's visits to Egypt in 1869 and India in 1875, it was invariably Russell who was appointed as the official 'historian'. On the latter trip, with some help from Disraeli, Russell was even appointed as the 'Hon. Private Secretary to the Prince of Wales'. He had a diplomatic uniform and, although the post involved no salary, he was paid £800 as *The Times's* correspondent.[104]

Unsurprisingly, Russell's preferential treatment provoked much hostility from the rest of the press, to the extent that, according to a letter Russell wrote several years later, his activities had to be curtailed: 'I was not to address the editor of the *Times*, or *The Times*, from the *Serapis* at all during the voyage, but if someone on board thought proper to send a letter on shore it would be surprising if the *Times* now and then was not "favoured with an interesting communication respecting the Prince of Wales's journey to India" etc., etc., etc.'[105] Such trite conventions replicate the protocol governing the invisible presence of reporters at the marriage of the Princess Royal. Russell's role, backed by the clout of *The Times*, emphasizes that there was an élite clique responsible for covering prestige occasions. Membership was self-perpetuating because the prominence of a few privileged reporters was constantly enhanced by their attendance at such events.

Alongside the efforts of the special correspondents at the wedding of the Prince of Wales, technical advances in photography meant that there was an attempt to capture a major royal event on camera for the first time. The advent of photo-journalism is the final strand in the cumulative news network around

---

[103] Vizetelly, *Glances Back*, ii. 61.   [104] Brown, *Victorian News and Newspapers*, 136.
[105] Quoted in Carol Chapman, *Russell of The Times* (London: Bell and Hyman, 1984), 164.

royal events—one that is obviously still very much in operation. T. R. Williams did take daguerreotypes of Victoria and the Princess Royal on the morning of the latter's wedding, but these pictures obviously could not be reproduced. The subsequent mania for *cartes* meant that the wedding of the Prince of Wales was the first royal occasion to be seamlessly covered by the camera. The photographic coverage began in November 1862 with Ghémar Frères's engagement photographs. When it came to the wedding itself, Mayall found himself sent for to take photographs of the wedding party, complete with ever-present marble bust of Prince Albert. The pictures of Mayall and Ghémar were similar in nature in that they were both series of standard *carte* portraits. Yet, what marks out the Prince of Wales's wedding is the impetus to photograph both the procession through London and the service at Windsor.

On one level, the wedding demonstrates that the communicative potential of photography was quickly appreciated. The camera covered each stage of the event, yet the differential nature of the photographic coverage replicates the experiences of the reporters and illustrators in attendance. Where possible, a strong policy of selected admission was in place. During the 1860s, the specialist photographic journals contained several complaints against the difficult conditions faced by the royal photographers.[106] They were expected to travel to wherever was required, denying to them the carefully controlled conditions of their glass-houses. It was an arrangement that was far from their liking. In 1865, an editorial in the *British Journal of Photography* claimed that photographers were sent for and honoured with royal sittings 'in a most thoroughly unsuitable room, or in full blaze of uninterrupted sunshine, or in the diffused shadowless light of the open air, and are then abused for not producing perfect results'.[107] Like the treatment received by journalists, such difficulties were more the product of a lack of consideration than any deliberate policy. Mayall, for example, received his command to take the official wedding photographs of the Prince of Wales only 48 hours before the occasion.[108]

Much was made of the opportunity for photography to prove its artistic proficiency through providing an accurate record of the wedding. In an article in the *British Journal of Photography* on the wedding photography, Alfred Wall, one of its most frequent contributors, proudly declared that future generations would be able to verify the welcome that was given to Princess Alexandra. They would have 'witnesses that cannot lie in a crowd of honest

---

[106] See Andrew Wynter, 'Contemporary News. Cartes de Visite', *BJP* 12 Mar. 1869, 151; 'The Late Prince Consort and Photography', *PN* 24 Jan. 1862, 38; 'Our Editorial Table', *BJP* 11 Aug. 1865, 419.

[107] George Shadbolt, 'Photography and its Critics', *BJP* 2 Mar. 1863, 109.

[108] 'At Home. Mr Alderman Mayall at King's Road, Brighton', *PN* 6 Aug. 1880, 375.

photographs'.[109] However, despite the epistemological weight attached to the camera's objectivity, the narrative constituted through individual photographs was far from impartial. Immediately following the wedding, Wall waxed lyrical upon the pictures that he enthusiastically envisaged to have been taken:

the future King and Queen placidly and fearlessly confident, though alone, in the midst of the surging and heaving mob, with rude, strong, dirty hands clutching the very sides of their carriage—the generous army of volunteer soldiers with their mutely eloquent salute—these and such incidents all doubtless photographed, will be witnesses which none can hereafter dream of dispatching or denying . . .[110]

Wall's written commentary, dripping with condescension towards the loyal hoi polloi, unravels his celebration of the objective properties of the camera. Like the *Illustrated London News*'s claim that its royal artists provided a daguerreotypic fidelity, Wall is using the realism of the camera to legitimate the narrative created by photo-journalism.

At Gravesend on 7 March, a whole coterie of notable photographers, including Francis Bedford and Valentine Blanchard, gathered to catch Princess Alexandra as she arrived.[111] At least two cameras were positioned along the Dover Road itself, and, in London, cameras were positioned on the Surrey side of London Bridge and in King William Street. Almost all of the photographers' attempts were none the less failures. Trying to gain pictures of an outdoor moving procession on a dull day in early March was a very different prospect from taking pictures in the highly controlled studio environment photographers were normally compelled to use. *Photographic News* summed up the disappointment of the day when it noted that, despite the preparations made by many photographers, their efforts 'turned out in the majority of cases comparatively useless'.[112] Beset by technical constraints, photographers were well aware of the photo-opportunities that the event provided, but were unable to take due advantage.

The procession through London was freely available to a host of photographers willing to try their luck. Access to the wedding ceremony at Windsor, however, was limited to only one photographer. Vernon Heath was stationed in the front row of the organ loft, yet, like the other photographers at the wedding, poor light meant that he had only a very moderate success.[113] None of Heath's photographs of the wedding were ever registered for copyright and it seems likely that they were not thought appropriate for public circulation. The

[109] Alfred Wall, 'The Royal Marriage from a Photographic Point of View', *BJP* 16 Mar. 1863, 123.
[110] Ibid.
[111] Frances Bedford was one of the founders of the Royal Photographic Society.
[112] 'Talk in the Studio', *PN* 2 Apr. 1863, 169.
[113] Vernon Heath, *Vernon Health's Recollections* (London: Cassell & Co., 1892), 144.

restricted admission of Heath is directly akin to that of the reporters. Like Mayall, Heath was only present with Victoria's express permission. Significantly, *Photographic News* lauded the encouragement that Princess Alexandra's public arrival had given to photography. *Photographic News* complained that the provision of royal pictures had been 'stagnating in a monopoly held by some one or two of the more eminent firms'.[114] The public opportunity that the procession offered was contrasted with the palace's patronage of a select clique of exclusive photographers. Both Mayall and Heath belong firmly to this category in that their relationship with the royal family stretched back to the early 1850s. They enjoyed eminent positions in their profession and there is a clear parallel between their admission and those of the favoured reporters. In the same way that special correspondents were far removed from penny-a-liners, Mayall and Heath were similarly exceptional and wholly outside the bounds of the cheap *carte-de-visite* studios. Indeed, Mayall would later move his studio from London to Brighton, becoming an alderman and then Mayor of the town.

From Victoria's coronation to the Prince of Wales's wedding, the memoirs and memoranda of royal reportage provide a counterpoint to the seamless ideology of most royal news narratives. The nineteenth-century press established a mode of journalism that was always a Pandora's Box. The royal family certainly benefited from the novel and fulsome attention it received. Yet, in so doing, it necessarily became subject to the demands of an ensemble of penny-a-liners, special correspondents, and photographers. Whether the British royal family desired it or not, they were the beneficiaries of a relationship that they could never hope to control. Moreover, the continued expansion of the press extended the double-edged nature of the dynamic. The New Journalism of the 1880s and 1890s, with its interviews, gossip, bold headlines, and extensive illustration, consolidated the human interest reporting of the royal family. Official access also increased in proportion with the expanding scale of the newspaper industry. At the 1887 Golden Jubilee, journalists were allocated ninety seats in Westminster Abbey for the commemorative service.[115] Conversely, though, the tensions within the relationship have continued to thrive, as has the intrusive and critical attention of the popular press. The mixture of prurient yet slavish coverage still given to the monarchy is the continuation of the contrary dynamics of royal journalism. The intrusions of the penny-a-liner are part of a genealogy that stretches forward to the paparazzi of the 1980s and 1990s. And, while the barrage of telephoto lens may seemingly dwarf the

---

[114] 'Notes of the Month', *BJP* 1 Apr. 1863, 151; David Lee, 'The First Royal Wedding Photographer', *BJP* 133 (18 July 1986), 840–3.

[115] PRO LC 2/114 5 'Jubilee Distribution of Seats'. I am grateful to Robert Lacey for drawing my attention to this point.

notebooks of the penny-a-liners, the court newsman has likewise been super-seded by a full complement of royal press secretaries.

To a large degree, the British monarchy remains within the news paradigm traced in this chapter. Indeed, there has been an increasing fusion between the disrespectful and deferential strands of royal reportage. As Wife, Mother, and, only thirdly, Queen, Victoria's feminine interest in her subjects was end-lessly lauded. Yet the intimate reportage that was so helpful to Victoria was not so forgiving to Edward VII. His mistresses and fast lifestyle did not go unnoticed by elements of the popular press; *Reynolds's Newspaper* maintained a love of royal scandal and the dissolute aristocratic life it confirmed. This impetus towards exposure still prevails in contemporary tabloid newspapers. Members of the royal family continue to discover that there is always more than one type of human interest story. In the news coverage of the British royal family, its exploits and sexploits, its philanthropy and philandering, have never been far apart. The contrary inheritances of the popular press explain why, depending on the oscillating fortunes of the monarchy, it treats royal lives as melodrama, fairy-tale, farce, peepshow, or—to use a more recent evolution—as national soap opera. And yet never abandons its delight in critique, exposure, or intrusion.

CONCLUSION

Queen Victoria established a successful and high-profile monarchical role that has been a significant influence upon subsequent members of the British royal family. During the latter decades of the nineteenth century, Victoria and Albert's civic publicness was enthusiastically copied, especially as imperial expansion opened up new and more exotic playgrounds for courtly patronage. Colonies had their loyalty rewarded and reinforced with an extended royal excursion by one of the increasing number of minor princelings. When Prince Alfred, Duke of Edinburgh, visited Australia and New Zealand in 1868, his tour lasted for seven months. On his outward journey, he stopped just long enough at the Cape of Good Hope to lay the foundation stone for a new dock. Similar tasks occupied his time in Australia. In Adelaide he was even presented with a gilded trowel to accomplish his civic work. For the pleasure of entertaining the Prince and his golden trowel, the governments of Victoria and New South Wales spent the appropriately royal sums of £35,000 and £10,000 respectively.[1] Later notable royal tours include the Prince of Wales's visits to Egypt and India in 1875, and the pomp of his imperial coronation in India in 1903. Importantly, though, both in Britain and the colonies, radicals continued to contest such visits. In 1908, Keir Hardie was temporarily banned from the House of Commons for orchestrating Labour's attacks upon Edward VII's state visit to the Czar.[2]

In terms of the media making of the monarchy, the precedents set by Victoria and Albert have continued to play an equally important role in defining the character of the royal family. Their relationship with the press meant that new media were assimilated into existing court practices and popular expectations. Thus, whereas Victoria and Albert's royal tours were broadcast via the new illustrated press, the imperial tours of their children and grandchildren received comparably novel coverage from the cinematograph. Victoria's Diamond Jubilee in 1897 was one of the first major public events to

---

[1] *Narrative of the Visit of His Royal Highness the Duke of Edinburgh to the Colony of Victoria, Australia*, ed. J. G. Knight (Melbourne: Mason Frith and Co., 1868), 24.

[2] Antony Taylor, *'Down with the Crown': British Anti-Monarchism and Debates about Royalty since 1790* (London: Reaktion, 1999), 213–14.

be filmed. It was a key event in the development of the British film industry. The Diamond Jubilee pictures proved highly successful and were a standard feature of many variety programmes in both London and the provinces. Films of Victoria's funeral procession through London reached an even larger audience. They received showings in cities as far apart as New York, Melbourne, Cape Town, and Paris.[3] When it came to the coronation of Edward VII, the dim light of Westminster Abbey and the noise of the cameras made filming the ceremony an impossibility. The desire for a recording of the coronation nevertheless inspired one early film pioneer, Charles Urban, who was head of Warwick Trading Company. Urban staged a massive reconstruction of the event just outside Paris, complete with mock-up of Westminster Abbey (see Fig. 43).

By the end of her reign, Victoria was the Great White Empress, the symbolic hub of the British Empire. Demonstrations of Victoria's personal concern for her multitudinous subjects continued to take place. Such displays were nevertheless only made possible by the communicative power of the international telegraph system. The first line between India and Europe had been opened in January 1856; Australia was linked with India in 1872, and Shanghai and Tokyo were reached in 1873. Before leaving Buckingham Palace for her Diamond Jubilee procession, Victoria sent a special telegraph message rippling across the empire reading 'From my heart I thank my beloved people. God bless them!' Contemporary writers and critics were well aware of the imperial role of the telegraph network. Rudyard Kipling's 'Song of the English' (1896) evokes a panoramic vision of the ties between the British colonies. Yet, typically for Kipling, it was the materiality of undersea telegraph cables, rather than simply love for the mother country, that unified the empire:

> Here in the womb of the world—here on the tie-ribs of earth
> Words, and the words of men, flicker and flutter and beat—
> Warning, sorrow and gain, salutation and mirth—
> For a Power troubles the Still that has neither voice nor feet.
>
> They have wakened the timeless Things; they have killed their father Time;
> Joining hands in the gloom, a league from the last of the sun.
> Hush! Men talk to-day o'er the waste of the ultimate slime,
> And a new Word runs between: whispering, 'Let us be one!'[4]

For Kipling, the silent operation of the cables has a quasi-mystical function. They dissolve the boundaries of space and time and pave the way for a higher imperial unity.

[3] 'Athenaeum Hall', *Melbourne Argus*, 16 Mar. 1901, 16; 'Huber's Museum', *New York Times*, 16 Mar. 1901, 19; 'Royal Biograph', *Cape Times*, 6 Apr. 1901, 6; 'Place Aux Dames', *Graphic*, 6 Feb. 1901, 16.

[4] Rudyard Kipling, 'Song of the English', *The White Man's Burdens; An Anthology of British Poetry of the Empire*, ed. Chris Brooks and Peter Faulkner (Exeter: Exeter University Press, 1996), 293.

Fig. 43. Cinema programme, Scala Theatre, London, *Through India With Our King and Queen* (1912)

Kipling's poem is similar to several published at the time of Victoria's death in January 1901. The telegraph network made the Queen-Empress's demise one of the first truly global media events. The latest bulletins upon her health were carried to every corner of the British Empire. Crowds gathered at telegraph stations as far apart as Melbourne, Bombay, and Montreal. One poem by

Bellyse Baildon envisaged the message of her death diffusing around the earth:

> Then thrilled the great globe like a sentient thing,
> Stung into life by sorrow, from there sped
> Along its swift electric nerves, that bring
> Together to one whole with heart and head
> Members and limbs of that vast realm that are
> By continents and oceans sundered far,
>   The words that said,
> *'The Queen is Dead.'*[5]

For Baildon, like Kipling, the telegraph system did more than create a collective and simultaneous grief. It provided individuals with a sublime awareness of their belonging to an imperial-wide mourning.

At Victoria's death and funeral, the dominance of the New Journalism meant that royal reportage remained a source of continuing controversy. As Victoria lay dying at Osborne House on the Isle of Wight, hundreds of British and foreign journalists gathered at the gates to receive the latest bulletins upon her condition. When Victoria's death was announced, their raucous behaviour provoked widespread repugnance. The journalists charged, en masse, to East Cowes telegraph office. Some ran, some cycled, and some were on horseback. Many of them shouted 'Queen Dead' in their headlong rush. Several newspapers also published fake reports of the events taking place inside Osborne House. The Press Association disseminated a spurious interview with one of the physicians attending the Queen, while the *Daily Mail* described a touching deathbed reconciliation between Victoria and the Kaiser. Court officials were assiduous in tracking down those responsible for the different fabrications. Having access to the telephone and telegraphic message sent from Osborne House, they were able to confirm which reports had been invented. At least two correspondents promptly found themselves recalled to their newspaper's offices after arousing the displeasure of court functionaries.[6]

All of these incidents were widely commented upon, accentuating the nature of Victoria's death as a media event. *The Times*'s correspondent noted that there was 'a good deal of the spirit and flesh of American journalism at large in Cowes'.[7] A poem published in Henry Labouchere's *Truth* denounced 'The Yahoos of Yellow Journalism':

---

[5] Bellyse Baildon, 'The Queen is Dead', *Poetical Tributes to Queen Victoria*, ed. Charles Forshaw (London: Swan Sonnenshein, 1901), 63.

[6] 'Authors of "Fakes" Punished', *New York Times*, 27 Jan. 1901, 2.

[7] 'Reckless and Untrue Reports', *Liverpool Daily Post*, 22 Jan. 1901, 5.

To be told, whilst the heart of all England was breaking,
How these Pressmen to still be offensive contrived.
How even the spot where the Nation was waiting,
As 'twere the last news of its Sovereign to learn,
These reporters—no jot of offensiveness bating—
Were into a bear-garden able to turn![8]

The cumulative effect of the disreputable incidents was such that a meeting of the Institute of Journalists was called. The Institute went so far as to launch its own inquiry in order to discover those responsible.[9] Amidst much moralistic huffing and puffing, the reporters concerned were condemned as falling below the rules of gentlemanly conduct followed by the general body of the profession. The various outraged commentaries were wholly similar to the opprobrium heaped upon Jenkins in the 1840s and 1850s. They prefigure the scorn endured by the paparazzi of the 1980s and 1990s.

Radical publications also attacked the role of the press in an equally familiar fashion. *Reynolds's Newspaper* inveighed against the Gutter and Garbage journals for their sycophantic pronouncements upon the national grief that Victoria's death had supposedly caused. It derided the journalists responsible as 'mere scene-painters and bill-stickers'.[10] The *Labour Leader*, then edited by Keir Hardie, and *Justice*, the organ of the Social Democratic Federation, expressed correspondingly sceptical sentiments.[11] *Justice* declared that her death was opportune for the daily newspapers because it 'provided them with a fresh sensation to fill the void left by the waning of interest in the [Boer] war'.[12] In 1901, *Justice*, *Labour Leader*, and *Reynolds's Newspaper* were perpetuating a series of customary anti-monarchist critiques. Their attacks look back to the Chartist press at the time of Victoria's coronation, and forward to the debates surrounding the mourning over the death of Diana, Princess of Wales.

With the development of new media industries like the cinema, the same concerns over press intrusion and loss of royal mystique resurface again and again. At the lying-in-state of Edward VII in 1910, special artists were permitted to sketch the lying-in-state, yet no photographs of Edward in his coffin were permitted. When it came to the funeral ceremony in Westminster Abbey, photography was again banned during the service and while any members of the royal family were present. A letter from Sir Schomberg McDonnell, Secretary to the Office of Works, to Arthur Bigge, the former Private Secretary

---

[8] 'The Yahoos of Yellow Journalism', *Truth*, 31 Jan. 1901, 254.
[9] 'The Institute of Journalists: Recent Incidents at Cowes', *The Journalist and Newspaper Proprietor*, 9 Mar. 1901, 10.
[10] 'Up to Date', *Reynolds's Newspaper*, 27 Jan. 1901, 1.
[11] 'Between Ourselves', *Labour Leader*, 9 Feb. 1901, 43; 'Khaki and Black', *Justice*, 2 Feb. 1901, 1.
[12] 'Are the People Asleep?', *Justice*, 26 Jan. 1901, 1.

to Queen Victoria, epitomizes the continued official ambivalence towards the role of the press. The letter was written in response to numerous requests requesting permission to photograph the funeral procession and service of Edward VII:

Personally I loathe photography, so that it is most repugnant to me to have to submit to such a proposal; but it must be remembered that photography in the case of great Ceremonials of public mourning is a popular institution. I use the word popular advisedly and in the best sense. What I want to convey is that it enables poor people who live at a distance and cannot afford to come to London to see in the illustrated papers photographs of what has taken place and that it would be a great deprivation not to have the opportunity of doing so.[13]

McDonnell's letter expresses both the official desire for a popular monarchy and the perceived ability of the press to further this aim. Yet it also demonstrates a condescending aristocratic reluctance to submit to its communicative power.

During the second half of the twentieth century, radio, television, and the telephoto lens ensured that the British monarchy's relationship with mass communications media became ever more overarching. Important episodes include the first Christmas Day radio broadcast by George V in 1932, the televising of the coronation of Elizabeth II in 1953, the two royal weddings of the early 1980s, and the celebrity status achieved by Diana, Princess of Wales, up to her premature death in 1997. Where is the ritual of these occasions? Does it stem from the pageantry or from the sense of national participation achieved via the media? Many people remember their first experience of television from watching the broadcast of Queen Elizabeth II's coronation. Around 20 million people watched her coronation, even though there were no more than 2.5 million working television sets in Britain. This enabling of participation via the media is obviously still very much in operation. At the funeral of Queen Elizabeth, the Queen Mother, for example, schools were invited to break their normal routines in order that pupils could watch the occasion.

It is impossible to gauge just how significant a role popular media played in helping the monarchy reinvent its position during Victoria's reign. Individual media functioned in multiple and contradictory ways, and continued to do so throughout the twentieth century. The extent of the various commentaries nevertheless suggests that we should be careful about reproducing a loaded political dichotomy that separates the popular character of the monarchy from its high-minded, heritage-bound, constitutional importance. Such a division is not only essentially flawed; it is already skewed in favour of the monarchy. The claims of figures like Bagehot and Disraeli reveal that Victoria's media

[13] PRO Work 21 20/7 242.

making was wholly bound up with the celebration of her constitutional position. Through the revolutionary ordinariness of the *carte*; the revelatory quality of news; and the press's promotion of Victoria's visits as her willingness to place herself before the approval of her People, there was a conflation between the media making of the monarchy and the conception of Victoria as a modern democratic sovereign.

The events around the death of Queen Elizabeth, the Queen Mother, coupled with the Golden Jubilee celebrations for Elizabeth II, demonstrate the ongoing appeal of the monarchy. Around 200,000 people visited the Queen Mother's lying-in-state in Westminster Hall. Republicanism remains muted and, with little opposition, the royal family continues to receive large sums of money from the Civil List. Nevertheless, the success of recent ceremonies has to be seen in the context of the far greater scale of previous royal events. At the funerals of George V and George VI, in 1936 and 1952 respectively, the coffins of both dead monarchs were taken through the London streets in an extended procession from Westminster Hall to Paddington. The coronation of Elizabeth II took place on a similar magnitude. The legacy and the remnants of British imperialism meant that it was celebrated at thousands of locations across the world.

Despite the historical potency of the relationship between the British monarchy and the media; despite the continuation of an inglorious dialectic that veers between fawning and fornication, the monarchy is fading from the fabric of national life. The decline is slow but it is sure and it is inevitable. It is a process tangential to the cyclical peaks and troughs of royal popularity. Claims of the decline of the monarchy are, of course, nothing new, and I am not predicting any imminent end to the royal family. My work for this book has none the less thrown into relief the myriad of institutional and aristocratic supports that the monarchy has lost over the last 150 years. Where now are the innumerable local processions and dinners that commemorated royal occasions? Where now are the obligatory parish sermons upon the latest royal birth, death, wedding, or christening? Organized monarchy, like organized religion—and the comparison is telling—is increasingly bereft. The walls of the House of Windsor, like those of the Church of England, are still standing. The congregation who come to worship are nevertheless increasingly sparse. The long link between Church and Crown, two mutually supportive pillars of the British state, remains strong: but the twentieth century has seen both institutions marginalized.

Much has been made of the reinvention of the monarchy in the late nineteenth century around grand pageants of pomp and circumstance; the creation of a tradition that literally set the stage for subsequent national occasions. Yet the concentration upon such centralized events, which were increasingly broadcast outwards by the mass media, misses the decline in the number of local ceremonies. Whereas a royal birth or wedding would once have occasioned the inevitable congratulatory resolutions from councils, parishes, and corporations, such official interventions now rarely take place. The comparative lack of enthusiasm for Queen Elizabeth II's Golden Jubilee was indicative of the way that the monarchy no longer inspires the same devotion. Regular national royal occasions have virtually been reduced to the monarch's Christmas Day television broadcast. It is a ritual that receives approximately the same disregard as the *Court Circular* did in the nineteenth century.

The institutional decline of the monarchy has gone hand in hand with a slow semantic loss. Victoria's tours and visits had a potent and evocative constitutional symbolism because they took place against a backdrop where the sovereign was still able to exert a large degree of political power and patronage. This constitutional charge has now been lost, as has the grand narrative of British industrial supremacy that was embedded in so many of the openings undertaken by Victoria and Albert. The validation for international state visits has been attenuated in a comparable fashion, reduced to a dogged utilitarianism. Royal tours have become promotional events in aid of UK PLC. Constitutional discourse is now focused around devolution and Europe. This shift is a significant index to the stress upon the nation-state and its corollary, a British national imaginary that was claimed to have the monarchy at its heart. To a large degree, this book has been premised on the impact of a national mass media, whether enacted through newspapers, photography, or the telegraph network. It was a development that was, on the whole, highly beneficial to Victoria. The traditional courtly pre-eminence enjoyed by the monarchy passed over into its dominance of the news values of a national press and the market for photography and prints.

The growth of the British Empire meant that such material and imaginative interpenetration did not stop with a photograph of Victoria in every British cottage and drawing-room. Upon the occasion of Victoria's death, memorial services took place across the empire to coincide with the passage of her funeral cortege through London. In South Australia and New Zealand, all trains stopped for 10 minutes as a sign of respect.[14] In Montreal, the fire bells of the city were tolled at 30-second intervals during the morning of the funeral day.[15] In an open air wake in Calcutta, thousands of Hindus walked past a large portrait of Victoria that was draped in mourning white.[16] The *Melbourne Argus* was typical in its declaration that 'Britons are realising now how the life

[14] 'Australasia', *Daily Mail*, 4 Feb. 1901, 4.
[15] 'The Brigade Parade', *Montreal Star*, 2 Feb. 1901, 24.
[16] 'The Death of the Queen', *The Hindoo Patriot*, 5 Feb. 1901, 5.

of their Sovereign was interwoven with the life of the world . . . Flags are half-masted, festivities are shadowed, in every country. There has never been anything like it before.'[17] The great expanse of such imperial modernity was the working out of an international dynamic that had already diffused Victoria as a ubiquitous yet intimate national presence. Thus, at the same time as the political influence of the monarchy was inexorably waning, we can begin to understand why Victoria was made into the hero of her own life and of the Victorian Age itself. In numerous biographies, poems, and editorials, she expanded to become the guarantor of industrial progress, individual liberty, and imperial greatness.

The insinuating nature of Victoria's presence, which was itself only made possible by much larger societal forces, helped to symbolize her as the Mother of her People and the Great White Empress. Its continuation, however, has created an imaginative atrophy. 'For Queen and Country' simply no longer has the same resonance. The inevitable and iconic existence of the monarchy is fading. It is losing its place as an unavoidable given of the national imaginary. The national is being permeated by the globalization of the twenty-first century. The fate of most dynasties looms over Queen Elizabeth II in that her head is indeed under threat. Victoria could find her own Patron Portrait staring back at her on stamps and coinage from across the world. Yet it is the survival of sterling itself that now threatens one highly symbolic removal of Elizabeth II from everyday life. Over the last 200 years there have been fundamental changes in the hierarchical structure of British society. These offer by far the greatest threat to the continuation of the Crown. The monarchy will not be abolished when it begins to arouse fervent political passion. It will become untenable precisely when it ceases to arouse the passion and the labour evident throughout this book.

---

[17] 'Wednesday, 30 January, 1901', *Melbourne Argus*, 30 Jan. 1901, 6.

APPENDIX

Queen Victoria in the Books of Beauty

William Beattie, 'Her Majesty, the Princes of Wales and the Princess Royal', *Heath's Book of Beauty* (London: Longman *et al.*, 1843), 1.

Countess Blessington, 'Lines on a Portrait of the Princess Royal', *Keepsake* (London, 1846), 49.

Annie Carter Hall, 'Victoria', The Book of Royalty (London: Ackermann & Co., 1839), n.p. (with a coloured lithograph of the Queen).

Henry Chorley, 'On a Portrait of Her Majesty Queen Victoria', *Heath's Book of Beauty* (London: Longman *et al.*, 1849), 1 (engraving after a miniature by Willaim Ross).

F.R.C, 'To the Queen', *Christian Keepsake*, ed. Rev. William Ellis (London: Fisher, Son & Co., 1838), 64.

Engraving after William Drummond, 'Her Majesty the Queen, the Prince of Wales, and the Princess Royal', *Heath's Book of Beauty* (London: Longman *et al.*, 1843).

Mrs Fairlie, 'Lines Written Beneath a Portrait of H. R. H. Prince Albert', *Keepsake* (London, 1842), 1.

Theodosia Garrow, 'On a Portrait of Her Majesty', *Heath's Book of Beauty* (London: Longman *et al.*, 1842), 1.

Laetitia Landon, 'To Victoria', *Flowers of Loveliness; Twelve Groups of Female Figures, Emblematic of Flowers* (London: Ackermann & Co., 1838), n.p.

Richard Monkton-Miles, 'Coronation Song', *Heath's Book of Beauty*, ed. Countess of Blessington (London: Longman, Orme, Brown, Green and Longmans, 1839), 247.

James Montgomery, 'To her Majesty Queen Victoria on her Coronation in Westminster Abbey', *Forget-Me-Not* (London, 1840), 9.

Bryan Proctor, 'A Song for the Queen', *Friendship's Offering* (London, 1839), 43.

'The Queen', *Fisher's Drawing Room Scrap-Book*, ed. Caroline Norton (London: Fisher, Son & Co., 1847), 5–7 (opposite engraving of Queen Victoria after portrait by William Ross).

'The Queen', *Fisher's Drawing-Room Scrap-Book*, ed. Laetitia Landon (London: H. Fisher, R. Fisher and P. Jackson, 1838), 3.

Agnes Strickland, 'Royal Christenings', *Forget-Me-Not* (London, 1841), 331.

Lady Emmeline Stuart-Wortley, 'To the Queen', *Forget-Me-Not* (London, 1845), 72.

Lady Emmeline Stuart-Wortley, 'On Her Majesty Landing in France', *Keepsake* (London, 1845), 125.

'To Her Majesty Queen Victoria', *The Gallery of Beauty; or, Court of Queen Victoria* (London: Tilt and Bogue, 1839), n.p. (with an engraving of Victoria after Richard Lane's portrait).

Camilla Toulmin, frontispiece, *Friendship's Offering* (London: Smith, Elder & Co., 1843), 1.

Richard Townsend, 'The Coronation; or, The Exiles of Siberia', *Finden's Tableaux* (London: Finden & Co., 1839), 49.

FURTHER READING

Albert, Prince, *Addresses delivered on Different Public Occasions by HRH Prince Albert* (London: Society of Arts, 1857).

Altick, Richard, *Punch: The Lively Youth of a British Institution 1841–1851* (Columbus, Oh.: Ohio University Press, 1997).

——*The English Common Reader: A Social History of the Mass Reading Public, 1800–1900* (1957; Columbus, Oh.: Ohio University Press, 1998).

Bagehot, Walter, *The English Constitution*, introd. R. H Crossman (London: Collins, 1963).

Barrell, John, *Imagining the King's Death: Figurative Treason, Fantasies of Regicide 1793–1796* (Oxford: Oxford University Press, 2000).

Beetham, Margaret, *A Magazine of Her Own?: Domesticity and Desire in the Woman's Magazine, 1800–1914* (London: Routledge, 1996).

——and Boardman, Kay (ed.) *Victorian Women's Magazines: An Anthology* (Manchester: Manchester University Press, 2001).

Brooks, Chris (ed.), *The Albert Memorial* (New Haven: Yale University Press, 2000).

Brown, Lucy, *Victorian News and Newspapers* (Oxford: Clarendon Press, 1985).

Cannadine, David, 'The Context, Performance and Meaning of Ritual: The British Monarchy and the "Invention of Tradition" *c.*1820–1977', in Eric Hobsbawm and Terence Ranger (eds.), *The Invention of Tradition* (Cambridge: Cambridge University Press, 1983), 101–64.

Colley, Linda, 'The Apotheosis of George III: Loyalty, Royalty, and the British Nation', *Past and Present*, 113 (1984), 94–129.

Dimond, Frances, and Taylor, Roger, *Crown and Camera: The Royal Family and Photography* (London: Viking, 1987).

Dyson, Anthony, *Pictures to Print: The Nineteenth-Century Engraving Trade* (London: Farrand Press, 1984).

Epstein, James, *Radical Expression: Political Language, Ritual, and Symbol in England 1790–1850* (Oxford: Oxford University Press, 1994).

Foot, Michael, and Kramnick, Isaac (eds.), *Thomas Paine Reader* (Harmondsworth: Penguin, 1987).

Fox, Celina, *Graphic Journalism in England during the 1830s and 1840s* (New York: Garland, 1988).

Homans, Margaret, *Royal Representations: Queen Victoria and British Culture 1837–1867* (Chicago: Chicago University Press, 1998).

——'To the Queen's Private Apartments: Royal Family Portraiture and the Construction of Victoria's Sovereign Obedience', *Victorian Studies*, 37.1 (1993), 1–45.

Jackson, Mason, *The Pictorial Press: Its Origins and Progress* (London: Hurst & Blackett, 1885).

James, Louis, *Fiction for the Working Man 1830–1850* (London: Oxford University Press, 1963).

Jones, Aled, *Powers of the Press: Newspapers, Power and the Public in Nineteenth-Century England* (Aldershot: Scolar Press, 1996).

Joyce, Patrick, *Visions of the People: Industrial England and the Question of Class 1840–1914* (Cambridge: Cambridge University Press, 1991).

King, Lyndel Saunders, *The Industrialisation of Taste: Victorian England and the Art Union of London* (Ann Arbor: UMI Research Press, 1982).

Kuhn, William, *Democratic Royalism: The Transformation of the British Monarchy 1861–1914* (New York: St Martin's Press, 1996).

Lee, Alan, *The Origins of the Popular Press in England 1855–1914* (London: Croom Helm, 1976).

Linkman, Audrey, *The Victorians: Photographic Portraits* (London: Tauris Parke, 1993).

McCalman, Iain, *Radical Underworld: Prophets, Revolutionaries and Pornographers 1795–1840* (1988; Oxford: Clarendon Press, 1993).

McCauley, Elizabeth Anne, *A. A. E. Disdéri and the Carte de Visite Portrait Photograph* (New Haven: Yale University Press, 1985).

Maidment, Brian, *Reading Popular Prints 1770–1870* (Manchester: Manchester University Press, 1996).

Munich, Adrienne, *Queen Victoria's Secrets* (New York: Columbia University Press, 1996).

Nash, David, and Taylor, Antony (eds.), *Republicanism in Victorian Britain* (London: Sutton, 2000).

Prochaska, Frank, *Royal Bounty: The Making of a Welfare Monarchy* (New Haven: Yale University Press, 1995).

—— *The Republic of Britain 1760–2000* (London: Allen Lane, 2000).

Seiberling, Grace, and Bloore, Carolyn, *Amateurs, Photography and the Mid-Victorian Imagination* (Chicago: Chicago University Press and International Museum of Photography, 1986).

Taylor, Antony, *'Down with the Crown': British Anti-Monarchism and Debates about Royalty since 1790* (London: Reaktion, 1999).

Twyman, Michael, *Printing 1770–1970: An Illustrated History of its Development and Uses in England* (London: Eyre and Spotiswoode, 1970).

Tyrell, Alex, and Ward, Yvonne, 'God Bless Her Little Majesty: The Popularity of Monarchy in the 1840s', *National Identities*, 2.2 (2000), 109–26.

Vernon, James (ed.), *Re-reading the Constitution: New narratives in the Political History of England's Long Nineteenth Century* (Cambridge: Cambridge University Press, 1996).

—— *Politics and the People: A Study in English Political Culture, c. 1815–1867* (Cambridge: Cambridge University Press, 1993).

Victoria, Queen, *Leaves from the Journal of Our Life in the Highlands*, ed. Arthur Helps (London: Smith Elder, 1868).

Williams, Richard, *The Contentious Crown: Public Discussion of the British Monarchy in the Reign of Queen Victoria* (Aldershot: Ashgate, 1997).

Wood, Marcus, *Radical Satire and Print Culture 1790–1822* (Oxford: Clarendon Press, 1994).

INDEX